for my loving fri
Mu

tenny
xxx

SHAKE
BEFORE USE

A BASIC GUIDE FOR HOW LIFE WORKS

This guide will explain everything we never learned growing up on how to easily overcome life's challenges and develop our full potential. It introduces a simple and practical framework that enables anybody to live consciously in order to enjoy a more pleasant and satisfying life full of happiness, love, peace and serenity. The principles and real-life experiences set forth in this book are designed to present both an educational framework as well as a spiritual one in order to empower and inspire all of us – mind, body and soul.

Written by **Penelope Morcillo**

Translated by Fernando Soni Ocampo

Original Title: "AGITAR ANTES DE USAR: Una Guia Basica de Como Funciona la Vida."

First book published in the United States of America by The Phoenix Servant Leadership For The World, LLC., under authorization from Ave Fenix, Servant Leadership for the World, S.L. Publication date: August 2018.

Written by Penelope Morcillo

Translation by Fernando Soni Ocampo

Graphic Design and Illustration by Signo Comunicacion Consultores, S.L.U.

Grateful acknowledgement is made to Rufina Santana for permission to print the Mural painting on the book cover: "El Viaje del Heroe" ("The Hero's Journey") by Rufina Santana © 2015. Printed by Permission.

Inside pictures and/or images in order of appearance in the book:
Mikael Damkier (Mikdam) / Depositphotos Inc. USA – page: 24
Signo Comunicacion Consultores, S.L.U. – page: 27
Tanya Beleshko (Catwoman10) / Depositphotos Inc. USA – page: 32
Michele Piacquadio (Olly18) / Depositphotos Inc. USA – page: 42
Sergey Konyakin (Artenot) / Depositphotos Inc. USA – page: 173

In this publication the company alone is responsible for statements of fact, thoughts, opinions, feelings, perceptions, examples, recommendations and/ or conclusions expressed.

ISBN: 978-1-7326408-0-1

THE ROYAL
HISPANIA
GROUP

DISCLAIMERS:

IMPORTANT! I am not a medical doctor or licensed mental health professional. This handbook is not intended to be used as a substitute for the advice of competent psychologists, or any other medical doctor recommendations, diagnoses or treatment plans. You should never delay seeking medical attention or psychological advice, or alter or discontinue any prescriptions and/or recommendations in matters relating to your physical health, emotional stability and personal well-being without first consulting a licensed health professional. The information on the following pages represents only my own personal life experiences and insights gained from trusted mentors and colleagues; hence, this book should be understood and used as such.

CONTENTS

ACKNOWLEDGEMENTS

To my parents, Maria Rosa and Francisco Angel,
To my sister and the rest of my family, and to all my ancestors,
To my teachers, professors, mentors and friends,
For believing in me and always giving me their best.
For their unconditional support, love, kindness and infinite patience.

I want to make a very special mention to my parents for their unceasing effort and dedication to our family throughout their lives. They have sacrificed their own dreams by always giving to their daughters the best of them. My love and admiration for both of them has no limits.

I also acknowledge the efforts of my main mentor, Alvaro D. Maldonado, who taught me, for the most part, the knowledge of other cultures and ancient traditions from India and other countries, as well as other general knowledge that has evolved over time. In addition, his particular way of seeing the world and describing it has given me a new understanding of the reality in which we live, and has allowed me to write this Basic Guide for How Life Works. Based both on his teachings and on my own personal experiences throughout the process, this book provides an educational framework for pursuing personal growth.

I also have a high regard for the meditations and training of Chakrasamvara Buddhist Center in Miami (FL) and as well as its Sangha (community of practitioners), and its spiritual director, Mai Pham. The Center introduced me to a new world and gave me access to its spiritual knowledge, practice and support. Additionally, it helped me to discover, listen and tune into my inner self that initially was totally undiscovered. This guide will also give you a personal and spiritual lens for how to begin understanding these deeper aspects of your own self.

Likewise, I want to thank Pilathon and Emily Bench for helping me stay flexible and strong, and for delivering Pilates classes with so much love.

Thank you to all those who have been part of my journey and to those who have contributed to my personal development. Because of you, I have raised my level of consciousness, opened my heart and unlocked my potential – and continue to daily benefit from it in such inspiring ways!

PREFACE

Despite having lived a relatively normal life for 36 years, I was always trying to make sense of my existence. It was only until recently when I was able to understand that I was quite confused and also totally unconscious. To put it simply: I did not know myself. I was not fully aware of what was happening within and around me, and I was experiencing tremendous amounts of pain in my life without even realizing it. My perception was blocked. I had a distorted view of my perceived and limited reality. I felt confused about my purpose in life. I was lost in terms of my direction. I was suffering – and I had no clue why. After a guided journey of self-discovery, however, I began to understand the causes of why I felt and behaved the way I did. I learned how to connect most of life's dots and eventually discover (and pursue!) my overall meaning and purpose.

I wrote this book because I feel the personal responsibility to pass on the knowledge that was shared with me. That insight brought me out of a dark and inhospitable world in which I lived (and where many people currently live, albeit unknowingly so!). With a very high level of commitment, and with a lot of work, perseverance and support, I was able to reach a higher level of consciousness – and it allowed me to live a more satisfying and rewarding life. After all, isn't that what we all want?

Learning life concepts as well as ancient and general knowledge, and then applying them, was certainly not easy because the information from my mentor was verbal and abstract. But when my perception began to change, I was able to understand and discover for myself that living – real living – was something else. By developing a higher level of consciousness and a better understanding of myself, I found that greater abilities and a genuine desire of enjoyment for life emerged.

Designing Life's Journey

It was definitely a long journey. Years earlier, at the age of 29, I remember counting the approximate time I had left to live. I did not feel depressed or sad, but I felt empty and broken, and even though I did not know it at the time, my understanding of reality was quite limited and restricted. Nothing fulfilled me in my life. Yes, I had a good job that afforded me a nice income and enabled me to live comfortably and hang with friends… but something did not quite fit. And at the time, I didn't know what was broken or how to fix it.

Overtime, I began to design a type of educational framework that also eventually took on spiritual overtones – for, as you will learn through this book, the body, mind and soul are all interconnected. It is result of a long empirical process through which I was the guinea pig in an incredible life experiment that not only was satisfactorily completed but also enabled me to raise my level of consciousness, elevate my level of living and enjoy a more fulfilling life. My process inspired this book, as I want to teach and encourage others who were in the same place I was years ago: lost, confused and uninspired. Life is too short to feel unfulfilled.

I have structured the book according to a visually conceptual framework I call the Pyramid of Consciousness (POC). This pyramid is the culmination of my own understanding and subsequent analysis of the process. It is comprised of sequential knowledge levels, each of which is described in this book as a lesson in order to facilitate learning and growth. I have also interweaved my own personal experiences, examples, comments, deductions and conclusions from my self-analysis and life introspection to show that ascending this pyramid is both essential and possible.

Why Read This Book?

The purpose of the book is to help people by informing them of some behaviors or responses that could potentially block their socio-emotional and mental development. It is a self-help guide. Its pages will provide a better understanding of the mechanism of how life works and the benefits of raising one's consciousness. It describes key situations, feelings and thoughts that I experienced before and during my own transformation towards a higher consciousness and deeper capacity to love, while also acknowledging that each person can experience different manifestations throughout each phase of the pyramid and during his evolution.

I tried to lay out the lessons as simply as possible so that no matter where you are in life, you can first understand the concepts and then apply them in your own life.

Ascending the Pyramid

This book will walk you through each Level of the Pyramid of Consciousness. The POC is comprised of 6 levels, from simple to complex, in the following order: 1. Ignorance, 2. Obedience, 3. Understanding and Comprehension, 4. Responsibility, 5. Conscience, and 6. Enlightenment (the summit).

Personally, the most difficult process for me was to awaken from the dream in which I laid dormant on the pyramid's two lower levels: Ignorance and Obedience. But once I started progressing through the levels and gained traction, I was inspired to persevere, despite the great internal conflicts and challenges I experienced. The rest of the levels were more bearable, easier, even enjoyable as I proceeded through the other physical, mental and spiritual practices. Reaching the fifth level in the pyramid, that of Conscience, has led me through a process of three years of my life. The summit, the sixth, is infinite, and although we technically will never complete it, we can continue to evolve and grow, and benefit.

Solving Life's Puzzle, Piece by Piece

It is my hope that by following this framework you will be able to create a greater level of individual consciousness and ultimately achieve inner peace, happiness and fulfillment. Personally, the most important part of my experience during this process was that it allowed me to fit together a lot of pieces of my life puzzle… and find my way out of the darkness and into the light. Leaving my self-imposed cocoon of fear and darkness was not easy, but applying the knowledge of the lessons made this task much easier for me.

Keep in mind that much of the information provided in this book is the act of my taking abstract concepts and turning them into concrete applications. It's only an introduction for beginning the journey of self-awareness and spiritual enlightenment, and as such this book should not be viewed as a comprehensive self-diagnosis or treatment plan. I am not a certified psychologist or a medical doctor. However, I have personally completed this process and have gained much knowledge and benefited greatly – and I would like to pay it forward. The following pages are a culmination of the insight and experiences I have collected throughout the past few years along with guidance from brilliant mentors in my life that helped me to synchronize my body, mind and soul.

This educational framework can be used to help others, raise their level of consciousness and open their eyes to what is both in and around them. This will eventually enable them to improve their mind, bodies and souls. I recommend progressing through this book sequentially, as each lesson builds on the previous one. Read this book daily and look for ways to apply the lessons to your life so that you can eventually stop old unproductive habits by developing new, healthier ones.

ABOUT THIS GUIDE

We all know that life can get pretty complicated sometimes. And understanding it can be challenging. Fully comprehending how life works requires much study and curiosity through deliberate observation, asking many questions, using a hypothesis approach, undergoing experimentation or testing, and analyzing data to arrive at general theories or conclusions that embody one or more learnings.

People who have lived a full life and are in the last phase of their lives often have many experiences and wisdom they have collected over the years and inspired very interesting specific and concrete conclusions. By applying the concepts laid out in this Basic Guide for How Life Works, we can obtain even greater insight into our own lives and draw our own conclusions not just about our present selves but also our future selves. To this end, three specific areas of study will be presented that will advise you on the framework to live and learn consciously. These are:

1. The Pyramid of Consciousness (POC): The structure that represents the different states of consciousness where one can identify his level of self-development
2. The Functioning of Love and Fear
3. The Lessons: Divided into six parts, with each corresponding to the evolutionary phases of the person that match with the POC levels.

This is where we will focus most of the object of study. Each teaching should follow a deep and sincere introspection of the individual

This system is applicable to anyone in any age range.

Best Practices for Benefiting from this Guide

This cumulative and linear knowledge framework utilizes a very easy-to-use methodology. It continuously builds on previously discussed insights and lessons. Therefore, it is very important that you follow the order sequence in the book and do not randomly jump from one topic to another or skim/skip parts; otherwise, it will negatively affect your comprehension of the subject matter.

To benefit the most from this book, all you need is the desire to learn, evolve and persevere – and be open to leaving your comfort zone. It will help light your way by giving you more insight, more awareness and more consciousness.

It is recommended to read the book for ten minutes, or review one lesson every day, always at the same time (before bed or at the beginning of the day, for example). Make it a daily routine. Then analyze these life teachings by practicing personal introspection or reflection. Decide to apply them in some way to your day-to-day activities.

In order to move on to the next pyramid level and make good progress, make sure you have gained a full understanding of the previous sections and are applying them in your daily life. Recall and reflect on them whenever you notice certain behaviors or traits both in yourself and in others. If it is difficult for you to get up in the morning to go to work, for example, evaluate what is happening to you and why it is happening. Likewise, if someone has responded to another person at work in a certain way, analyze what is happening, and identify which patterns and tools they are using, etc. In order to learn and understand, you must first observe.

It is advisable to review this guide's lessons as many times as necessary before moving on to the next pyramid level to ensure that all concepts became fully clear. Even if you have read this complete guide, it is ideal to leave it on your bedside to continue learning and improving your behaviors and patterns instead of falling back into the old habits that do not support growth and development.

Are you ready? Good. Let's begin!

PART 1

THE
STRUCTURE

A Helpful Reminder

All individual observations, although can often seem obvious, should be seen as fluid and temporal since people are always struggling with relative truths that eventually become clearer. Therefore, the concepts that we will review in the following pages may at first appear somewhat rigid and overly simplistic, but will eventually help create a much more complete reality. Everything we perceive, understand and comprehend is temporary and depends on our state of evolution at a given time. This is why evolving oneself can be so valuable and rewarding.

PART 1
THE STRUCTURE

LIFE'S LEVELS: ASCENDING THE PYRAMID OF CONSCIOUSNESS (POC)

The structure of the "Pyramid of Consciousness" or POC, is developed as a result of observation, experimentation and analysis of the process to increase one's consciousness. It is the basis for understanding this entire book. It serves as an internal guide and structure that will allow us to understand the stages through which we will go as we progress on our path towards self-awareness, enlightenment and evolution. Each section will provide corresponding lessons to facilitate this process.

The pyramid works just like a video game. When passing from one level to another it is very important to put into practice what has been learned and apply it whenever and wherever there is an opportunity. This way, you can consolidate all concepts and jump to the next stage, since the level of knowledge is cumulative and difficulty increases.

The level of the pyramid in which we are on is proportionate to the level of required effort or difficulty. For example, the lower level might necessitate greater effort but will be relatively simple, while the middle to upper levels will likely be more difficult. In either case, the important thing is not where we are but where we are going. We could aim to reach the top or, even better, we could measure our effort according to how much we have evolved. However, whatever our strategy, we will have to ascend it alone because our path of personal and spiritual enlightenment is a "DIY"(do-it-yourself) job. Nobody can carry you.

This framework will help us recognize and internalize our own observations and insights. With practice, we will be able to see that each lesson brings its own challenges and benefits. Some will be easier than others. The key is to try your best to absorb the concepts and persevere through the pages, while continually applying the knowledge gained wherever and whenever possible. This will increase your consciousness.

As we move forward, the new knowledge gained will allow us to connect with our original essence and help us strengthen our own inner spiritual connection. We'll be able to better understand ourselves and motivations – who we are, how we can improve ourselves, what we like/dislike and how we can reach our goals. Our approach to life will be motivated by either love (positive) or fear (negative), both of which exist within us. Before we move on to the next lesson, we need to understand how the pyramid as well as the love and fear base works. Only then can we discover (and embrace!) our authentic self.

The shape of the pyramid of consciousness represents the general percentage of people in the world who are in the different consciousness stages or evolution, with the bottom base being the biggest. Most people are in the lowest levels. The summit (the top of the pyramid), where there is enlightenment, is where we begin to transcend into the more spiritual realm.

Visual Representation of the POC

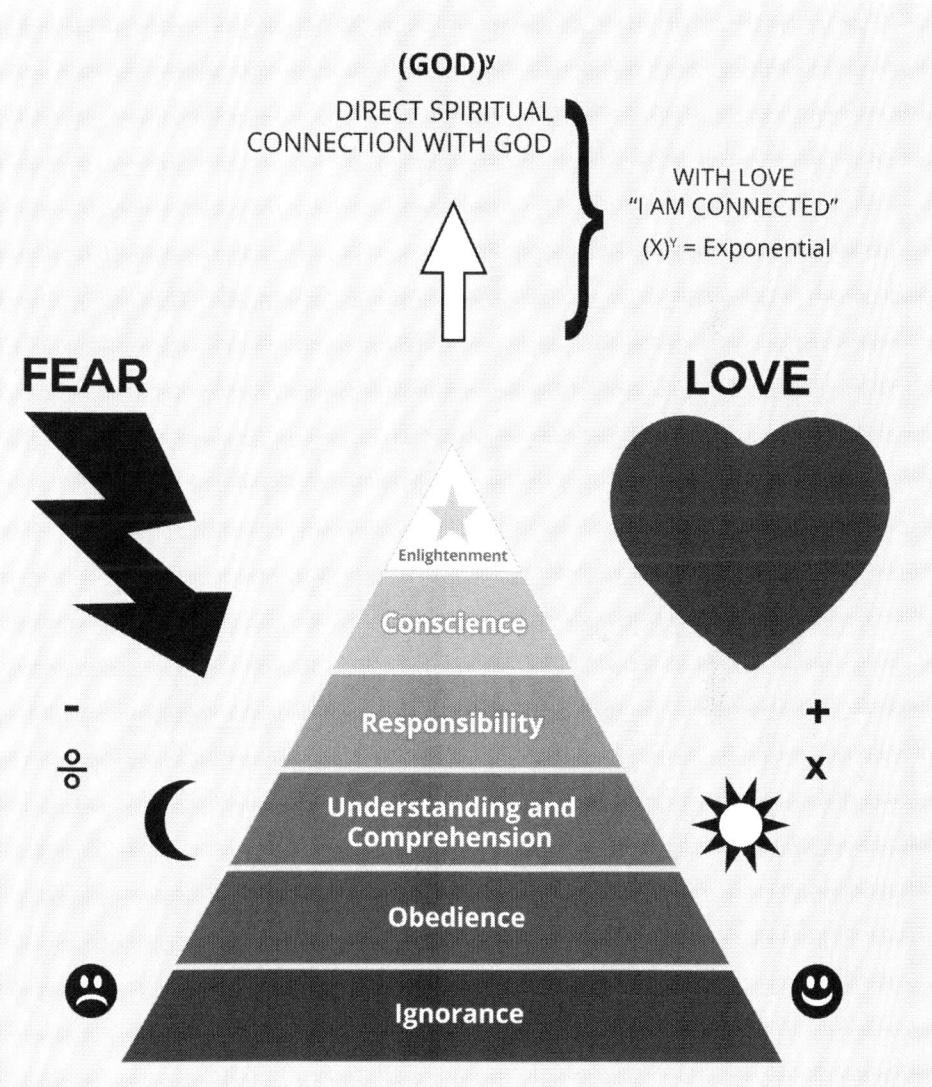

From the point of view of the reader, on the right side, is where the heart representing love is located. On the left is fear, which is symbolized by a thunderbolt. Starting from the base, the first two levels refer to ignorance and obedience and are related to our animal instincts and innate/primitive desires.

The pyramid is made by five levels plus the summit. It means that they comprise a total of six levels that follows the order of the rainbow colors (or chakras). The individual who wishes to raise his consciousness – and intelligence – a significant amount will need to advance at least to the next level. The higher up the pyramid, the more insight gained about how life works – and the greater likelihood to feel better, independent of situations or circumstance. Hence, the ultimate goal is reach the star of this communication and information system, which represents complete enlightenment.

The first main goal is to reach the "Love" stage when evolving or moving towards the top of the POC where the enlightenment is found. The six levels of the pyramid from most basic to most advanced:

1. Ignorance
2. Obedience
3. Understanding and Comprehension
4. Responsibility
5. Conscience
6. Enlightenment

Descriptions for each are as follows:

POC LEVELS	DESCRIPTION	EXPECTED RESPONSE
1. Ignorance	It is represented by our gut, and is guided and strongly influenced by our most primitive instincts. There is an innate lack of awareness. It is at this level when our instincts, desires and feelings predominate. Think of it as the animal part of the human being involved in eating, sleeping and reproducing. The general feeling associated with this can be apathy, survival or suffering, probably unconsciously so.	"I do not know anything."
2. Obedience	It is similar to Ignorance, but it takes into consideration that strict societal rules and norms — also applied to education to guide and rule us — produce a kind of short circuit in an individual, limiting his ability to think for himself and inhibiting his development process. It also represents the animal part of the unconscious human being.	"Whatever it may be, I will do it."
3. Understanding and Comprehension	It is personified by the mind. The individual is able to recognize, discern and interpret his internal and external stimuli.	"I understand and comprehend, therefore I am."
4. Responsibility	This level is located in the heart. The individual feels an obligation to take ownership over what he says and does.	"I will do the best I can" (usually for me).
5. Conscience	It is embodied by the soul. The individual is able to have a more holistic view of not only what affects him but what affects society as a whole.	"I will do my best for all."
6. Enlightenment	It is symbolized by the spirit which we connect with when we are aligned with the common good. The individual feels compelled to act in the best interest of others.	"I will do the best for others."

There may be concepts in the following lessons that might seemingly conflict with each other, but as we move towards the POC summit, you will gain more clarity and know how to discern the appropriate use in each case. For example, you will learn more about how "our reactions are our teachers" (first POC level) and we have "the right to speak," (third POC level), and how best to respond in any given situation, just like how you would instinctually know when to use a knife or a pair of scissors when doing a craft. The more you practice, the more skilled you will become and the right life tool you will be able to select.

The concepts in this guide need to not only be understood and analyzed but must be internalized, put into practice and perfected, as is the case of having less jealousy and less resistance each time. This type of learning depends on the person and a period of time suitable to each individual through understanding and personal spiritual practice. In addition, because some terms are initially obtuse or temporal, always continue practicing to understand and apply them.

Generally, I also considered that each level of the Pyramid of Consciousness (POC) develops its equivalent in conscience whenever the lesson are owned and applied at all times. It also includes the body, mind and soul practice.

In cases when individuals stop using the lessons learned from this guide, they will risk the advantages of living on a higher level of the pyramid, as they are likely to render some of the skills they have acquired unusable. Think of it like muscle memory. If you don't use it, you lose it. This can negatively impact their state of consciousness, while the newly acquired or discovered abilities become blurred or lost.

CREATING A STRONG FOUNDATION

PART 2

CREATING A STRONG FOUNDATION

HOW LOVE AND FEAR WORK

When I was creating the structure of this book, I realized that I was missing a fundamental piece of the puzzle that I had not yet managed to decipher. It was not until I was able to comprehend the general functioning of love and fear — and the polarity between them — that I could begin to analyze and describe how it applied to personal relationships. The rest of my understanding in terms of how it all worked together came through the questions I asked and learned about it.

It is important to understand how love and fear work, and identify the consequences and responses of living in one side or another. In order to truly know ourselves and move forward, we need to be very honest with who we are. This means asking questions that we may never have considered, and trying to really find out in what base (approach from love or fear) we find ourselves most of the time. This will enable us to then set goals for improvement by recognizing the moments in which we act according to the basis of love or fear.

The lessons we will see later on in this book will help us clarify and better understand which behaviors lead us to love, such as supporting someone's development, or towards fear, such as criticizing an acquaintance or creating negative rumors.

It is important that we do not judge ourselves throughout this process and to simply be as transparent as possible in order to accurately identify which self-improvement areas need more focus or more effort.

Love

Love is an energy of openness, expansion, affection, compassion, transformation, happiness, serenity, gratitude and growth, which is replenished from the universe. Whenever we express love, we receive its energy. True love is genuine, does not have an agenda, and does not require reciprocation from another. Love can also be associated with terms such as freedom, responsibility or consciousness.

When the feeling of love overflows and is transmitted to all, it is characteristic of unconditional love. Individuals who are purely motivated by love will always win in the end, with expansion of their mind as its reward. This is where we would all like to live, although only a few actually know it.

Fear

Fear is an energy opposed to love, of disconnection, anger, pessimism, stagnation, limitations, oppression, anxiety, sadness and jealousy that is very easy to multiply if we let the feelings, emotions and experiences that we go through trap us.

Fear is subjective, and we create it ourselves when we have experiences that we do not like. It is also the instinctive function of the body that can inhibit learning.

The Process

A) Our Objective

The objective of our life plan is for us to go through certain experiences and expand our knowledge on how life works. Along the way we will find support and encounter challenges, which together with free will, enables us to define our life's path.

B) From Fear to Love

The spiritual purpose of life is to move from fear to love. Just like a butterfly must first exit its cocoon before it can fly, people need to go through the experience and then learn from it before unfolding their wings entirely. Likewise, those who have better guidance and orientation can move faster towards love and learning.

It is more difficult to learn something when we are controlled by fear because we repeat the same experiences over and over again. This prevents us from gaining insight, which traps us in fear. There is great difficulty in moving from fear to love; however, it is easier to escape from fear to a state of peace (an intermediate state between the two), to finally reach love.

C) The Dance between Fear and Love

Individuals can live in two opposing areas: love or fear. Both areas are not always stable in an individual since we fluctuate between one and the other. Therefore, the oscillations between the two mean that the way we face life is not something fixed, but is flexible and involves choice.

We tend to live part of the time in love and the other part in fear, and there are few who live 50% in love and the other 50% in fear. For the purposes of this book, we will assume that people have their base or are motivated primarily by love or by fear.

Choosing one or the other leads the individual to understand life from two different points of view that will influence his behaviors, thoughts, feelings and even his abilities. In other words, people can view the same reality very differently depending on their lens.

Along the way, our tendencies towards love and fear become balanced as we all fluctuate. Therefore, something can happen that completely changes the dynamics of the experience, and shift our view to the opposite side. You can start with love and end up with fear, or vice versa. For example, if we plan to spend a nice weekend with a new partner but if the event ends with physical or verbal aggression, the experience moves from love to fear.

The good news is that those whose lives are predominantly based in fear have the ability to migrate to love. There are little moments in which rigidity disappears whenever they connect with love – when they take advantage of the opportunity to transmit light to individuals, or find meaning in their experiences and expand their mind. It may also happen during these moments of light when the individual discovers his own path for the first time.

Nevertheless, it is also during these moments and openings when we change temporarily towards love, where great intellectual and scientific advances are achieved. It means that although those individuals who remain in fear most of their time, they can use these moments of observation and reflection to reach great discoveries, despite not having a strong base of love.

Innate or Learned?

It is an interesting debate about whether we are innately bent towards fear or love and the role that determining circumstances play in our life plan. However, during the course of life the experiences we go through can cause two situations to arise that potentially alter our approach or our emotional base:

1) Adaptation: Adaptation to the environment, conforming and acclimating to the situation. For example, if I travel

to Canada, I adapt to the cold environment by buying warm clothes, but I continue with my normal ways of life (seeking out like-minded people, enjoying my favorite foods, speaking my language, etc.)

2) Transformation: Implies a change (metamorphosis) as is the case of turning from a worm to butterfly. For example, I travel to Canada and immerse myself in their customs, traditions and culture, and I also leave behind my own norms so I can fully embrace new ones

Throughout life, one can experience the adaptation stage and then progress to transformation.

The Formative Years: How Life Perceptions Develop

Childhood plays a crucial role in the formulation of perceptions and attitudes. In their first years of life children are like sponges, and the composition of their fundamental pillars and general emotional motivations form a very important part of their worldview and approach. They can even be negatively impacted in the womb by stress, which may predispose them towards fear. These situations in which the child experiences physical, emotional or sensory stress may cause him to perceive life as a struggle or feel the need to continually defend or protect himself. It might make him more sensitive to physical or emotional triggers.

It is also possible for the child to move into fear whenever he is confused or frightened by experiences he does not understand or does not know how to manage. His survival instincts then kick in and trigger fear and angst. This is because our children, in their early childhood years, have a limited ability to understand what is really happening around them and the consequences their initial choices might have. Experiences lived by children do not have to be bad per se, but in some cases they can be misunderstood or misinterpreted when fear takes over. It is necessary to take into account that when they are so young, their actions are influenced by instinct and impulse, which can trigger fear very easily.

At times, the way parents, caregivers, tutors or educators teach children may also create confusion. Therefore, if we as adults have not learned to manage ourselves responsibly, and we let our feelings and thoughts flow when we want to, provoking unconscious responses to our children, in the form of yelling or beatings, these could also frighten the child. Children tend to absorb the emotional fears and instability of other individuals around them from an early age.

Personal Experience

I will share a story of happened to me when I was a child so I can better illustrate this earlier point about how the instinct of fear can easily be triggered in a child in a completely normal situation. I remember one day when we were on vacation in Portugal, my parents put my older sister and me in the car of a man and a woman who appeared to be a couple. I did not know them.

We were about seven and five years old, and had climbed into the back of the car and sat down comfortably. So far so good, except for me, because in my mind I attributed what was happening to a single conclusion: My parents had given us to these people to become their new daughters.

At that moment I remember thinking that my parents did not want us anymore because sometimes we behaved badly or they had grown tired of us, and this was our punishment. Obviously, my parents had a very complex and sensitive daughter. Something had caused me to be afraid in this moment, yet my sister was not. She was calm and happy, like always. Even though we were in the same predicament, and had grown up and were educated in very similar ways, our views of this experience differed in the same circumstance. And so did our reactions.

The difference was that I had a bias towards fear and was an obedient girl who did everything everybody told me, and yet my sister had a bias towards love and was rebellious, so she never accepted rules. I obeyed without questioning yet internalized my emotions. She questioned everything and externalized her emotions.

Opposites Attract

It is common for people to be attracted to others who are polar opposites. For example, there is a great majority of people who become a couple when they have a different polarity, that is, one whose predominant base is in love and the other's whose based in fear.

I've found that those with a higher level of consciousness usually seek out the other person for a specific purpose that goes beyond what they like about the other person. That is, individuals look at whether the individual with whom they want to commit is a relatively "good" person, instead of focusing only on those other qualities or attributes that attract them. For those based in love but whose partner is based in fear, I highly recommend stepping up (and away) – from your significant partner – , at least one level of the POC. This way the relationship works much better and is more balanced.

Food for Thought

The overall lesson is to always be mindful of your (and others') motivations in terms of thoughts, decisions and behaviors. Even a young child can be taught to become more self-aware and as a result make better choices. It all starts, though, with taking a moment to self-analyze.

Rather than instantly reacting to something (words, behaviors, etc.), stop and think. Perform a self-check. What impact will your response have on that person? On yourself? Will it help them or harm them? Is it a quick fix, or does it promote healthy long-term development? Ask yourself those questions, and you will become clearer in terms of how life works and how you can benefit from it.

PART 3

LESSONS TO RAISE ONE'S CONSCIOUSNESS

Our operational (mental, emotional and physical), and spiritual level of evolution depends exclusively on our attitude and the level of commitment that we are able to have in terms of understanding ourselves. Continually thinking that our development depends on the people who raised us or on those we meet on our life's journey will never get us very far. If we get stuck in habits, such as blaming others instead of ourselves and not owning responsibility, we will hardly evolve or improve our overall well-being, if at all. We can change ourselves and our path in life to reach a higher evolutionary level – but we need to be strong, courageous and fully committed in order to do so.

PART 3
LESSONS TO RAISE ONE'S CONSCIOUSNESS

FIRST PYRAMID LEVEL: IGNORANCE

"Ignorance is the mind's night;
but a night without moon or stars."
Confucius

THE ROLE EDUCATION PLAYS IN CHILDREN'S PERSONAL DEVELOPMENT

- *Mom, I don't want to eat anymore.*
- *Aren't you hungry? All right, pick up your dish.*
- *Mom, may I eat dessert?*
- *If you want dessert, then it is not because you are not hungry.*
  Mary, what do you think is the responsible answer to your
  question? Please think about it and explain to me your reasons.

Child education has changed considerably throughout the years. For the most part, it has evolved from a more strict and traditional framework to a more relaxed one. Children need love, support and wisdom from us. They demand different answers depending on each moment in order to consciously interpret and understand their circumstances. Dedicating some time to really talk with them, and teaching them how to be responsible as early as possible, are crucial to their long-term development as well as can increase their feelings of stability, security and self-worth.

It is my view that traditional education takes away students' freedom to make decisions and disempowers them to reach their full potential, and instead restricts them to rigid standards and rules so they won't behave in a certain way or be considered "bad." Therefore, part of what we are taught in traditional education could limit our ability to be strong in who we are and what we become. This differs from educational frameworks in other advanced countries where they empower children to increase their consciousness, build self-confidence and take responsibility for their actions. These teaching frameworks are centered in the discovery process and encourage students to open their eyes to the world of experiences and draw their own conclusions.

People are generally products of their origin, history, culture and circumstances, and parents tend to teach their children in the best way they can while drawing on what they themselves were taught from their parents. And while it is all well intentioned, it is often not effective or enough.

If we compare our current level of conventional knowledge, let's say scientific, with the level of knowledge about education applied to children, there is often a considerable gap. The reasons may not be fully clear why a country is more conscious than others but it is a fact that Spain (Europe) existed longer than other countries under a dictatorship (1939 – 1975). Hence, historical circumstances, such as being isolated from the outside world and having an authoritarian government, could have meant that the country and its citizens had not finished stripping off the old typical frameworks of traditional education, and were therefore slower to evolve than others. However, there are many countries today that follow the same system of traditional education based on cultural, political or religious reasons.

In their formative years, children need to truly understand the world in which they live. Parental help can act as a fundamental decoder to enable a child to view and interpret his world and develop perceptions, make better choices, and utilize coping mechanisms when faced with potential threats or challenges.

Pointing our Internal Compass in the Right Direction: Forward

Children store information from their experiences, which together with their genetics, culture and what is taught to them, guide their development in one way or another. Each of us is born with a different compass, similar to the phenomenon of fingerprints, where none is equal to another. However, sometimes if we do not investigate exactly how each internal compass works, we will not be able to fully nurture each child according to their needs in a responsible way. This is not optimal, of course. On the contrary, sometimes we decide to impose on children what we want or believe works, and in doing so strip them of their power and of the opportunity for them to pursue their own paths. Children are not robots, yet some people treat them as if they are.

When we teach children to develop their consciousness, punishing discipline in the form of scolding or shouting is not necessary. Sometimes educators do not know any better and so they resort to teaching through punishments or rewards. Punishment is counterproductive to helping others increase their consciousness. These punishments can leave a lasting mark on children and reinforce detrimental reactions and behaviors, such as the natural tendency to be motivated by fear.

Empowerment is Stronger than Discipline or Rewards

In other situations, some educators will implement a system that focuses so much on teaching children what they can and cannot do, and expects them to blindly follow all rules and obligations, the students will not build good judgment, reasoning and problem-solving skills. This presents a child from being able to understand situations later in life and think for himself. As they become adults, they then lack the ability to evaluate their situation or develop their consciousness. All they have learned to do is to simply obey rules (represented by the Obedience level on the POC), which is controlled by animal instinct.

Conscious (enlightened) children, on the other hand, will gradually take control of their lives by being aware, responsible and accountable. Overtime they develop their own power (the ability to exert change). However, responsibility must be taught in order to be learned. Educators and parents can enable children to learn such important life skills by explaining to them why and how things work – instead of just telling them that they work. Children can then evaluate matters themselves by weighing the costs versus the benefits of a decision, and then choose the right action. By doing so, they are empowered to think for themselves and not rely on others to think for them.

During this educational process, negotiating with children might be necessary if after evaluating a problem/solution, they choose the "wrong" action. Instead of forcing them to choose the right action, it is ideal to persuade and reason with them. The main objective for them is to feel good (valued and empowered!), grow their sense of responsibility, and develop a strong sense of stability, security and unconditional love. By allowing them to be their own person, and teaching them they're responsible for their own actions, we are encouraging them to develop their own consciousness and self-worth.

Much of today's society likes to reward children's behaviors with tangible rewards, like money or gifts, even bribes. But those are only shortcuts to achieve short-term results. It is their long-term development and life lessons they have learned that should matter most.

Children are not Robots

Sometimes, if children are overly restricted, they rebel or develop unhealthy patterns. This can lead to anxiety, resentment, even rage, which can be very damaging in the long run. Feeling continually oppressed, obligated, constricted and punished only generates negative energy that builds over time – until it finally becomes part of them or explodes.

Similarly, those children who have not reached a certain level of consciousness and are not motivated to be responsible or accountable will struggle with even the simplest of tasks, like good hygiene practices, chores or studying. The only way they will complete those tasks is if they're required to, instead of being motivated to take care of one's self. They only do things because they robotically follow rules or obligations. Obedience instead of personal responsibility drives them, which stifles their ability to be self-governing.

As a child, my energy was fueled by fear and rules, which diminished me over time and made me feel small. It negatively impacted almost every aspect of my life. I started to struggle with academics and studying. I stopped feeling passionate about learning and became apathetic. I stopped being the girl who loved to develop her mind and study. Rather than trying to learn and comprehend things, I simply memorized. Everything became more difficult and more boring. The Spanish educational system at the time did not promote active learning, yet somehow I managed to progress forward.

It is important to note that I recognize that parents and schools generally have good intentions and want children to receive the best possible education. However, we can develop our conscience (and consciousness) at the same time we lose our internal guide due to the confusion that others can generate to kids. I use my own experience as examples not to criticize or reprimand, but rather to offer insight and ideas that can improve our current educational system – worldwide.

THE GAP BETWEEN EASY AND DIFFICULT

- ROBERT: Mom, this is very easy.
- PATRICIA: No, it is difficult. I am not getting it right.
- MOTHER: Try again Patricia and you will learn it. What is
happening to you is that you still don't know how to do it. Here
is another button and more string. Practice and you will see that
very soon it will be easy for you too.

When people refer to something as "easy" or "difficult," what are they essentially saying? *Easy* means that we know how to do something (i.e., I know how to do it). When it is *difficult*, it means that we have not yet learned it (i.e., I do not know how to do it). Humans learn from experience, so as much as we're told how to do something, sometimes we just need to actually do it where it makes sense. For example, if we want to ski we can collect information from books, videos, specific programs for beginners, but until we find ourselves on a snowy mountain trying to keep our balance and sliding, we can never truly learn to ski. We can admire the sand on a beach, but we do not truly know what it feels like until we wiggle our toes in it.

Neither do we learn if the event is experienced by others, no matter how close it is to us. We must experience it ourselves. When we are on the higher levels of the Pyramid of Consciousness, our comprehension of our own life increases, but we can only observe and theorize that of others. Each person's development towards consciousness is different and personal to them. We all must travel our own journey in life. And we must be courageous to seek out new adventures and challenges.

THE BALANCE BEAM OF LIFE: HOMEOSTASIS AND MOTIVATIONS

- Lucy, get up, you have to go to the university.
- Yes, I know. Five more minutes and I'll get up.
- Lucy, come on! I'm about to leave. You have five minutes to get out the door.

The body is governed by fight-or-flight instincts that are programmed to survive and reproduce. It also has an internal animal preservation system called *homeostasis* that tries to maintain a stable equilibrium.

There are times when the body wants to stay as it is and not spend energy to preserve its current state. Sometimes when we're feeling "lazy," our body is telling us to rest. There are people who fight every day against homeostasis and overcome it, just like there are others who succumb and let animal instincts win the game.

The problem is when you remain in one state for a very long time. Constantly doing nothing, for example, prevents people from important learning opportunities that can come to them through life experiences. However, on the other hand, continually being on-the-go without ever stopping to rest and being consumed with so many things can distract you from valuable insights and lessons you could have picked up along the way.

When we develop a higher sense of responsibility, we also increase our level of consciousness and as a result can learn things faster and easier. But it's a process for many, with the first challenge being to push through the Ignorance stage (which can cause confusion and hardship) in order to eventually reach the light and learn what life is continually teaching us.

Understanding What Motivates Us

Ever wonder why some people are inspired to work long hours while others would rather spend that time relaxing on the couch? It is because people are motivated differently depending on their values. There are two different types of motivation: extrinsic and intrinsic.

Extrinsic motivation occurs when we do something in order to receive an external reward (money, grades, praise) or to prevent something from happening (fear). This exchange of something for something else is referred to as *transactional*. For example, if I pass with good grades, my parents will reward me with a summer trip. This type of motivation generally works best with individuals at the bottom of the pyramid.

Intrinsic motivation is where one does not need to be externally rewarded because he receives internal pleasure or satisfaction from it (enjoyment, fulfillment). People who are intrinsically motivated tend to complete things by themselves – without nagging or threats – and do not expect anything in return (similar to the act of unconditional love). For example, when I was in school, I studied many hours for an exam and felt good about my strong work ethic. Actions are performed conscientiously and responsibly. This motivation usually works best with individuals located in the upper part of the pyramid of consciousness.

The type of reward system applied to education plays a key role in the development of consciousness. Implementing strict rules to try to improve and control what children do, for example, could cause them to become dependent on extrinsic motivation factors. The negative impact is that they will then only complete things when they expect rewards, which might work in the short-term, but in the long-term, it prevents them experiencing the inner joy and satisfaction of a job well done.

Living Purposely

Without proper instruction, guidance and inspiring motivations, we as human beings tend not to evolve much beyond the comforts of homeostasis, which keeps us stuck. However, when we experience enthusiasm and inner motivation in our work, as well as know our purpose and passions in life, fighting homeostasis becomes much easier. Eventually the urge to do very little fades out of our lives because we learn to live fully, with meaning and responsibility, and apply our mind, heart and soul to everything we do.

Life is wondrous and offers many insights and growth opportunities; its journey is personal and different for each person. Depending on his innate traits, environmental circumstances and basic needs/desires, each individual will define his own life's path. Life does leave many clues along that path, but the problem is that many of us are not good disciples (i.e., desire to be taught) and we prefer to shut our eyes and ignore what happens around us. We develop tunnel vision, and instead of looking for the lessons from challenges we face or mistakes we make, we look elsewhere – and do not grow.

THE ABCs OF HOW LIFE WORKS

> - *STUDENT: Why did this happen to me again? I do not deserve it. I do not understand it. I study, I do all my school chores and I behave well. Why do the same things that I do not like always happen again and again?*
> - *PARENT: It is obvious you are not learning about life. You go through experiences without learning from mistakes, and so they happen to you again. How many times do I need to tell you?*

As explained in the previous section, current parenting and educating practices can (and should) improve. Of course, this is not to say that there are many wonderful ways in which today's students are learning not just about academics but about life; however, the typical educational system is convoluted and plagued with incorrect teaching frameworks – many of which forget that the ultimate lesson is the life skill that is taught. This makes learning more complex and slows down growth development. The focus is on where we are going (the destination) but not on where we start the journey.

The Natural Progression of Learning

We are largely conditioned to think a certain way and accept things for what they are, for many of us have simply inherited the thinking patterns and beliefs that were passed down to us by previous generations. In some ways, we are taught what to think – not *how* to think. But as the world continues to evolve, so must we, and I have fortunately found that society is starting to shift towards empowering children to have more of a say in what they learn and do, which is inspiring to see.

Still, for the most part, many individuals are unaware of how the learning process about how life works is actually carried out: how one must first push through moments of confusion into moments of clarity, effectively moving them from darkness to light. For that reason, we must first embrace this challenge by getting lost and experiencing a period of turbulence and suffering (emptiness, pain, hunger, depression, sadness) in order to then make sense of *what* we experienced and *why* we experienced it. Ideally, we would analyze the experience in depth from different perspectives in order to acquire more knowledge, and fully comprehend and react accordingly.

To better understand this concept of how we learn, consider the parable of the prodigal son that appears in the Bible. In this case, one of the sons asks the father for his inheritance, which is eventually spent in its entirety during his stay in another country. The boy then suffers through a period of hunger and misery until he decides to finally return home so he can apply for a job as a day laborer and ask his father for forgiveness. With grace, the father receives him with open arms. Feeling blessed to have recovered his son again, he organizes a great celebration for his son. The father explains it very well with a few words when he says: "He was lost and has been found" (Luke 15, 1-3, 11-32). When we learn from experiences and understand all the factors that played into them, we can better understand motivations, actions and life lessons – and move closer to the base of love.

The life choices can make our learning process longer or shorter. Therefore, it will depend on how we manage and react to moments that will move us closer to either the darkness or the light. Our choices depend on whether we are spiritually guided or innately guided, and our own free will decide the final choice.

The problem is that sometimes we prefer to ignore life's guidance or clues because we simply do not want to make the effort (homeostasis) that it requires to actively stop, look and listen to what is around us and within us. Sometimes we are distracted by outside influences or factors that prevent us from analyzing and understanding our situations, and so we stay in the same place with no possibility of progress. It is not until another moment or opportunity arrives when we can see it again and decide (or not) to learn from the experience and perhaps evolve into the next consciousness phase. If we were more responsible we could evolve more quickly instead of waiting for similar situations to come to us – some of which can be so intense, we wonder how we can ever move on from them.

"THE LAWS": CAUSE AND EFFECT VS. REVELATION

- JASON: Alan, you fell down again. You are so clumsy! I mean...
You are not good at anything ... hahahaha!
Two seconds later, a soccer ball hit Jason directly in the face. The
consequences were a black eye and a broken nose.
- ALAN: Are you OK, Jason? Can you hear me?
Alan immediately went to help the passed-out Jason and ensured
that he got his friend to the hospital as fast as possible.

Whether or not we believe in the fundamental laws of life (unseen laws that influence our lives), the idea of them is very interesting. Two of them are the law of cause and effect, and the law of revelation.

You Get What You Give

The universal law of cause and effect, also known as *karma*, essentially means that what we sow is what we will end up collecting. For every effect, there is also a cause – and vice versa. This law is also related to Newton's third law: "For every action, there is an equal and opposite reaction." Therefore, all our thoughts, behaviors and acts have consequences. For example, if we treat our friends with love and respect, they will likely respond to us in the same way; or if we mistreat a person, at some point they may do so to us as well. Think of a boomerang. If we throw it hard, it can go very far, but sooner or later it will return to its origin.

Karma does not start only with negative acts, but also with positive ones. Every action has consequences: good or bad. The law of cause and effect is also set in motion through words, thoughts and even feelings. Therefore, it is crucial to be very careful about what or where we put our mind and feelings, for often we become what we think.

The law of cause and effect is not absolute, however. Regardless of what happens, people still have free will, that is, they decide how to proceed or what to do in each situation. They have a choice. Imagine that we are about to have dinner with family and our hungry selves start eating before everybody has joined the table. Later, when we realize we were rude, we try to amend it by cooking or preparing some tasty sandwiches for them. In this case, a wrong was corrected with a right. Let us always try not to do to others what we would not like them to do to us.

If we did something wrong we could, of course, try to solve the problem and/or apologize. However, the best thing in all cases is to always act in good faith, with good intentions and without wanting to hurt anyone. Preventing the wrong act is always more ideal than repenting (or regretting!) one.

Another example: Suppose we get fired from work. As we have free will (choice), we could opt to: 1) stay home, cry and send bad feelings towards the company and our boss, or 2) decide to get up early the next day and hunt for work with a smile, seeing this as an opportunity to get something better and try to create a more beneficial future.

Ride the Wave

The law of revelation means that the teachings that come to us from life will only be learned if we are ready to receive them. Therefore, being a proficient student has its rewards, since it allows us to be prepared to surf the corresponding wave whenever a lesson rolls in. This way, we can face the situations that happen to us and find the lesson, instead of simply letting events happen to us without realizing it and then wondering why we feel the way we do. Remember to always be prepared and ready to catch life's wave.

The way we view situations or events influences our behaviors, which when repeated over and over again becomes conditioned patterns (or habits). Similar to muscle memory, those habitual behaviors are done automatically or without thinking. For instance, telling ourselves "what a fool I am" when making a mistake, or always taking the same route to the supermarket, are patterns. There are constructive habits, but there also destructive ones, which can, if unchecked, harm us. And over time, we are unaware of these automatic thoughts or behaviors. Our inner voice that always tell us we're fat or stupid is a conditioned destructive thinking pattern, for example.

THE MONKEY'S MIND

- I'm sorry, Emma, today I am really preoccupied. I know I need to concentrate on my work, but I am dealing with some personal problems right now and I cannot get them off my mind.
- Don't worry, Allison, sometimes it is better to put a project aside and do something else. It can wait until tomorrow.
- Thank you for understanding! I will start checking the designs that are pending.

Our brain loves to be active and is always searching for something that keeps it occupied – it never stops thinking. But sometimes, especially at night, when the mind becomes uncontrollable or overwhelming, it can cause us to feel agitated or restless or confused, which can be described by the psychological metaphor, "monkey mind." This state of mind can cause severe distress and is often difficult to calm or silence, especially without the proper training to do so.

There are ways we can tame the mind to observe, focus and discern. This process is key to developing the capability of consciousness. We are born with unconscious minds, in that we have not learned yet how to control our mind and focus it. Sometimes one never learns how to do it, but the good news is that through the right training, it is possible no matter the age.

Specifically, *monkey mind* is a Buddhist term to describe those times when we feel our head has so much going on in it that we feel dizzy or that our mind will explode. It is as if we have several people speaking (and even shouting!) all at the same time in our brain. Sometimes the conversations or questions generated by the brain itself are so absurd or mundane that, if it were not something almost involuntary, we would make sure to stop doing it so that we could feel calmer and less anxious.

How many times have you wanted to stop thinking about something – and couldn't? This type of restless thinking can plague us any time, at work, at home, right before bed. It becomes problematic when these thoughts are negative or counterproductive to our own development, and so it is important to learn how to change this pattern of thinking.

The monkey mind is like a wild horse that we cannot stop if it is not deliberately trained. If we cannot control the behavior and repeatedly run those thoughts in our head throughout the day, it is not uncommon to feel bad at night, beaten up, guilty, or mentally exhausted. Continually thinking about a mistake we made is enough to make anybody feel like a bad person at the end of the day. And even though we go to sleep, the monkey mind still persists.

Taming the Monkey

When we cannot control our mind and we feel like "we're losing it," there are several ways to reduce its intensity. Many people use breathing and relaxation techniques. To do this, in a sitting position, close your eyes and begin to inhale and exhale, counting the number of inhalations performed. Sometimes, the mind starts to wonder and loses count, and in this case, one should start over from scratch. Fifty inhalations at a time is an ideal target. The main thing is to keep trying to relax the brain as many times as possible and only stop until your mental state has improved and you feel calmer.

Other people prefer other mediation or spiritual practice techniques, like reciting verses or praying the rosary or listening to a phrase or mantra that helps calm and focus the mind. I prefer the method of focused breathing, although I sometimes use alternate techniques. Also, I find comfort in reading a spiritual guide that helps me to center and align my energies in ways that are more constructive. Occasionally I listen to some music, with the genre depending on what I need in the moment.

It is very rewarding to me to help children calm their monkey minds. In order to help them develop the ability to recognize (and respond to) a monkey mind, I explain to them that their brain is very active and has not learned yet how to be focused, which can cause them to feel anxious or fearful or out of control. In particular I tell them that if they feel bad about something for a long period of time, it is because the "monkey" has taken control of their brains and is causing negative self-talk to spiral out of control. The monkey has taken over and is in charge. At this point, I reassure and empower them that they can take control back by telling themselves that they are not this monkey.

In some cases when the monkey does not cease, I encourage children to visualize locking the monkey in a mental cage. Sometimes the monkey figures out how to escape, so it is important for the child to realize that he might need to continually return the monkey to the cage as many times as needed. When the child eventually realizes the power of the mind to distort reality, he becomes enlightened and discovers he can control that power. It is the monkey making him feel bad, not himself. And now there is something positive the child can do about it.

THE POISON OF RESENTMENT

- Martha, you have to be home at ten-thirty.
- Mother, until eleven o'clock, please. That is the time my friends arrive.
- Do not contradict me. I told you ten-thirty, end of story.

Resentment is a feeling of displeasure or bitterness that is felt more than once (re-feeling). When we get upset or angry about something, for example, such emotion causes us pain. It is a negative feeling, possibly in the form of anger that we have towards an individual. In this case, it means the act is not forgiven and we hold onto that emotion for a period of time, until the anger turns in resentment. It is common to experience resentment with regards to love, for example. The pain of lost loves or old wounds can often stay with us, causing resentment towards the current or former partner.

Resentment can also occur in situations in which a family, partner or authority member tries to control how we behave, think or live. Our freedom to speak or act is taken away, and we have to sacrifice our own rights and expressions in order maintain relationship "harmony" with the other. In these cases, there is no negotiation between the parties to reach an understanding, since one imposes himself on the other. Meanwhile resentment grows.

In relationships in general, forced cession of personal liberties tends to build resentment and internally damages us, often without us realizing it. We do not recognize it is happening at the time, and so we express our feelings through various behaviors. Think of an old-style pressure cooker. If it is left on the stove for too long, it eventually explodes to release that pressure. Rather than continually bottling up resentment, we unconsciously or consciously turn our pressure valve to release some of the pressure buildup. In some ways, these outlets to release steam are healthy, such as getting in touch with nature (walk outside, etc.), going out with friends, watching or playing sports, or being intimate with our partner.

There are, however, negative actions that result from pent-up frustration and resentment. These actions could result from feeling unloved, for example, or experiencing too much mental/physical stress. Sometimes they materialize into rebellious or even disturbing behaviors like, for example, drinking excessive alcohol daily or physically hurting others. However, many times we do not connect these actions to our internal feelings, and are therefore not conscious of how our mind directly affects our behaviors. Over time, this can destroy us.

This concept is often illustrated with the proverb: "It is the last straw that breaks the camel's back," which means a seemingly small or routine action can cause an unexpected large reaction – not because of the small act but because of the cumulative effect of repeated small actions. Often, we continually (and unconsciously) internalize resentment and continue to compound it in our imaginary receivable account. Meanwhile pressure builds. At the most unpredictable time, that account will reach its maximum limit, and the negative effects that follow (or explode!) can be toxic.

To protect ourselves from the harmful effects of resentment, we can responsibly and consciously decide to react to others' words and actions without anger. Instead of holding a grudge against that person, we have the power and freedom to choose to let it go and, thus, not create resentment against him. This way, we can use it as an opportunity to learn and grow. It is important to remember that we have a choice in terms of how we respond and what we take away from the experience. We choose to be angry or choose to be tolerant. The key is to become aware of our feelings and emotions, recognize their influence on our way of living, and learn how to respond in a healthy way. This is how we move closer to the light.

EGO, PERSONALITY AND INNER WAR

- Be careful, General, they are going to shoot at us!
- What are you saying, Lieutenant?
- They are shooting! Watch out... Take cover!
- They hit you ... General! You are bleeding! Don't worry. I'll send the doctor right away.
- What are you saying, Lieutenant? Don't send anybody. I am not injured. It must be somebody else's blood. I am fine, I don't feel anything. Let's keep moving!

As part of our animal instincts, we all have the same inherent basic need to survive; however, we as human beings differ in our level of mental, emotional and spiritual development. From a spiritual perspective, we either have an open or closed heart. Those who have open hearts are generally kind towards others and demonstrate empathy and compassion. Their heart, much more than their mind, decodes reality and shapes their worldview.

On the other hand, those with closed hearts live in fear and are socially disconnected from the world. It is as if they live in a confined and dark place, surrounded by walls. Most of them are still in the most basic states (lower part) of the Pyramid of Consciousness, and find it very difficult to see or move forward, as they are lost and blocked.

Me, Myself and I

It affects how we see ourselves and others, which is shaped largely by our ego. The ego is part of one's mind that mediates between what is conscious and what is unconscious, which defines their perception of reality and their personal identity. The problem that exists when speaking about ego is similar to what happens when one talks about karma – they only see the negative side. Ego (self-identity) and personality (expression of that identity) go hand in hand. Hence, both are the same as well as the interplay of how we manifest and interact with the world. This book will later discuss how our mental and physical bodies can coexist and optimally interact with the world around us.

Meanwhile, it is important to recognize our internal war, which creates conflict within us that we may or may not be aware of. An example of internal warfare can occur when we become angry with or jealous of someone (thereby disrupting our inner peace), and we react accordingly. However, since we typically do not externally articulate these inner conflicts, third parties do not understand these reactions. Passive aggressiveness, which we will explore later, is a great example of how unexpressed anger or resentment can manifest.

This emotional war may have one or more internal conflicts occurring, perhaps in different phases, and is located within one's ego. If there was no ego there would be no inner wars; therefore, internal warfare is a manifestation of the ego. For example, somebody with a disease will likely have physical symptoms. You cannot see the actual internal disease, but you can recognize its physical traits. Just like others cannot see our emotional wars but they will notice and judge us by our actions. However, when an individual becomes self-aware of his internal conflicts and increases his level of consciousness, he can better manage his emotions and behaviors.

The external symptoms of a turbulent emotional war can manifest in headaches, sleeping problems, skin issues and other ailments. These conflicts can come from multiple sources, but the important thing is how we unknowingly trigger them to occur. Therefore, what is important in understanding what is happening within us is not necessary who/what created those emotions, but how they are being expressed outwardly. Over time, if we do not resolve our inner struggles, we can become apathetic, numb or even ignore them altogether, just like a closed heart.

The Outward Expression of our Ego

Our personality is essentially our projected image (character and traits) to other people. This image is composed of a "higher self" (emotional intelligence) and a "lower self" (animal instinct). There is often internal conflict between the two. For example, what we want versus what we need, or knowledge versus instinct. This means that sometimes our interface/personality is focused on one side or the other. Sometimes what we have been taught is right is different than what we feel is right, for example. Internal conflicts are what causes us confusion or stress us.

To help me better understand this concept, my mentor shared with me the following hypothetical. Imagine a country (the person) that is in the middle of a civil war, where neither side (ego1 and ego2) wants to understand the other and would rather internally struggle.

The fact that inner war appears in us means that there are two opposing sides, each operating at its own level with its own desires and goals. The result is often lack of understanding or comprehension because they cannot agree to find a "middle or neutral point" or compromise. There is no willingness/ability to negotiate, and therefore no middle ground. Expressed in another way, a conflict also occurs when our anger prevents the inner peace we want so much. One side of our ego is fighting the other side. In other words, our "higher self" (which is more evolved with higher emotional intelligence) battles our "lower self" (less evolved and fueled by animal instincts). The consequence: No side prevails because no compromise is reached. Division in the form of conflict appears.

Internal struggles can occur when we are conflicted between the motivations of love and fear, although as we move toward love the internal struggles virtually disappear. In the end, like most wars, if we are not self-aware and continue to battle without finding the source of our problems, we cannot fix them. In the event that internal conflicts blind us, this will mean that we are fighting a war that someone has imposed on us or we are applying someone else's rules.

Distorted Perceptions of Reality

In general, our internal struggles can at first manifest themselves in seemingly healthy behaviors. For example, an adult can sleep a lot and very "well," which might be interpreted as a positive pattern. However, it might actually be a sign that the person is suffering from prolonged internal stress and is not only mentally but physically exhausted because of it. When the person is sleeping, the brain starts cleansing and repairing. Sleep regulation is actually a healthy brain mechanism we are born with, but it could be manipulated and damaged partially at any point in our lives. In fact, one of the signs of depression can be prolonged periods of sleep.

An individual on the first level of the Pyramid of Consciousness who is continually experiencing inner strife does not yet know how much it distorts his reality and influences his behaviors. Because he is unaware of the internal conflict with his ego, he naturally assumes he is accurately interpreting his surroundings and others' motivations/behaviors. He believes he is intuitive and is in the right, and so he judges and blames others for mistakes and situations. He believes that his truth matters more than that of others, which gives him self-permission to do as he pleases without consideration of others. He does not think he needs to change and therefore dismisses any opportunity to learn or evolve. Of course, others recognize his distorted sense of reality but realize they cannot change what he cannot see.

Using this same example, the man also decides to separate certain feelings from his situational context, rather than acknowledging that those feelings are influencing his surroundings. Instead, he blindly blames the person or persons who he thinks made him have those feelings. The result: anger and/or resentment against those whom he believes, directly or indirectly, have hurt him. And so he plots his revenge.

We have the ability to prolong various conflicts within us, either by continually interacting with people we have argued with, or even incessantly thinking about it. Sometimes the conflict can last for several weeks (or months or years!) until resolved. If we continue to see it only through our lens and maintain our ego is always "right," our pride and lack of empathy will be our undoing. The problem will never be solved, and the pressure-cooker of resentment will build.

However, if we work to change our mindset and become more conscious of our internal struggles (motivations, feelings, etc.), we can more easily assess situations, find healthy coping mechanisms and respond accordingly in a matter of minutes. As we become more self-aware, it is important to remember that self-analysis skills always need to be practiced and improved. Whenever we feel we have evolved to a healthy mental and emotional state, we should be mindful that life is always throwing us curve balls and we need to prepare ourselves for the next game. Learning is infinite, and life makes us actively practice and consciously evolve by putting us in new positions or challenges, some of which can cause internal conflicts.

In any case, the key thing is that we continue to learn more and more even though there will be times when we face new challenges and will feel discouraged. The more insight and experience we collect, the faster we can understand people and situations because we likely know what to expect and how to react to avoid suffering.

DISEASES: HOW OUR EMOTIONAL STATE AFFECTS OUR PHYSICAL SELF

I do not know how I could treat him so badly yesterday; I mean, he has always helped me out when I needed him. Why was I so angry? I don't know, but I do know I regret it. Well, I will see this as a learning opportunity and will not allow this to happen again. I have to control my sudden mood swings more. I can only hope that he will forgive me when I apologize and tell him what I really feel and that no matter what happens, we will always be friends.

It is common at funerals for people to eulogize the deceased. However, I have noticed that some people who speak well of that person have actually criticized him every day while he was alive. Is it because they now have put aside negative feelings and reflected on the person's merits and what truly matters? Do they just feel guilty? Why wait until people die to realize that other human beings are very similar to us and that what we don't like about them might actually be a reflection of what we don't like about ourselves? It is up to us to change our thoughts about others – not at their funeral, but at this precise second! We often choose to direct love or fear towards others based on what we direct towards ourselves. If you do not like yourself, for example, chances are you will not like many others.

Being (and feeling!) alive, especially when we are in good health, is a gift many of us do not value until we lose it. We should be continually grateful how scientific and technological advancements have come a long way and can remedy diseases that were incurable a few years ago. We have medicines and knowledge that were previously unimaginable, such as cures for fatal infections, and extraordinary surgical procedures, such as heart transplants. We are extremely fortunate, yet many of us are still so grumpy and so ungrateful.

There are theories and much debate today, especially those that deal with alternative medicine, discussing claims that diseases are often created by our own selves. For example, personal conflicts of some sort are translated by the body in various ways and manifested in physical symptoms, pain, illness or even chronic diseases.

In my view, illness is often an indicator that something does not work well within us. We can try to discover it through personal introspection or internal analysis of our thoughts, feelings and actions, with the goal being to solve the conflict and perhaps be able to heal our body, if possible.

Finding the Good in the Bad

I have found that diseases can teach us something. Analyzing our symptoms and drawing connections between them and our internal struggles can provide guidance in helping us detect what is wrong with us, and perhaps point out clues towards a solution. In fact, the famous phrase "mens sana in corpore sano" (or "healthy mind in a healthy body") could be reinterpreted literally by changing the word order to "healthy body in a healthy mind." That is, if we have a clean mind and no internal personal conflicts, the body will be healthy.

Nowadays there are some training guides, self-help books and ancient knowledge practices that tie specific illnesses to their possible causes that can help us better understand diseases. It is also believed that certain fatal cancers in adults can result from great personal dilemmas or "life-defining moments," which adds to the sense of urgency of why there is currently so much focus on understanding the connection between the body and the mind.

Health problems that plague older generations are sometimes the universe's way of teaching them to address things (i.e., longstanding stressful issues) they might not have wanted to face or accept in the past. As "old age" begins to set in, some of us tend to become more self-reflective, and rather than thinking we are invincible, we begin to realize that the older we become, the faster we need to learn more – maybe to avoid suffering in the form of diseases. This newfound vulnerability decreases our pride and opens our eyes to the possibility that we may not understand our physical/emotional self as much as we had thought.

The Purpose of Pain

Diseases often culminate in pain (sometimes great pain!) that serves two primary functions. The first function is to challenge our ego (our sense of invincibility, for example), and the second has a more physical function, which is to warn us that something is wrong in our body. If we have intense pain, the body lowers both our mental and physical resistance, and can often make us feel less powerful and more vulnerable. This can humble us and prompt a self-investigation into what is happening to us. However, if we sense only physical pain, but still felt healthy and strong, we might push past the pain, ignore the external information and not bother to find what is wrong.

In my experience, I have found that when the mind is not positively balanced with the body, there can be internal and physical stress. The pain grows and in some cases can become quite intense. I used to experience much mouth pain whenever I visited the dentist for a simple cleaning. However, as my mind continued to be enlightened over the years and I have become more aware of my emotional triggers, I have created more internal balance. As a result, my pain receptors are not as sensitive, and I am happy to report that now when I visit the dentist, I feel no pain. Definitely something to smile about!

The same thing happened with my menstrual period. When I used to have a lot of internal stress, emotional issues and negative thoughts, I experienced unbearable cramps and related pain. But just like my trips to the dentist, I greatly reduced my menstrual pain. In fact, my menstrual cycles taught me a lot about the strong connection between mental/emotional pain and physical pain. The better I treated myself (reduced stress, let go of resentment, etc.), the milder my physical pain became each month. Also, pushing through the intense pain literally brought me to my knees sometimes and reminded me to stop resisting, and instead relax, rest and reset.

Moving from intense pain to absence of pain was a conscious process. At first, I was completely unaware how my internal state affected my physical self. But as I became more self-aware and looked within and around to identify triggers of emotional stress, I began to find ways to reduce personal problems. Nevertheless, now, I notice that when I have an internal conflict, it very quickly triggers a strong headache – insight I was never conscious of before. Because I am now a lot more aware of these patterns, I can quickly reduce, prevent, modify or process them. As time goes on, I will continually learn how to avoid stressors and, as a result, likely increase my health and improve my overall sense of well-being.

THE SELF-DESTRUCTIVE TECHNIQUE OF THE "POOR LITTLE ME"

- Mary, did you hear what happened to me? I still don't believe it. Who would have thought? I would have never imagined it. I supported him in every way for many years, and he betrayed me!

- Well, John, don't look on the bad side. Remember that you are in good health, and you are a very intelligent and capable person. Let it go. Life goes on, and this is a fantastic opportunity to show the world and yourself that you can do what you set out to do. Look for the lesson in this experience. What happened to you no longer matters – unless you let it.

- Yes, but listen. It's just that he's done things to me that I can't let go. What am I going to do now?

- John, did you even hear what I said?"

The experiences that come our way can challenge us and even push us down. For that reason, we have to pay close attention to the lessons that these experiences can bring so that we can gain the insight to be better and do better the next time. Looking for a solution instead of focusing on the problem takes work. Sometimes, it is much easier to fall into our learned thinking pattern of "poor little me."

In these cases, we complain. We feel sorry for ourselves. We crave attention and pity. Meanwhile, we stay stuck in our predicament, with no chance for a solution. There is a popular saying that one should never bring a problem without offering a solution. It is great advice. Instead of "poor little me," one can say "I am empowered."

The universe sends us signals or warnings all the time. The question then becomes: Do we pay attention to them? Some of us ignore its warnings until the last possible moment in which there are no longer options available.

I teach this concept to children using this analogy about teeth:

1) If you do not brush your teeth, you will probably get cavities.
2) If you still do not wash them, you may have to get several cavity fillings.
3) If your poor dental hygiene continues, you will have to get a root canal and maybe, over time, some of your teeth will fall out due to bad gums.

This behavior is typical of someone who decides not to take responsibility for his actions and ignore the consequences until they get so bad, and so painful, that they realize they have to finally address/correct them. But sometimes it is too late. In the case of improper teeth brushing, you cannot save teeth once they have fallen out.

In cases where the person continually plays the helpless individual and tries (intentionally or not) to provoke pity through complaints or crying, he fits the persona of those who think: "poor little me." The problem of continually feeling sorry for oneself – and essentially acting as a masochist who finds pleasure in pain – is that the person develops a habitual negative thinking pattern that prevents problem-solving or any personal growth. He stays stuck because he does not look outside of himself or try to learn *why* he feels this way and what can be done to fix it. There is no self-discovery process, not even an attempt to try.

It's like a little boy who has a tantrum, blaming everybody except himself, kicking and screaming "why me and not them?" There are many reasons for this type of behavior: a sense of entitlement, conditioned negative thinking, selfishness, not self-aware, to name a few. However, a person who is enlightened, tuned into his motivations and is responsible for his actions would be able to solve his own problem.

Using Feelings as an Excuse to Avoid Responsibility

Thinking patterns or habitual behaviors – good or bad – can last a few moments to many years. The duration depends on the level of self-consciousness, motivation to change and ability to release internal negative feelings that hold us hostage. These deep-seated feelings could be the result of never wanting to study again due to failing a college entrance exam. Or, not overcoming the loss of a loved one in a car accident. Or, feeling resentful because somebody did something that was unfair or disloyal. These feelings are then used as excuses to explain negative behaviors and not accept responsibility for one's own actions.

Responsibility means responding with ability ("response" plus "ability") that is, "the right thing to do" in every circumstance. For example, assume a child living in a third-world country unexpectedly passed away. Of course, his mother would want to take time off her job to properly grieve her loss, but she knows that if she does, she will lose her job and so she decides to do the responsible (and very difficult!) thing to work the next day in order to feed her nine other children. Necessity, in some cases, throws out the "poor little me" temptation and forces our hand to behave responsibility.

Suffering and persevering through challenges can often lead us to new insights, new opportunities for growth. It has often been said that if it doesn't challenge you, it doesn't change you. In difficult situations where we feel apprehensive about our ability to overcome, it is reassuring to remember the saying: "Every cloud has a silver lining." Expect and embrace suffering, for in the end it can transform our life – but only if we learn from its lessons. If we focus only on the misery and get stuck in "poor little me" thinking, we will never move forward in life.

One's "poor little me" thought pattern can be controlled or prolonged depending on factors, such as others' enabling of it and its rewards. Why would somebody want to stop thinking that way if he continues to receive the much-desired attention and benefits from it?

HOW CONSCIOUSNESS AND CONSCIENCE GUIDES LIFE'S PATH

- Look what that man is doing! He is sticking his hand in that lady's handbag. He must be stealing from her! ... Madame! They are stealing your wallet. Watch out!!!
- You did well to warn her. We should never look the other way even if it is not happening to us.

Our Compass: Navigating the Map of Life

When we are born, each of us comes into the world with a kind of compass or internal guidance (also called conscience), which helps us navigate this world and make better decisions. It is often referred to as our "inner voice." This inner compass can be influenced by our individual preferences, desires and motivations. Generally speaking, this compass is grounded in our spiritual origin and shapes our perceptions and ability to discern (i.e., identify and assess what happens to us). Internal compasses can differ greatly in their scope and power, with some people having a more precise compass and orientation than others.

The challenge is then to recognize and understand each person's internal life compass. I have found that some parents and educators do not take the time or the effort to investigate each child's unique compass and consequently do not give them the knowledge, life skills and tools to thrive. Instead, they usually assume all compasses are identical and fixed, and therefore assign the same expectations and rules regardless of what can motivate or empower a child. Furthermore, young people can lose their internal guide due to the confusion that others can generate. them.

If the Shoe Doesn't Fit, Don't Wear It

Children are often educated according to a standard set of principles and lessons that is the same for everybody, without factoring in individual and distinctive personal traits and strengths. It's a one-size-fits-all approach. It is like trying to fit all different sizes of feet (our individual compass) into a one standard shoe shape (educational system) in order to facilitate walking (behaviors). This approach to stifling one's inner guide and requiring different people to be accountable to the same standards prevents them from developing self-awareness (consciousness) and responsibility for their own thoughts and behaviors. Consciousness allows us to realize what is happening around us, and without it, we are merely cogs in a machine.

Just like a compass, our conscience orients us and guides us, but it needs to be developed, nurtured, even corrected throughout life. At birth, our inner compass is immature and must be expanded and fine-tuned through deliberate practice and the process of discernment between the good and bad.

Discerning between the Good and the Bad

Discernment involves acquiring consciousness and choosing between two or more alternatives. In our case we will also evaluate the options according to a deeper personal reasoning, whenever possible, which leads to a logical conclusion instead of a shallow preference. It is our ability to judge well and make wise decisions. It also involves obtaining spiritual direction and understanding in order to evaluate what is good or healthy for us, and what is not through our conscience. If we are taught only to adhere to strict rules or live a life imposed by others, we are not empowered to develop the important ability to make careful or correct distinctions in our thinking about reality (our truth).

Life can act as a mechanism to teach us how to make better decisions through our own experiences. Although, sometimes we ignore the lesson and instinctually react to the experience, which does not elevate our ability to effectively discern in future similar experiences or events. In these cases, we simply act without thinking or reflecting.

The Experiment of Life

This approach to life means we are experimenting but are not truly discovering or learning. It is like reading a story simply for entertainment, without looking for any fable teachings or moral guidance. But we can only grow if we gain those insights. The act is secondary to the learning from it. This is why it is important to see every challenge, every hardship as an opportunity to learn and grow.

We need to experiment and go through specific experiences so that we can build our knowledge base. When we encounter similar challenges we have faced before and learned from, we can overcome them easier and faster. If you have found your way out of a maze before, it is simpler to complete it the second time. The key is to actively look for the connection between the experience and the lesson, which increases our level of consciousness and our ability to mitigate future hardships.

For example, a scientist or researcher goes through a similar process in order to gain insight and form conclusions. This process involves theories, discovery, research, tests, experiments, analysis and reports to eventually prove or disprove those initial theories. By being able to study and learn from experience (data) along with study and introspection (information), we have more clarity and light (evidence, enlightenment, conclusions).

Of course, each experience brings its own challenges and even similar ones that are not identical; some are seemingly benign or might actually contain multiple layers or depth that we learn about from only as we go through them.

Therefore, we have to complete a process of personal discernment with both consciousness and conscience, and develop responsibility (i.e., to be able to respond) so we can build our knowledge base. For discernment to occur, we pull information from both our internal knowledge base and spiritual experiences. If there is no discernment capability, there is no development of neither our consciousness nor our compass; therefore, we will repeat the same actions and behaviors that are counterproductive to personal growth – and direct our children to do the same.

Which One: Choice A or B? What about a C?

Typically, when we have to make a decision, there are two forces at play. First, we factor in what we instinctually like and do not like. For example, I like political party "X" and I choose to vote for them. But then we consider other factors (emotional, social, spiritual) that influence our decision. For example, I belong to political party "X", but the country would be better served by party "Y" for the various reasons I already mentioned to you in the previous report, so I should probably choose to vote for "Y." Nevertheless, sometimes we just judge and/or blame without much rationalizing, which becomes a weak justification to choose one or the other. For example, political party "X" always lies, so that's why "Y" received my vote.

A high level of consciousness leads to better, wiser decision-making. It does not feed on judgment or outside influences, but rather analyzes facts and discerns between what is better or worse (conscience). An expanded consciousness (communication and information system) allows the individual to observe life from a higher level ("higher self") in each moment, instead of resorting to mere instincts, feelings or desires, like the "lower self" that the subconscious tends to do. What happens is that the "lower self" imposes itself over the conscience and/or consciousness and rules unconsciously. Therefore, it is crucial to continually move up the Pyramid of Consciousness (POC) where our "higher self" is in order to avoid making bad decisions based only on instinct or emotions.

There are times, however, when we do make decisions utilizing either our lower or higher self, as shown in the following example. Imagine that a friend invites you to her college graduation. There might be several reasons why or why not you will attend, but for the purposes of this example, we will focus on two of them:

- Option #1 (where the "lower self" is imposed on the undeveloped or the unconscious mind): You decide to attend the event to avoid hurting your friend's feelings. This decision is influenced primarily by feelings without much consciousness of other factors.

- Option #2 (where the "higher self" leverages a higher level of awareness and greater responsibility): You decide to attend the event because you want to support her, make her feel appreciated, and help validate her effort to excel. This decision involves discerning what is a better option.

As we move up the Pyramid of Consciousness and become more self-aware and responsible, we can avoid many of the pitfalls and emotional setbacks of unwise decisions. For the untrained and unconscious person, it is much easier to simply react based on instinctive feelings or desires. However, the more conscious person will step back, assess the situation, and consider all sides before making a decision, which typically pays off in the end.

"The God within the Dog"

There is a common saying that represents the duality of the divine and the human quite well: "the God within the dog." It means that on the one hand our body has an animalistic nature that is naturally instinctive, basic and unconscious (lower part of the POC), hence the reference to the dog; but on the other hand, we have characteristics similar to "God" that allow us to develop our "higher self" at the top of the POC. Consequently, there are times when the "lower self" or instincts influence our conscience and/or consciousness, and other times in which our conscience and/or consciousness leans toward the divine or "higher self" where our mind and soul are integrated with our physical body.

Generally, instead of approaching experiences and decisions from a holistic view where we form analysis based on our mind, body and soul, we tend to isolate various parts of our self and act in ways that merely satisfy one aspect of our personality. For example, we want to reduce a specific painful feeling, so we act this way. Or, we desire a certain behavior in an individual so we flirt to get what we want. Rather than practicing discernment from a "whole self" perspective, we respond based on an individual emotion or feeling or desire. As in the case of the "God within the dog" analogy, we often find that our intellect and moral compass conflicts with our instinctual desires. For example, we want to be a "good" person but we constantly crave sex.

Being aware of what influences us (increasing our consciousness) has inherent benefits. Some of us are very driven by intuition and common sense, while others of us just ignore it. Similarly, our conscience has an internal mechanism, which often is unrecognized, that warns us a few seconds before we are about to do something wrong. It acts as a type of alarm ("warning bells") that pings our senses of the impending consequences of a particular act. We choose whether to listen to or ignore that warning.

WHY WE PASS JUDGMENT ON OTHERS

- Dad, look what the neighbor is doing. He is sawing the tree in front of his house that gives him that wonderful shade. He must be out of his mind.

- Son, do not judge him. You do not know what his reasons are, and in any case, he is free to do what he pleases as long as it does not harm anyone.

- Yes, but I can't see any reason why he would want to do that.

- Probably the roots are breaking the pipes of the house; it already happened to him with the swimming pool. In any case, it is not up to us to judge whether cutting the tree is a better or worse option. We do not judge, for we do not know his reasons, even if some seem obvious. Why don't you go over there and ask him directly instead of just assuming?

As noted earlier, we are born with an internal compass that can guide us. However, our decisions are greatly influenced and fed by our existing knowledge base and other factors (emotional, mental, spiritual). It is important to understand that judgment is not the same as discernment. When discernment is practiced after investigation or discovery, we can gain greater knowledge, which also helps us choose between what is better or worse for us. When we pass judgment on somebody or something we are essentially evaluating whether he/she/it is simply good or bad. When we move into a "higher self," we forego judgment for enlightenment, which gives us more awareness and clarity and leads to a deeper understanding of the situation or others. Our internal compass does not judge but rather guides our path and lights the way for a more informed and deeper understanding of the situation and ourselves.

Generally speaking, to judge means to review someone or something according to the facts (or how we see it) and then formulate a personal opinion of that person or thing. Our evaluation is often based on a good/bad scale and is seen as either positive or negative. However, judgment is not based exclusively on what we observe at the moment but is also formed according to our inherent biases and prejudices. For that reason, I recommend using the words *better* and *worse* rather than passing judgement as blatantly *good* or *bad*.

We also project our own self-image, motivations and desires, which influences our judgment. Sometimes gossip, rumors and other people's judgment affect our perceptions and evaluations. Our "lower self" especially relies on all these factors to formulate judgments; however, our "higher self" is less likely to judge because it perceives people and events through a more conscientious, more informed lens.

Whether aware of it or not, we often judge everything from situations, to behaviors, to people, to ourselves. Sometimes judgments about a situation automatically turn into assumptions or opinions about somebody's character. For example, if we say that "it is not right to hit a child" we are expressing our judgement that the behavior is bad. But, if we say "that lady who beats her son is doing something wrong and is therefore a bad mother," we are using our judgment to assume that because her behavior is bad, she must be bad as a person.

Judge Not Lest You Be Judged

Unfortunately, the judgments we make are often negative against ourselves or other individuals – and can often even be wrong. We can inaccurately judge people or situations based on false assumptions or predictions about thoughts or actions. It is why the act of judging based on limited information as well as on our own preconceived notions can be detrimental in terms of family, relationships, careers and on our own personal development. While we likely try not to judge or criticize others, it can be difficult not to naturally evaluate whether something/someone is good or bad. Making hasty conclusions based on limited information can negatively impact us, and therefore it is ideal if we can deliberately suspend judgment until we have more informational input (awareness). Removing habitual judging from our lives will help us eventually develop compassion and maintain inner peace.

Only God knows the absolute truth for any situation and can see what is in somebody's heart and head. Therefore, ask yourself whenever you pass judgment: Do you really know the full story? Are you forming your opinions based solely on facts and void of emotions or motivations? Do you know what that person is thinking or feeling, what his internal motivations are? Would you put your head in the lion's mouth for it? If the answer is "no" or "not really," then consider not judging at all. Remember that everybody – including you – is fighting some type of battle in their life. Who are we to judge others?

Perpetually engaging in gossip and criticism of others only distracts you from looking within and identifying and solving your own problems. This is typically referred to as: "seeing the mote in another's eye, and not seeing the rafter in your own." Imagine how much more time you would have to focus on evolving and improving yourself if you stopped wasting hours worrying about others.

MEET GUILT – IT'S INFAMOUS FOR MAKING YOU FEEL BAD

- It was you, I saw you.

- That's not true! Okay, well, maybe it's true. But I did it without meaning to. I took the cup and it fell. A complete accident. I am sorry.

-You aren't sorry. You did it on purpose. You are the guilty one. From now on I will not leave anything with you ever again. Get out of my room right now!

- I'm sorry, please forgive me.

- I said no! Go, and do not speak to me again!"

- Forgive me. I feel terrible.

In today's society, the concept of guilt is often misinterpreted in our collective understanding of it. Some of us feel it traps us in despair and there is no relief in sight. However, if instead of drowning in guilt we seek forgiveness and use it as a learning opportunity, we can push past toxic feelings like shame and move towards the light. A simple three-step approach will be discussed later in this chapter to empower you to prevent or overcome the detrimental effects that guilt can cause.

Many people view "guilt" as the result of doing a bad thing and can become an automatic and learned response or defense pattern, just like instinctually responding to a karate kick. We don't plan to (or want to!) feel guilty, but it just happens. When we experience guilt, we internally reprimand and/or punish ourselves on an unconscious level. However, fortunately, there is a healthier, more productive and beneficial way to respond to situations that have the potential to make us feel bad.

Choose Your Path

Guilt has two distinct paths, each yielding different results. We can never walk both paths at once; we have to discern which is a better option and is more ideal… and then choose to follow it. The first path leads towards the mistake's learning opportunity, while the other is a worse option, merely plagued with negativity, blame and shame. Which path sounds better to you? And although you likely picked the first one, we tend to automatically travel the second one, for many of us are not yet empowered by the awareness that we are in control of which path we take. We have the power and freedom to choose how we will feel and respond.

To better understand this important point, consider the following illustration. A man decides to use a carton of milk to make butter and cheese. However, butter and cheese cannot coexist in the same bowl with the milk. He must choose which product to make (butter or cheese). Something very similar happens with guilt; either we learn or we suffer, but both can never happen at the same time, and it is our choice to decide what we take away (positive or negative) from the experience.

The problem is that many of us continually choose the path that makes us feel worse instead of the one that can enlighten and empower us. Why do we do this over and over again? It could be that we are unaware that we have a choice. We can decide to not dwell in destructive feelings. It also could be that we feel it is too hard to accept responsibility, learn from it and move on, as it takes deliberate discovery and honest reflection.

When we feel disappointed, remorseful or uncomfortable about something we have said or done, it can be difficult to let go of shame and move towards enlightenment. It is far easier to fall into the distributive "poor little me" mode, which keeps us stuck in our experience and prevents any type of beneficial learning or awareness.

Feeling bad is a seemingly perfect excuse for not taking responsibility, that is, until we either dwell in those negative feelings or continue the bad behavior for so long that we always feel deflated, ashamed and weakened (emotionally, spiritually, even physically). But, there is hope and much we can do to reverse this pattern and… take our power back!

Course Correction

I have discovered (and successfully used!) a simple, yet effective three-step technique (examination of conscience, act of contrition and commitment to change) that can help us course correct whenever we find ourselves traveling down the wrong path. As will be explored more in the following lesson, adopting this technique will empower all of us to cleanse and correct what happened without feeling guilty; this makes it possible to rectify what we have done. In this case, the person takes an active role in reconsidering, repenting and repairing – and ultimately learns and grows in a healthy way from a negative event.

Imagine walking into the kitchen, pouring a glass of milk and then accidentally dropping it. Looking at the broken glass all over the floor, we are faced with a choice. Choice A is to select the negative "poor little me" path, feel sorry for ourselves that this happened to us, refuse to face the consequences and leave the spilled milk and broken glass there. Choice B is the more responsible, enlightened path that prompts us to examine how/why the milk was spilled (*Was the glass slippery? Were we tired and just tripped?*), figure out how to avoid a future accident... and clean up the mess! Choice A is about playing victim; Choice B is about solving a problem and taking responsibility. Which would be your choice?

Always self-checking our thoughts and behaviors is a great way to ensure that we are not traveling down guilt's destructive path. For example, if you catch yourself having or saying repeated thoughts or phrases like "I apologize again for what I did to you, I cannot get it out of my head," it means you are allowing guilt to self-inflict punishment or encourage negative thoughts. Consider this: If you have already asked for forgiveness, or have already been forgiven, what is the purpose of continually apologizing or feeling guilty? You can and should break this thinking or behavior pattern as soon as possible. Acknowledge, accept and then move on. It is the only way you will continue your evolution and improve your overall well-being.

HOW TO ASK FOR FORGIVENESS AND DISINFECT THE EFFECTS OF BAD BEHAVIORS OR NEGATIVE KARMA: INTRODUCING THE THREE-STEP TECHNIQUE

- Justin, sorry that I took your motorcycle without asking.
- You know that I do not like when you borrow my motorcycle, so why did you do it?
- I let myself get carried away, and I did not think it through. I really wanted to ride it, but I was so scared of you finding out that I actually rode faster than I should have and fell. I apologize – I will not do it again. I have learned my lesson.
- Don't worry Joe; the important thing is that you are safe and have learned from it. Thank you for your apology; I forgive you.

During my initial phase of spiritual growth, I was taught to cleanse myself from the negative effective of bad actions or karma. The Catholic Church advocates for the following three steps that have been shown to help us repent and rectify our bad behaviors. However, it is advisable to first drop to your knees or do a prostration (lie stretched out on the ground), with the sole purpose of putting your ego (self) physically aside so that you can focus better spiritually.

To cleanse karma, these three steps are recommended in sequential order:

Step 1: Examination of Conscience

This step requires a full analysis of what has happened and what specifically we want to rectify so that it does not happen again. Let's say, for example, a person did not study or pay attention in class and consequently failed school. He decides he wants to change what happened. In this case, he must first look at his situation from an objective lens. Where and how was he not responsible? What distracted him? What were his motivations for not studying? Answering these types of questions helps him to examine where he went wrong and therefore become aware of the problem he needs to rectify.

Step 2: Act of Contrition

This step requires that we repent for offenses we may have made or pain we might have caused. But careful, though, not to dwell in feelings of guilt, which as discussed earlier, closes us off to key learning. Instead, ask for forgiveness – directly from the person if possible.

Using the example in Step 1, the boy would say something like the following to his parent: "I am sorry I did not study enough; I know I wasted your time and money you sacrificed for me to go to school. I regret what I did, and I am sorry." At this point, it is up to the parent to decide whether or not to forgive; however, that should no longer be on the shoulders of the boy. He asked for forgiveness, which is the important thing. Through grace, God always forgives if one's repentance is authentic, for only God knows our hearts and He cannot be deceived.

Also, remember that there will be times when we face the temptation to feel guilty, but we should not give into those feelings and rather see those mistakes as opportunities to learn and grow.

Step 3: Commitment to Change

We need to purposely decide to change; it will not happen otherwise. It is helpful, for adults especially, to verbally declare our commitment to learn and evolve (change). An ideal declaration, for example, could be: "From now on, I will not allow this negative or bad behavior to continue. I plan to be more responsible with my studies. Therefore, I have decided to hold myself accountable." Being conscientious about improving ourselves (thoughts and actions) involves awareness, declaring our intents, and planning an optimal course of action to stop the behavior and make wiser decisions.

HOW TO BUILD ONE'S SKILLS – LITTLE BY LITTLE

- Susan, I have to tell you a secret: I cannot watch scary movies. I'll never watch them; they disturb me.

- I understand, but maybe we can see one that is not too scary. This way, when you want to go with your friends to the movies to see one, you will be prepared. Try to think like the director; do not get caught up in the movie; look at it from an objective or distant point-of-view. Watch it from another perspective and always remember that nothing is real and it's all just special effects. It's just images on a movie screen.

It is best not to wait until the last minute to do or achieve something. It is ideal to develop a good long-term habit of reviewing everything you learned each day and planning how you can efficiently complete your tasks (e.g., studying) in a timely manner. Otherwise, you might cram a lot of knowledge in your head right before an exam, and then forget it days later.

The sample dialogue at the beginning of this section represents one person's attempt to teach her friend a new skill: how to be comfortable watching scary movies. Rather than teach her all at once, the friend suggests a small first step, which is to change her perception of the movies. Similarly, any personal skill we want to learn in life is best acquired little by little so that we understand each step and can practice accordingly. It is most ideal to learn skills when we are young, as our brains tend to be more resilient during childhood.

The Skill of Managing Emotions

Processing and managing one's emotions follows a similar pattern of learning. We can begin to understand them even when they cause us pain or confuse us. Of course, it can be overwhelming to process different emotions all at the same time, but try to recognize each emotion, one by one, to figure out its triggers and evaluate their impact on the mind, body and soul. This does not mean we should allow ourselves to be carried away by our emotions, but should rather validate and study our feelings so that we can learn how to better manage them.

One technique for trying to get in touch with our emotions and feelings is to ask questions like:

- What is their origin or cause?
- What are my repeated emotional triggers?
- What are my typical reactions?
- How do I feel when I encounter this emotion?
- How am I making the emotion/feeling increase or decrease?
- What can I learn from this?

A simple action step is actively observing (monitoring) our internal state whenever we experience the emotion and whenever that emotion dissipates. These emotions will come and go, as in the case of a summer storm, where after the rain comes the shining sun. Once the specific feeling has passed, we can then analyze and think about how we felt during its onset and whether or not other mental states followed. We should also reflect on whether we dismissed the feeling or tried to control it. With practice, self-examination can also be achieved at the same time we are experimenting.

This type of insight enables us to develop more self-awareness… more consciousness. By simply studying specific moments when feelings occur and testing our reactions in real-time, we can step by step (or moment by moment) develop the skill to identify and connect our feelings with our emotions and responses. This will help us to better manage emotional triggers and resulting actions in the future – and hopefully get to a point where they do not affect us at all. What then begins to happen is that the greater the expansion of our mind (knowledge), the greater the challenges (tests) we will likely face in life; however, we will be able to leverage our "higher self" to react in much healthier and more productive ways.

Barriers to Growth

Despite our desire to grow our skill sets and improve ourselves (mind, body and soul), there are various internal and external barriers that can slow or stop personal development.

The way we were raised can affect our propensity to experiment with life and try new things. For example, if you were like most children growing up, your parents did not let your young self play with sharp knives. Chances are it was not until you were older when you learned how to properly use knives, and because of that, some of you are currently fearful of knives or lack the skill in using them. Undoubtedly, parents always seek the best for us and therefore try to protect us from all kinds of dangers, like a knife, but it can also take away the opportunity to learn and grow. Using the knife scenario, if a parent teaches a young child, little by little, in a supervised environment how to use a knife in a responsible way, that child will develop the skill earlier and faster, gaining confidence along the way.

In general, the sooner we expose ourselves to new experiences and challenges, the sooner the opportunity to learn and the better ability to develop a higher level of consciousness. Many of our current fears were developed during childhood or as a byproduct of the educational system or through specific encounters or experiences in our life. Inherent fears (i.e., fear of the unknown, fear of rejection, fear of failure, fear of death) can prevent us from embracing change or new adventures. It can produce anxiety or mistrust, and prevent us from moving forward in life.

Other factors that can act as barriers to growth are our mental capacities, attitude, personality and values we developed throughout the years. For example, maybe we were taught to deliberately avoid dangerous situations or stay in our safe zone, and therefore automatically said "no" to anything that seemed risky. Or maybe we value comfort and security, and therefore avoid anything physical that has the potential to hurt us.

WHY YOU SHOULD "FEAR" YOUR FEAR

- *Mom, I do not want to sleep without a night-light. I keep having nightmares that there is a skeleton in the tub and that it attacks me.*
- *Relax son, no one's going to do anything to you. You're here at home with me. I will take care of you.*

Think of fear as an emotion that we create artificially whenever we have experiences we do not like and do not want them to happen. Fear is often irrational and is influenced by our desires. For example, when there is something we really want and feel that we will not get it, we become scared of the perceived loss. Fear is personal and is different for every person. What scares one person might actually be craved by somebody else. Some people love jumping out of planes, while others would not even consider it.

It is not rational thinking but rather emotions that create fear. When we encounter a new experience or situation, our brain often initiates the fear response by first sending signals that communicate our displeasure or apprehension. We then allow those signals to turn into negative and fearful thoughts that lead to certain emotions towards that experience. Together with our brain and emotions, we build our own level of fear and, if unchecked and not effectively managed, enable it to grow.

There are several types of fear, such as physical, mental and emotional. The physical refers to something happening to or in our body, like someone literally hitting us. The emotional refers to feelings and emotions, such as grieving a loved one or experiencing heartbreak. The mental refers to our state of mind; for example, the fact that we cannot solve or perform something intellectually, like failing an exam, for example.

The Good and the Bad of Fear

Historically, fear has served a very specific purpose, as it is important to have a healthy sense of fear in order to perceive threats and avoid danger. When we perceive a threat to survival, our fight-or-flight response kicks in and can often be life-saving! And in case of a potential animal attack, it is not only typical but advised to fear such a situation. But when it comes to managing our feelings and thoughts in our everyday life, fear only gets in the way. Let's be realistic: no beast is going to try to eat us today or any day.

Fear is energy governed by the animal part of our self. It is instinctual, and we can react to it in various ways. Either we try to prevent fear by avoiding situations perceived to produce it, or we push through fear so that we can learn from it.

Fear exposes us to two types of situations, and causes us to continually fluctuate between them:

1. Paralyzing Fear: In this situation, we literally become so paralyzed—mentally more than physically—that we cannot move forward. We are stuck because we have allowed fear to hold us back.
2. Fear of Movement: In this situation, fear acts as a physical reaction (as opposed to proactive behaviors, such as love). Sometimes when we perceive a real threat, we literally move away or against it in order to survive. For example, somebody threatens us with a pistol, and so we likely turn and run in the opposite direction so that he does not kill us.

Paralyzing fear constantly prevents us from personal growth as it stops us from moving forward. It can be fluid, though, in that it often depends on what situation faces us and what we choose to do about it. For example, we can choose to let fear continue to incapacitate us, or we can choose to create opportunities for learning. It is also increased or decreased by other factors (environment, people, etc.). This concept of fear is illustrated by the physical state of water, which can be in either liquid form or frozen into ice – it all depends on the internal and external conditions in the moment.

Think of fear in this way: it represents our selfish desire(s). Unlike love that we give to others (or is given to us), fear grabs or holds hostage one's thoughts and feelings, eventually controlling his reactions and behaviors. It is a by-product of what we want or do not want. Fear is subjective and can negatively affect our entire well-being.

When it comes to moments when we face fear, our main objective should be to seek opportunities to learn from them and develop a higher level of consciousness. The benefits of progressing up the Pyramid of Consciousness (POC) are motivating and inspiring. For example, once we have experienced what it is like to live in love and benefit from inner peace, we will likely never want to live in fear again and will therefore deliberately try to avoid the pitfalls of fear and eventually slide back down the pyramid. This pertains not only to individuals but also cultures. There are cultures that are trapped in fear, just like there are those, like Nordic countries, that are based in love.

THE TEETER-TOTTER OF EGO
AND AGAPE LOVE

> - *Manfred, you did not eat breakfast today; that is not good*
>   *behavior. I have told you that I love you when you behave well.*
> - *Mom, then when I misbehave, you do not love me?*
> - *No, when you're bad or yell at me, I do not love you. Mothers*
>   *should be respected and loved at all times – not screamed at. They*
>   *should constantly receive hugs, affection and love. You owe me an*
>   *apology.*

To show love, you first need to know how to receive it. Love manifests itself in many different ways, and it is important to learn to accept it as is, instead of trying to force or change it. Love can give us what we need: affection, understanding and support. It should not be conditional based on what we want or desire. If we do not accept that principle, it will be difficult for us to fully receive love without expectations.

Love does not demand physical things, but it does require a sense of responsibility. Since love is the act of giving, not receiving, it should not expect anything in return. We can only fully understand the power of love if we unconditionally give love to others. This may see like common sense, but this simple concept is often confused as equating the act of receiving love to the satisfaction of our desires; however, they are two totally different things.

Love is giving, and it also always involves understanding what each person needs. Love answers the question of how we can support someone's development. In this sense, we think about the well-being of the other individual and not in terms of what we want. That is love.

For this reason, many individuals do not provide the kind of unconditional and responsible love that we really need. The ability to love and receive love relates to the person's level of consciousness. Sometimes we love others based on a false or distorted view of them and/or misunderstanding of the relationship, and so our love then comes with unrealistic assumptions or expectations.

Love is an energy that manifests itself in different ways, such as sexual love (animal quality), sentimental love (emotional quality), intellectual love (mental quality) or pure love (spiritual quality). In fact, there are two main types of love that will be discussed in this section: Ego and Agape.

Ego: It's All About Me

The ego, as its name implies, is a kind of selfish love that we give so that we can receive. This type of love taps into one's "lower self" or towards the bottom of the Pyramid of Consciousness. Usually this love creates an expectation and a dependency, since one needs to receive from the other person before completing the love cycle or transaction. It is about us loving somebody with the primary objective of being loved.

It is important to be mindful that just because some of us might currently be on the lower part of the Pyramid of Consciousness, we should not see that from a negative lens. It just means that we have opportunities to learn and grow – ideally, while we ascend the pyramid. We need to be patient with ourselves, for we would never blame a young person for not having the years of wisdom and experience that an elderly person likely has. In addition, each person has its own evolutionary rhythm. We are not perfect and we make many mistakes, but if we always view them as learning opportunities, we can improve ourselves more and more every day.

Agape: It's All About Giving (You)

Agape is the other type of love, which is satisfied merely by the act of freely giving it. It does not expect reciprocity. It is usually given by those whose "higher self" possesses a great deal of consciousness. This love is completely unconditional and is pure, without an agenda or expectation of special treatment, benefits, favors, payment, etc.

As mentioned, in agape the person is connected with his more conscious "higher self" and typically puts others before him. Moreover, this love is free and not linked to any dependencies. It is not transactional, for it feeds only on the act of giving. A key benefit of those who embrace the agape type of love is that it helps to open their hearts towards others and change them in a positive way.

Demonstrating Love in Everyday Life

Consider these types of love when it comes to relationships. If we love our significant other because we want him to love us back, that is not part of agape. It is a "business" transaction: I give you something (love) in exchange for something (more love). Therefore, it is not "free", but is rather transactional and comes with strings (conditions).

If a child is given love, and understands it as unconditional, he feels secure, accepted and valued, which are very important towards creating a solid foundation for his personal development. The key is to properly teach him the differences between ego and agape love in simple language, since his young mind cannot understand or process information like adults.

It is always important to show him what unconditional love is and what it is not, for a child can often become confused when he faces discipline, punishments or is triggered by fear. Their ability to discern between love and discipline, for example, is limited at that age, which is why parents should help them understand actions and situations, and be mindful of the messages their words or body language communicate to children. In the hypothetical conversation at the beginning of this section, the child has been told that his parent only loves him when he behaves, which shows that the adult is communicating the ego type of love (conditional).

Love's Power

The type of love determines the ultimate effect on a person. For example, the Ego type is exemplified in conditional phrases like: "I'll show my love after you do this," or "If you do "X", I will give you "Y." When this type of love is communicated to children, its consequence is the increasing (and counterproductive) dependence on the parent regarding the formation of the child's self-image, confidence and values. The child then feels he has to "earn" his parents' love, which does not motivate him to develop his own unique self and rather performs in ways that "please" his parents so that he can receive their love. This prevents healthy personal development and causes anxiety and insecurity.

On the other hand, a child whose basic needs are met but also receives physical affection (kisses, hugs) and encouragement (attention and constructive feedback) from his parents is more empowered to increase his levels of self-confidence and security, enabling him to thrive in his personal development.

To help children develop into confident, responsible and productive beings, through the lens of love, we can facilitate this process. There are simple and seemingly "little" things we can do that can actually have a big (and positive) impact on their development while making them feel loved. For example, treating a child in a respectful (adult-like) way and bending down to talk to him at eye-level. Instead of yelling or wildly reprimanding, we calmly yet firmly talk to him in an even tone. Because we have treated him in a respectful and mature way, he will be more likely to model our action and reciprocate it, instead of talking like a baby or throwing a tantrum. By gently guiding (and showing!) children how to behave like an adult, we empower them to want to change and then feel confident to do so.

Love's Sweet Bliss

One of the most important goals in life is to learn more about how works – and love is a big part of understanding ourselves and others. But the act of giving and receiving love is a process, one that we must continue to nurture. While we love others, it is important throughout to be mindful of our thoughts, feelings, emotions and actions on both sides. Consistent self-checks are necessary, for if we do not accurately and consistently observe, analyze and reflect on what happens to us, we will miss the amazing opportunities to learn and grow. The longer we live life without being self-aware and not learning from our mistakes, the more challenges we will face, the less problem-solving skills we have, and the reduced capacity to experience all the wonders of love. When we do not learn from our life experiences, we are typically exposed to greater amounts of needless suffering. *Why delay the benefits of consciousness and love, when you can start experiencing them today?*

Love can give us the support and motivation we need to move forward. Think of love as necessary fuel. It is always flowing; it is always building relationship bridges; it is always healing – love is the energy that metaphorically feeds the world. I have made the act of nurturing love a passion project of mine and have studied the effects of giving and receiving love in my life these past few years. And I can now confidently say that showing love, helping others and having an attitude of gratitude are healing to the body. These behaviors have empowered me to feel more in tune with my body and understand feedback cues. I have learned how to calm my mind, sooth my soul and create inner peace.

When I modified my base from fear to love, what happened next initially took me by surprise – an extraordinary wave of love crashed over me, followed by gratitude from the Universe (and I was able to feel it fully for the first time!). It was just like the most ideal bottle of Champagne (pure bliss!) had been poured into my cup (my soul). I think it was at that precise moment when my new approach to life had reached a point of no return – I was hooked! From then on, my understanding of what love was and could be made total sense. It was something I never knew existed, had never experienced before, and it lasted for weeks. This was a wonderfully intense and overwhelming experience that felt like shockwaves of bliss throughout my entire body. It was like an overflowing fountain or the sea waves breaking on the shore, where amazing feelings and emotions of love and gratitude wash over you to the point you never want that feeling to end. One peek at a happier, more fulfilling life through God love's lens can inspire even the most stubborn person to want to change and find inner peace. At that point I asked myself: *How had I missed out on all this in the past?!* From that moment on, I began to look for ways to fully align and connect with the world and receive this bliss in small doses.

When we begin to raise our level of consciousness and evolve in many ways, we begin to embrace love more fully and can better prioritize what matters most in our lives. Many of us discover that we actually need less material things and less emotional or social baggage (toxic people, stress, etc.). When we make a concerted effort to rid ourselves of anything that they do not need or that weigh us down, we experience the joy of freedom. We have released the heavy luggage of negativity and material/emotional waste, and are now lighter, stronger and better.

As noted earlier, agape love is authentic, genuine and nurturing; on the contrary, the ego type of love makes us dependent and weak. If we have to force ourselves to love somebody, or only give love so we can get love, that is not agape love – or even love at all. Genuine love provides support, freedom, trust, responsibility, and is unconditional and never forced.

What Love is ... and What Love is not

Love is not something we should have to ask for. We cannot make somebody love us. Love should be given freely and without any kind of judgment or evaluation. Love can provide a strong foundation for helping one transform. Just like food, love can nourish us… if we let it.

Love is also not jealous. When we feel that a person, in appreciating and loving us, brings out the best in us, it does not matter if that person shares love with others, because if we are blessed by it and others can also be blessed by it, that is what matters most.

People can change their heart, if they really want to, and in turn their heart can then change their lives and everything else – what they think, feel or act. Just as when we put a toy boat in a river and it follows its course to the sea, sometimes when we set love free, it finds it path. It just happens. Love has a multiplier effect that is transmitted and propagated.

Love can also be supportive not only on a social level but also in helping us with our learning process. It plays a role in shaping the lens through which we look at life and relationships. When there is an initial attraction between two people, that is not love but is instead chemistry (animal nature). With true love, however, there is a conscious appreciation of the other person that goes beyond falling in love (i.e., chemistry + mental and emotional connection).

Its Evolution

The initial attraction to the person dissipates as one moves towards agape love – and loves all people regardless of gender, background, etc. This means we appreciate all people and fully accept them for who they are, regardless of their differences. In agape love, we view and love people as equals. Of course, this is harder said than done. And although the ultimate goal of agape love is to love everybody, our evolutionary state, inherent biases and desires make that a very difficult, practically impossible task.

In today's society, our collective concept of love is typically shaped according to the current cultural/moral norms and social structures, which can remarkably differ from each other depending on the country. As society changes its values and customs, the institution and manifestations of love will inevitably change. It was only until recently, for example, that couples were expected to get married and live together for life. But the past decade has seen an increase in divorce, same-sex marriages and unmarried couples living together. Everything and everybody evolves over time.

BROKEN IN PIECES

> *- I do not understand why you say that about my daughter! She is a very good student and very educated and obedient. She has never given me any problems.*
> *- I see, ma'am, but the reality is that we caught her burning some of the classroom bins with a lighter. I made an appointment with the psychologist to talk to you.*
> *- I do not understand because she does not behave like that at home.*

The separation process between child and parent is usually initiated during childhood, when the child's individual personality begins to form and he tries to figure out the world. During this time, there can be a disconnect between what the child does in the home and how he behaves in society. Children are often discovering which behaviors can please their parents, teachers, friends, caretakers, or even themselves, as they try to conform to societal norms and to make loved ones proud of them. Meanwhile, however, some become so focused on impressing or pleasing those around them, they create a persona that does not reflect who they really are. This becomes especially problematic as they lose a sense of their self-identity independent of their parents and thereby begin to act out in negative ways.

Even at a very early age, the child has likely learned how to line up his behaviors with traditional customs, societal expectations, fixed rules or stereotypes. He is typically categorized and perceived according to a certain role. For example, the good child, the successful student, the overachiever, the genius, the clown, the flirt, the troublemaker, the shy one, the funny one, the brain, the nerd, the lazy kid, etc. It can sometimes become a self-fulfilling prophecy where the child starts to believe and act like the role society assigned to him. As a consequence, his confidence wanes. And as he continues to compartmentalize his personality to fit specific stereotypes, he starts to lose a sense of himself and becomes confused about who he is, who he wants to be, and who society expects him to be. It creates internal conflict between "who I am" and "who I want to be" and "who they want me to be." It can cause much stress.

The Metaphorical Hand

The following demonstration illustrates this concept. Stretch out your hand and spread your fingers as if making the sign for the number five. Each finger performs a different role or represents a personal stereotype (the smart one, the funny one, the serious one, etc.). Notice that each finger points slightly in a different direction. There is no alignment.

Apply that to everyday life. Imagine that each situation you face requires you to conform to only one part of your personality (one finger). How can we be our true and complete selves, if we can only show one part of it in order to please somebody? How do we fully leverage our strengths when we are limited to utilizing only one side of us? It is like trying to walk on only one foot when you have two good legs. It is a lot easier to fall that way.

Now, close your hand so that all the fingers are touching, and imagine using our full hand to hold something heavy instead of just a finger. Feel the strength? When we leverage all parts of our self (personality, abilities, etc.), there is a synergy that can empower us. In this case, we no longer feel broken or disjointed. We do not feel as though parts of our self are confined in a box or on display, but instead feel whole – strong and powerful.

Polishing the Lens

Human beings tend to view and judge others' imperfections – no matter how seemingly small or unimportant – and usually through a negative lens. Judgment often goes hand in hand with gossip, which just reinforces negative thinking and behaviors. Both the acts of judging and gossiping are usually practiced by those on the lower part of the POC, for as they increase their level of consciousness, they begin to develop a greater capacity to see and understand all sides of a situation, and therefore become more broadminded, compassionate and accepting.

All of us are far from perfection, for each of us has strengths and weaknesses. A big part of our evolution process is then to become aware of those and then learn how to turn a weakness into a growth opportunity. It is how we can continually polish our lens so that we see more clearly and react more responsibly. As a society, we tend to be ashamed of, or frustrated, with any perceived weaknesses, and so we often hide or dismiss them. This stunts our personal growth. However, accepting that we have faults or flaws, discovering what they are and how they impact us, and then learning how to turn them into strengths, are key to successfully overcoming challenges and creating a healthy balance in our life.

Becoming Whole

We begin to become "whole" when we recognize and accept all parts of our personality, including our flaws, instead of ignoring bits of ourselves we do not like. When we seek understanding in terms of all our motivations and behaviors, we develop a more complete (and realistic!) view of ourselves. This not only increases our awareness of negative behaviors but enables us to manage them in more positive ways.

This type of thinking pattern can be applied in many other aspects of life. Consider, for example, when we blame life circumstances for happening to us and reject any role we might have played in causing or responding to them. Instead of dismissing personal responsibility that we often exercise our own free will and are accountable for our actions, we should educate and empower ourselves to recognize what we can/should change … and then change it! (This book is a step forward to receiving that education.) *What we want*, *what we need* and *what we should do* types of thoughts often conflict with each other; however, "higher self" awareness, consciousness and conscience give us more clarity to discern.

In short, it is very important to also accept people as and where they are – and holistically support them. In the case of children, for example, it is essential for them to be strong (both mentally and physically) and to be allowed to be their wonderful selves instead of being forced to become a replica of their educators or fit the ideal of perfection model their parents set forth. Think of the yin and yang (bright and dark) philosophy when it comes to people's virtues and weaknesses. One cannot exist without the other; therefore, always accepting one's entire being – even when they are a child who seems to have a lot of flaws at the moment – is key to being able to view and treat them respectfully. When we change our view (lens), we change our approach.

Seeking Self Authenticity

When we pretend to be what we are really not, it can cause much confusion and internal conflict. Consequently, we can begin to lose ourselves and act out accordingly (consciously or unconsciously). Reflection can help reorient us. I remember that at several moments in my teenage life I tried to make sense of why I had such conflicted and confused thoughts, which eventually influenced my behaviors. Now, upon reflection, I understand that I was essentially torn in emotional pieces with my only internal compass being a sense of duty to be obedient.

It is typical that people make decisions based both on what they believe to be true at the time and also on their motivations. For instance, children might choose a certain behavioral response simply to avoid conflicts with his parents or punishments. This role of absolute submission or avoidance without understanding can be so stifling and confining that the child's internal pressure cooker builds and eventually explodes into behaviors such as fighting and rebelling when authority is not around in the streets with friends. The child then believes he has "won" and that he is now behaving the way he wants when nobody is looking. He thinks he has empowered himself with his own thoughts and his own actions. However, the opposite is true. He has the illusion of empowerment and freedom, but in fact, he has only tapped into the fragmented negative feelings and emotions of his personality and acted out accordingly.

Today, for myself personally, I am pleased to share that a lot of the mixed thoughts and feelings I had in my youth have now disappeared in my life. Through hard work of self-discovery, I am now able to recognize and accept all aspects of myself – and realize what I can change and what I cannot. Seeing myself as "whole" has given me much inner peace to know that I do not crave the approval of others in order to feel good about myself. I do not need to act a certain way so that a certain somebody will like me. I have found that this awareness is both empowering and inspirational for me. It is why I hope my story (and this book) will help all those who have lost their way because they have essentially lost themselves. There are answers. And I have found that most of those answers are within one's self.

THE FLUX CAPACITOR OF DISINTEGRATION

> - *I don't know why you're so submissive to your mother – that's not you.*
> - *Yes, but it makes things easier for me at home, and I don't like arguing. I do what they tell me at home, but when I'm outside I do what I want.*
> - *Yes, but you know what that represents. If you continue to sacrifice your own needs and desires in order to please somebody else, it will be difficult to evolve into your own person as an adult. Change is not easy, especially when you prolong it.*

Individuals come into the world as an integrated (whole) system, but the impact of society, culture, education, experiences and/or fear often isolate their thoughts, feelings, personality and behaviors into silos. There is a separation that occurs that breaks down one's system into smaller parts. It is called disintegration. Although the goal is to view ourselves as whole and act accordingly, there are valuable lessons that we can gain from the process of disintegration, for the experiences (and challenges) it brings provide us with insight to change. If we recognize them and learn how to persevere and overcome them, we will be able to transform our way of thinking… and our way of life.

This process can provide trial-and-error experiences and learning, in which we encounter a specific emotion, person or situation that affects us (negatively or positively). We then have a choice: to overlook/dismiss that experience and continue our way of life, or to pause for a moment and look for the lesson. To simply dismiss the experience, we run the risk of continuing our patterned behaviors and conditioned responses. To acknowledge and address them, we build our knowledge base and increase our consciousness, which takes us one step closer to the light (enlightenment). For some of us, this process is easy or fast; for others, it can be more challenging. It really depends on our ability to assess situations (which is improved through the right education and training) as well as on our motivation and commitment to learn.

As mentioned earlier, our fragmented selves can often struggle between "what I am" and "what I want to or must be" thoughts. This internal conflict can produce fear of not knowing who we really are. However, if we view fear as an opportunity to learn, we can turn the feeling into a powerful awareness about ourselves. The primary way to turn fear upside down is to migrate to love. Believe it or not, there is a healthy side of fear, which is the non-paralyzing type of fear that keeps us in constant motion, provoking experiences and, as a result, lead to new learning opportunities to find the light of love. Therefore, do not dismiss moments when you feel tempted to give into homeostasis (a form of resistance) and succumb to your ego telling you to escape from the learning opportunity. Instead, proactively take control of your thoughts and learn from the experience! This continuous state of flux helps us to change life dynamics and move between fear and love in ways that help us personally grow over time.

OUR REACTIONS ARE OUR TEACHERS

- CHARLES: Austin, that move was foolish.
- AUSTIN: No, Charles, you're the fool!
- CHARLES: No, the only fool here is YOU. When you did that careless action without thinking, you messed things up for yourself.
- AUSTIN: Arggggh! Shut up, Charles! Leave me alone once and for all. You're an imbecile, so get out of here!

In the above conversation, when Charles confronted him, Austin lost his patience, allowing himself to get carried away by anger. It had lit the wick of the rocket (figuratively) and there was no way to turn it (his temper) off. Charles, on the other hand, was a bit calmer as he watched and analyzed what was happening between them. He was secretly pleased he provoked Austin to lose his temper and be distracted from the game. Anger caused Austin to lose focus… and Charles was able to finally win the game because he had discovered Austin's Achilles' heel.

There's so much to learn about life, which is why we should always look for its lessons and analyze our reactions to situations and experiences – even the uncomfortable, annoying and undesirable ones – because sometimes they lead to the most valuable insight. When somebody congratulates us for a job well done, it typically means we leveraged enough learning to have mastered it. If we then did that exact same job and also performed well, there was no higher level of education and learning involved… only the confidence-boosting feeling that we excelled again. How can we learn and grow if we are always doing the same thing with the same behaviors and the same responses?

In order to continually challenge ourselves to evolve, we need to seek new experiences and opportunities. We need to sometimes push past our comfort zones so that we develop new insights and skills. We need to be discerning about what we like and what we don't like, and then analyze how we respond because we all respond differently. Some people when faced with a hardship respond with negative coping behaviors like excessive alcohol consumption, while others might opt for more positive outlets, such as yoga or taking a fun vacation. Just like a baby who cries when he doesn't like something or laughs when he does, no matter our age, we all exhibit responses to any type of stimuli, whether we are conscious of them or not. This book advocates that we should deliberately seek consciousness in all situations.

Danger of Dependence

If our personal happiness is directly dependent on somebody or something else, we give up control over our own sense of well-being. Let's say, for example, you love hanging out with this particular person because she is always happy, always positive and always builds you up. You depend on her to share her joy so that you can have it too. But, what if one day she shows up and she is… grumpy and negative. What then? In this case, you might find it difficult to find your own joy when your longtime personal joy trigger (your friend) has temporarily broken.

The challenge (and lesson) then becomes how to control your own state of being – without depending on other situations or people. If we do not consciously control our responses to situations, we are giving those situations permission to control us. The first step in taking the control reigns back is to first decide that you will not let anything or anyone control your thoughts and actions, and to remember that everything (good *and* bad) happens for a reason, which is to teach us. Your role is then to learn.

The Relay of Reactions

If we look beyond our reactions to consciously analyze and understand our patterned response mechanisms, we will begin to feel more empowered with homeostasis harmony, emotional stability and inner peace. Through the process of active observation, reflective analysis and introspection, we obtain the knowledge and ability to then change our responses to future events. Sustained peace of mind happens when we realize we may not be able to control events in our lives, but we can absolutely control our reactions to them.

Therefore, we should never dismiss, avoid or fear a reaction, because it can often be the best teacher. And just like better and worse teachers, there are good and bad emotions that inspire positive and negative responses. Some we will want to hold onto, and some we will want to give away. Think of emotions like runners in a relay; they need to continually pass the baton until the last runner holds on to the most important one for the finish. Ignoring or dropping a baton disqualifies the team, just like skipping an uncomfortable emotion or reaction you do not want to handle will prevent you from learning the complete lesson.

Inner or Outward Lens

Our view of behaviors and reactions differs based on whether or not we are directly involved. In general terms, if someone is insulting another, for instance, we would likely label it a negative act, judge accordingly and decide not to replicate the behavior. But, we can emotionally distance ourselves from it since we know we cannot control what others do. The event happened, but it did not affect us. However, when someone does or says something hurtful to us, we have the tendency to personalize it as an attack against us and suddenly become angry. We enable somebody's action towards us to affect us – mentally, sometimes even emotionally. However, if we instead are able to perceive the aggressive behavior as a hindrance to the attacker's ability to learn his own lessons, we can develop compassion for him and react accordingly. This last part I adapted from the Buddhist teachings. In this case, we control our emotion, instead of giving him the power to invoke an unwanted emotion within us.

How many times have we heard on the news how one person killed another because of jealousy or rage, and we barely blink? It is like our society has become desensitized and learned to distance itself from bad or negative news. And yet, if the jealously is directed towards us or loved ones, we experience anger, which can ignite strong emotions and reactions. Anger can act like a drug that inhibits any form of logical or sensible thinking, and compels us to react to situations. We tend to focus on outward rage while forgetting it is the anger within that is manifesting itself.

Therefore, it is crucial to always monitor both our outward and inner responses. In fact, the antidote to anger is active consciousness – continually being vigilant and analyzing what is going on inside (desires, feelings and thoughts) and outside of us (reactions, responses, others' actions) so that we can correctly read the situation while avoiding the temptation to make snap judgments or wrong assumptions based solely on our emotions, like anger or frustration. Just like in a courtroom where both sides are presented and all pieces of evidence are carefully considered, we should first seek all the facts and perspectives instead of instinctually reacting. This way, we are more able to respond to people and situations in more productive and beneficial ways.

More Insight Produces Higher Understanding

Understanding other perspectives and seeing events and people through a multidimensional lens helps us to develop the capacity of understanding and compassion. Let's say, for example, somebody tries to make us feel bad or says something hurtful to us. It is very tempting (and likely!) to have a lack of compassion for him, and maybe even insult them by giving them a taste of his own medicine. In this scenario, we have reacted without thinking about the consequences because we are upset. Our negative emotion creates a negative response.

However, using this same scenario, a more self-aware person would first try to figure out why insults were being thrown his way before reacting. He would calmly assess the negative behavior and try to connect it with a possible motivation. Why is the man so angry? Is his anger really more about feeling hurt or frustrated? Maybe this attacker had a bad day. Maybe he is suffering from a lot of personal or family issues and therefore lashes out. This analysis enables the "higher self" to better comprehend the situation, possibly develop some compassion towards the attacker, and restrain from returning the insults.

As mentioned earlier in this book, anger is a primary coping mechanism for those who are in the "lower self" and rely on instincts and desires to generate responses. If we take a moment to analyze and understand the situation, we can then develop more positive, more beneficial responses. It is important to also factor in the possibility that maybe this anger is the body's way of unconsciously asking for help. There is always a cause behind an effect; the challenge is to identify it.

Breaking Old Patterns to Create New Ones

Anger has a similar pattern of development to that of pain. Just like pain management, there are different levels and different timeframes to overcome anger. Sometimes it can get out of control and we need to treat it to make it better. Other times we can prevent it or manage it. Or, we might have to stop it altogether, or ask for help to make the effects go away because its aftermath has become uncontrollable or unmanageable. For example, when it comes to pain, various scenarios are: 1) preventing a child from touching the boiling water in the pot; 2) managing the slight pain after the kid quickly dipped his finger in and out of the pot; or 3) driving him to the hospital after the pot falls on him and causes second degree burns.

The recovery time varies per case and per level of pain. This concept applies to anger. Let's try not to let anger get out of control or rise above a certain level – or drown us. Let's decide to not allow anger to hurt us or cause scars. The important thing is to prevent anger whenever or wherever possible; once triggered, anger demands our time and effort to dissipate. Wouldn't you rather be spending that time on something more productive?

When we consciously choose to change our behaviors, we can begin to break patterns. Instead of treating somebody the same negative/bad way they treat us, we can decide to respond by showing compassion and kindness. This is no easy task, of course; it is easier to insult somebody after they have insulted us. But, our "higher self" knows better. Be mindful that "our reactions are our teachers" because they can enlighten and instruct us. Remember to look inward and not just outward whenever faced with a challenging person or situation, and take the time to think before reacting. This way, we can better monitor ourselves and manage others.

Find the Core Cause or Reason

There is always a reason behind every action, whether it is conscious or not. And sometimes that initial reason might seem obvious, but it might actually be hiding the real reason why somebody behaves in a particular way. A big part of increasing our awareness is to find the core cause or reason behind the action. For example, somebody who is suffering himself might be lashing out because he is externalizing the pain he feels inside. Just as he feels bad, as a way of coping, he tries to make others feel bad. It is like an escape valve or compensatory behavior where he deals with the inner pain by making others – typically those who are weaker than him – feel that same pain.

So, whenever you feel slighted by somebody, tell yourself that their words and behaviors are because of them… not you. Do not take it personally, and instead try to find the cause behind their action so that you can better understand and then adjust your response accordingly. It can help to visualize this concept as a billiard game where one ball hits all the others. The white one will shoot against the ball that is strategically in the best place to be able to sink it through one of the six available holes. In other words, sometimes we will be the unintended target of somebody's anger or frustration. If they just found out really bad news, for example, and you were the next person whom they talked to, you might experience their emotional outburst – just because you happened to be in the "right" place but at the "wrong" time. They will share their suffering with anyone who crosses their path, and unfortunately that can be you. Therefore, it is better not to take things personally and give them the benefit of doubt.

There are occasions when someone says negative things to us, and even though we know they are not true, it feels like *they* believe it is absolutely true and so we become naturally defensive. We resort to our primal instincts of reacting without thinking because what they said touched a nerve or emotional trigger, and it overpowered our mental capacity. It is like a hook being thrown at us, and it is up to us if we bite onto it. If we do, we will get pulled into the mess of negativity. Even though it might feel that individuals are throwing "bombs" or hooks in the form of fighting words to use throughout the day, let us choose not to give them power or control over us (our thoughts or behaviors). Let us not fall in this emotional power game. Recognizing our behavioral pattern when faced with negativity is an important first step in the process of increasing our consciousness.

Our reactions will teach us much about what we need to do in order to improve ourselves not only mentally and emotionally but also spiritually. Therefore, we say that our reactions are our teachers, since they are teaching us all the time. You just have to observe them and analyze what has happened to learn and grow from the experience.

A renowned pastor and educator, Charles R. Swindoll once said: "The only thing we can do is play on the one string we have, and that is our attitude. I am convinced that life is 10% what happens to me and 90% of how I react to it. And so it is with you. We are in charge of our attitudes."

Once we recognize our attitudes, we have the power and the opportunity to change them.

FREEDOM AND RESPONSIBILITY

- Sara, are you already watching TV?
- Yes, I will leave the shower and homework for tomorrow morning.
- Are you sure? Won't it be more difficult to get up so early in the morning? Do you have a moment to talk about this? I would like to understand your reasons and your point of view a little better.
- Perfect. Let's talk.

Human beings are naturally intelligent and their physical environment is shaped and influenced by them. God has given each of us gifts and abilities to develop our full potential in life, but we need to first discover them and then learn how to use them. Increasing our consciousness gives us a deeper insight into who we are and what we do so that we can decide who we want to become and know how to get there. This process of self-discovery starts during childhood, and so the education we received and the experiences we go through play a huge role in terms of developing both our academic and socio-emotional intelligence. As society continues to learn the direct (and powerful!) impact of education on children, new academic curriculum and training frameworks are being considered and implemented for the next generation.

As discussed earlier in this book, society, parents and educators can impose on us dogmas, rules or obligations that use discipline and punishments to govern our lives – from the moment we are born. But, what would happen if we discovered that this traditional system did not fully enlighten and equip children, and was actually counterproductive to what was originally intended? What if all this time, our educational system built on rigid rules and strict policies of obedience was flawed and was inhibiting children instead of empowering them?

We can greatly improve the way we instruct and guide children if we first realize that each has an internal compass, and that each one is different. Our role as parents and educators then would be to discover that compass and then teach frameworks that nurture and refine it. When we help children develop their conscience along with consciousness, we give them the life skills of discernment, responsibility and accountability, which empower them to make wiser and better decisions (conscience). With our help they can receive guidance toward where they should operate. Children must learn them not just at school, but also in the home.

Teaching responsibility is the foundation on which personal consciousness and conscience is developed. Such responsibility is something that is not learned in and of itself, but through others demonstrating it. Children will learn to be more responsible by watching their parents be responsible. As noted earlier in this book, responsibility means "the ability to respond," and once children learn they are responsible for their choices in life and also have the power to make decisions, they will realize they are free to define their life's path. That realization is empowering! However, if one feels that he cannot control his life, he will feel confined to a self-imposed cage of rules. It is why we say without responsibility, there is no freedom to be ourselves.

Navigating a Child's Compass

To effectively educate children in ways that grow their conscience and/or consciousness and sense of independence, it is very useful to ask specific questions that guide their thoughts and responses. The goal: to inspire deep self-reflection and enable them to carefully observe and reason. Through our clear guidance and thoughtful explanations, children will gain the insight and encouragement to begin creating their own path, with their compass guiding them. If we see that our child is not being responsible, instead of telling him to do something, we can ask him if he thinks he is being responsible and, whether he says "yes" or "no," then asking him why he believes that.

Help children see what their options are and why they have chosen a specific one. When they learn they have options, they learn they have a choice. Show them how each option leads to a specific result or consequence, and they will weigh the options and hopefully choose the wisest or beneficial one. Instead of them doing something because we forced them to do it, they are empowered with the knowledge that they are able to choose their path and therefore become more responsible for what those decisions may or not bring.

Suppose (again) a child does not want to brush his teeth, for example. To help him change this attitude and become aware of the consequences of not taking care of his teeth, we should ask him questions to lead the conversation. What are the benefits of practicing good hygiene? What might happen if he does not brush his teeth? What specifically is the reason he does not want to brush them – time, effort, pain? He likely has not thought about *why* he does not want to do something; he just knows he does not want to. Our job as parents and educators is to enlighten him.

For example, we could talk about the bacteria in the mouth and the process of how teeth get cavities. We can mention the bad odor of the breath, and the economic cost of going to the dentist for not brushing them. If he complains that he does not like the brushing sensation in his mouth, we can assure him he will like the pain of oral disease or surgery much less. We can educate him about all the methods and foods that will help keep him healthy, maintain the white color of his teeth, etc. The child begins to learn how to assess the benefits and consequences of a behavior and create his own criteria, which then enables him to make an informed decision. With practice, this ability to think critically before making a decision will be a very beneficial lifelong skill.

Responsibility is Taught

It is also important not to forget that responsibility is taught, and is not just learned by itself. Responsibility is exercised only when there is the awareness of freedom of choice because it is directly related to the person's intrinsic and/or external motivations. Consider the analogy of a father who teaches his son to ride a bicycle by himself (responsibility). Initially, the father has to hold onto the bike and guide him. But at some point the father lets go and the child will ride without supervision.

When the child becomes an adult and decides to ride a motorcycle, he may or may not decide to ask for help depending on the learning experiences he had when riding a bike. It also depends on his motivation to learn. The point is, yes, the child could have maybe learned to ride a bike on his own, but his father was able to facilitate that process by guiding him and teaching him how to become independent.

Freedom of Choice

We all have basic human rights, yet sometimes our individual freedoms can be removed – even by force. Unknowingly so, educators can often take away a child's freedom to have a voice in their own learning process. The act of effectively educating others requires our focus, energy and continuous effort; there is a lot involved. For example, staying alert, monitoring social cues, testing hypotheses, analyzing results, etc. It is a combination of commitment, effort, determination and perseverance that enables an educator to act responsibly in every situation with a child.

However, we must always be mindful that the most ideal educational process also demands our ability to give children the freedom of choice. This means experimenting with the best way to enlighten the child from a positive and well-informed perspective. It means not judging or blindly assuming, but rather teaching and guiding from the point of view of learning. Do not simply tell them what it is; *show* them what it is. Instead of telling them what to do, *explain why* to do it. Of course, there will be moments when you will have to push through unpleasant experiences or resistance with the child, but be mindful of your influence over their long-term development. Decision-making and problem-solving are key skills to have as an adult, and their learning process is part of our role and responsibility as educators (parents and teachers) in their life.

Think of every child like a fruit tree (orange tree) that is planted in seed form. It will gradually evolve but will need certain foods, supplements and water from us to properly flourish and grow on its own (responsibility). It must mature before the actual fruit (oranges) appear. We cannot force the tree (child) to bear fruit whenever we want it. It will be when it has to be – and when they are ready, not when we are ready. However, we can nurture the development process along the way.

The Ability to Fail Forward

We all know that nobody is perfect; therefore, we cannot expect the child to be perfect or the learning process to be perfect. So, expect mistakes and mishaps. Expect the process to be difficult. But, welcome those challenges. See every mistake, every challenge as a learning and growth opportunity. Encourage the child to "fail forward" – make mistakes, learn from them and then improve as a result. It is how they will increase their level of consciousness.

We as parents, aunts and uncles, brothers and sisters, teachers and spiritual leaders, etc. can guide this process by offering questions, suggestions and thoughtful explanations. Remove judgment and reprimands. Toss out punishments, and leverage the power of intrinsic motivation instead. The most difficult part of this entire process will likely not be felt by the children, but rather by you as it will require the ability to adapt to children's ever-changing minds, bodies and attitudes. Stay focused, be vigilant and remember your influence on their long-term development in life. Do not casually dismiss experiences or behaviors you do not like or that make you feel uncomfortable. Sometimes it is those types of moments where the most insight can be gained.

Remember It's a Process, Not a Fast Fix

If a child does not want to do something on his own initiative, or we encounter resistance to our teachings, try to figure out the reason why, instead of reprimanding him or forcing him. It may be because we have not yet found a way to motivate or persuade him properly. Or, maybe it is because society's rigid system of rules and regulation that command blind obedience and rely on punishment to motivate has caused him to lose the desire to learn and grow. Change is not easy, especially when there is a fear of or resistance to it. In order to overcome the challenge, we must first seek insight and understanding.

Learning is about the journey, not just the destination. However, every journey should be towards something or lead someplace. Usually when one starts a journey, he defines an inspirational vision of success. He sets goals and then spends a lot of time working towards those goals while also making personal sacrifices. Consider Olympic athletes, for example. The typical athlete follows a very strict and intense physical training routine of six, even seven days a week. Some train between five to eight hours (or more!) per day. Sustaining that type of schedule requires an inspirational vision, intense focus, and a lot of sacrifices in terms of time, money and family. What motivates these athletes to stay on the right path and push through challenges is their ultimate vision: making the Olympic team and earning a medal.

Now, apply that same concept to teaching children. In a sense, children have already started a lifelong journey to increased awareness and enlightenment. But like any journey, it needs a destination. Goal-setting is crucial to any type of education (academics, playing instruments, sports, etc.). It is our role as educators to help them set short-term and long-term goals that will motivate them towards the ultimate "pay-off" of hard work and perseverance. Helping our children develop and exercise their power towards their goals plays a very important role in their fundamental education and personal growth development. In doing so, we empower them with the responsibility, know-how and confidence to be masters of their lives – and to own their future. What an inspiring thought!

This sense of responsibility can then be extended into other areas of life as well (i.e., personal hygiene, personal safety, household chores, managing their own property, etc.). It is all about reminding them they have a choice, training them to look for options, and then guiding them on how to make the best decision. I remember a friend telling me once that his father encouraged him to always choose the most challenging option in life (the one that required the most amount of work) because life worked better that way and grew that person the most.

The Art of Negotiation

Discipline and obligations imposed on the child should always be monitored and modified and only be applied with an emphasis on responsibility, dialogue and negotiation. This way, the child can correct his behavior while also increasing his level of consciousness. The ability to negotiate and dialogue with the child will be key to overcoming challenges. Negotiation should be used whenever there are differences of ideas or opinions, or a lack of understanding. During the process of negotiation, each side is free to express his views and desires, with the goal of calmly helping the other see and understand his perspective (lens). The ultimate goal is then to empower the child to choose what to do, as our role should not be to force but rather guide. We are not dictators, after all.

After the negotiation process, if we then observe that the child does not organize himself properly or does not make a wiser or better decision (i.e., continually goes to bed late or skips showers), it is an opportunity for us to talk with him again to point out our observations and seek understanding of why he is behaving as such. It is important to reason with him without losing control of emotions or passing judgment. This way, he will be more motivated to recognize and learn from the consequences of his behaviors, and ultimately make more informed, more responsible choices.

Helping him create plans of action is another way we can teach responsibility. For example, guiding him to make an after-school to-do list with timelines as to when he will do his homework, have dinner, play sports, watch television, etc. Rather than us just telling him what and when to do things, we can empower him by involving him in the planning process. When he participates, he will feel more motivated and more accountable in terms of following that plan. Negotiation will also play a role in this planning process. For example, if he expresses his desire to play video games or use technology for hours at a time, we can negotiate with him in terms of better balancing his schedule that accounts for his desire for entertainment but also fits in time for other essential activities, such as doing homework or practicing an instrument.

Ask the Right Question

At all times, it is very important to connect with children through genuine love. Otherwise, we will focus on using obedience rather than understanding to guide our instructions and responses. The following questions are helpful to encouraging awareness and self-reflection:

- What do you plan to do to become better organized?
- What time are you going to bed?
- How long are you going to play?
- Why is a better option for you?
- What could you do to improve next time?
- Is there a wiser decision?
- How can you continually improve your body? Your mind? Your soul?

In order to create an effective plan with children, be specific in terms of times and responsibilities. Remember you are helping them set up guidelines, not dictating rules or laws. Instead of saying "Do what I say," it would be more productive to say, "While in this house we always tell the truth as well as pick up after ourselves." Once the child has learned to be responsible, the need for rules goes away, as they are self-aware and self-sufficient to behave more respectfully, constructively and consistently.

Over time, as there is an increase in mutual respect, you will be able to see they do things not because they have to (or because they fear punishment), but because they want to. Intrinsic motivation instead of extrinsic motivation drives them as they elevate their level of consciousness and responsibility and are free to make choices. This type of freedom is crucial to their long-term growth and development.

RESISTANCE AND THE FIGHTING FORCES

- Connie, you need to stop what you're doing because you have an exam, and you need to study.

- Yes, I know. But I do not want to start studying right now. It's such a nice day and I'm enjoying something at the moment. Besides, I hate physics.

- Connie, the sooner you begin, the sooner you will finish. You still have to take that exam and, if you do not start studying now, you will finish very late and you will be too tired to remember anything.

- Yes, yes, give me 20 minutes more because I want to finish this movie.

When we love what we are going to do and it excites us, such as eating ice cream (yum!), playing a sport, going to a concert or traveling, starting the task does not require any effort or need any convincing from others because we like doing it. Nobody needs to nag us or threaten us to complete it because we delight in the task and want to do it as soon as possible and as much as possible.

However, when there is something we do not like or do not want to do, or we perceive it as an obligation, the easiest thing is to make up any possible excuse to procrastinate or not even do it at all. For example, when faced with homework or household chores or family obligations, some of us complain. We pout. We argue. We cry. We ignore it. Or we don't give it our best effort. These are all forms of resistance (pushing back/against). A visual example of physical resistance is the difference between running on grass or running in a pool. In which case does one experience the most resistance? The pool, of course, since the water makes us move much more slowly. As a result, we spend more energy and more time in the pool than we would walking on somebody's lawn to achieve the same distance.

Acknowledging the Resistance in and around Us

We face resistance in many aspects of our lives, which can make moving through life faster or slower, or harder or easier. Resistance (emotional, mental, physical or social) can often inhibit growth or expansion and prevent us from reaching our goals or obtaining the insights we need to evolve. To oppose something is to resist it, as resistance involves two opposing forces. Mass is a manifestation of energy that produces resistance. If there is no resistance, there is no mass or form, so there can be no experience since we would not exist. A bookshelf, table, chair or bed causes resistance because it has mass, so you can store your books, sit or sleep.

The strategy behind personal growth is to continually push beyond our limitations. Meanwhile, the opposing force of homeostasis (resistance) wants us to stay where we are and not advance. Resistance is a force of the "human will" that opposes something we do not want to do because of homeostasis. We need to fight resistance and persevere if we want to evolve. We need to understand that we have to overcome the human duality of the animal and God, where we will sometimes be closer to one part or the other.

The Lessons of Resistance

When we are in our lowest moments, maybe closer to the animal part, and we feel weak or in constant pain during difficult times, we can ask God to help us rest and recover. In this case, the purpose of resistance was suffering so that we can humble ourselves and ask for guidance and help. In these moments we can simply kneel and call upon God for help – to give us a reprieve from our suffering and help us learn the lesson from it.

The level of resistance depends on the individual. We cannot permanently conquer it or ignore it, so we will have to learn how to manage it as best as we can and minimize any negative impacts. The force of resistance varies depending on the intensity of the moment, our internal state of mind and environmental/social factors. Sometimes it can be managed well; other times it can get out of control.

Forces Vary

It is somewhat like the view and attitude we have when we get up in the morning. Every day is different and we cannot know completely what we will face or experience, or how we will feel and respond. Sometimes we wake up in a good mood and feel powerful, but other times we are looking forward to the end of the day because we got up on the wrong side of the bed and we want it to end. Then there are times when life throws us an unexpected curve ball, which can either improve or dampen the day. Life is adventurous like that.

In situations where we do what we are passionate about, it seems that everything goes effortlessly. We do not even know that time has passed, as we are so engrossed in what we are doing, we do not notice anything else. Like when we read a fascinating book, for example. Ever accidentally stayed up all night because you just could not put down the book and had to see how the story ended? Some of us concentrate so much on a task we love that we do not even hear when somebody is talking to us.

But then there are things we do not like doing. For example, if we hate school, depending on our level of resistance, it might take us four to five hours to prepare for an exam instead of the typical hour we would spend on a similar task (but one that we actually enjoyed). The good news, however, is that in these types of cases, if we are in our "higher self" and are conscious of why we need to study, we will become more mature in our ability to effectively face and overcome resistance. It is a constant journey to be able to manage resistance (internal and external) and it takes deliberate focus and hard work, but it is a worthwhile endeavor. Resistance is itself a very important evolutionary force.

The Ultimate Neutralizer

Motivation can overcome resistance. Being motivated towards some-thing helps balance and eventually overtake the opposing force of resis-tance. Love (not fear!) is the primary motivation to neutralize resistance. Through love, we give the best of ourselves and leverage understanding and compassion to lessen the power of resistance.

Also understand that, as we increase our knowledge and skills about life and move up the Pyramid of Consciousness, we will become more la-ser focused in our thinking patterns and behaviors, and not be weighed down by all the forces in and around us. Instead of spreading ourselves thin multi-tasking and responding to various things coming at us, we can focus our efforts on achieving one thing or responding to one person. This is a lot less overwhelming and enables us to become more proficient or more effective in a specific task or situation. With consciousness and love, everything flows and works differently. This is the process towards spiritual awakening in which individuals are more present and conscious in their everyday life.

The goal is to create more balance and inner peace for ourselves. Just like it is not ideal to be weighed down by the burdens that come with multi-tasking, it is also not ideal to be so focused on one thing that it becomes an obsession or addiction or escape from reality. Thus, often choosing to travel life's middle lane (gray zone) and vary focus from one thing to multiple things, and then back to one thing, will depend on your motivations, state of mind and forces you encounter. This middle point can be reached with practice once we reach the upper levels of the pyr-amid.

"ADULTING:" LEARNING TO MAKE RESPONSIBLE DECISIONS

- *Well, so what are you going to do?*
- *I think I should study medicine, but what I really want is to pursue music, which is what I'm passionate about.*
- *They why don't you study music?*
- *Because my parents want me to study medicine.*

There are three main roles we can take on when we interact with others: child, parent or adult. Each one has distinct characteristics, traits, thoughts and behaviors. Of course, we want to always behave as an adult, but the reality is that some adults still behave as children. Regardless of age, however, we should always seek enlightenment and maturity.

Each of us, no matter how old we are, should always assume the adult role. This means treating everybody equally and respecting them as human beings. We should think as adults, and act as adults – even when conversing with children. Although their bodies are small and their minds are young, babies and children still deserve our respect. Instead of treating them like a baby, we should treat them as an adult in terms of showing them love and sensitivity since what we say and what we do can directly impact their development in either positive or negative ways.

Interaction with Babies

Of course, we cannot expect babies to treat us as adults – they cannot even talk yet. But we should still talk to them from a position of respect, and actually make a conscious effort to communicate with them. Babies, in fact, need more positive attention than any adult because they are forming their foundation of self and will absorb both our verbal and nonverbal cues. We definitely do not want them to adopt any neurosis or emotional instabilities we might have.

When those babies turn into toddlers who are learning how to talk, they might interrupt our conversations with their own babbling or simple questions. This might annoy us at first. However, instead of telling them to be quiet or ignoring them, the respectful thing would be to listen to them. They are building their foundation of language and speech and are still learning the most optimal ways to express themselves.

Which Role: Child, Parent or Adult?

In life, you will find that some people will tend to adopt a specific role, such as that of a child, depending on those who enable it, or on the rewards received from it. If a grown woman knows she will get her way if she acts like a child to her parents, she will take on the role of a child. Additionally, others will continue to see somebody according to a specific role. For example, a mother might continue to view and treat her grown son as a child, even though he is physically an adult. The man then has a choice: to act as a child so that his mother will do everything for him, or as a man/adult who is not dependent on his mother. Role playing becomes very important in the context of relationships. Ideally, there would be equal roles (adult versus adult), but often people take on different roles at different times, which causes conflict for both the self and the relationship.

As discussed, the basic roles are:

1)   Role of Child: Speaks – sometimes – with the voice of a small child, acts based on impulses and instincts, does what he wants and when he wants without considering the consequences, pouts when he doesn't get his way, and focuses on quickly satisfying his current desires.

For example, a person playing the child role would say: "I want to eat some cookies, so I'll take them from this person's kitchen and eat them." He does not think it through or consider the consequences, but rather acts on instincts and impulses. If we asked him why he took the cookies, he would say, "I think it because I want it, so I do it." Although the cookies did not belong to him, he justifies it in his mind and excuses his behavior.

2) Role of Parent (Father): Thinks, acts and behaves through the lens of what one "should do" or "must do." His actions are influenced by what society or his parents have conditioned him to think and do. This self-imposed behavior is memorized and then passed on to others. He does not think for himself but merely thinks and does what he believes he should do – or what society tells him is right or wrong. It may seem ideal to play the role of parent, but it is actually the opposite. In this context, the parent role manifests in behaviors, actions and decisions that are void of real self-consciousness or responsibility.

For example, assume a child plays the father (parent) role. He is governed by how he thinks he should act and obeys without asking questions. Before making a decision, instead of evaluating things himself, he considers what his father, mother or authority figure would tell him. It is their voice in his head instead of his own voice. For this reason, he would try to think and behave as his parents would, with repeated phrases in his head like, "I have to …" or "I must …"

In the case of the cookies scenario, he would think, "I should not eat chocolate cookies before dinner, so I will not." To reach this conclusion, he thinks what his own father would tell them to do, and by doing so, assumes no responsibility or control over his thoughts and actions.

3) Role of Adult: Behaves in more balanced, mature and responsible ways. The Adult role gives us more control of our own lives by enabling us to make decisions with conscious insight and reflection. It is aware of society's learned rules, but does not use them as the basis to form thoughts and decisions. The "Adult" usually speaks in a normal voice using a calm and cordial tone, but modifies it accordingly based on the situation.

The Adult analyzes the situation and is not deceived by or oblivious to external factors. He recognizes and accepts the consequences – whether positive or negative – and looks for the lessons in them. He is empowered with both the knowledge and the ability to make changes in his life after carefully weighing the pros and cons of each situation at any given time. He consistently takes responsibility for his decisions.

In the same example of the cookies, he will think: "I know that cookies of any kind will take away my appetite if I eat them before dinner, but today I did not have a snack and I could use a cookie, and I also fancy it a lot. I will savor it very slowly so that I can reduce my hunger pain but will not let it fill me up for dinner. Once I have something in my stomach I will see how I feel and, if I need another, I will eat it too; otherwise I will just wait for dinner."

Being an Adult does not always mean we have to be "right" or choose the "best" option. In order to learn responsibility, we have to practice making good choices, knowing that sometimes it might not be the best one for us. However, in those cases, it is important to reflect on the decision and action, recognize and accept the consequences, and learn how to make a better decision next time. Instead of resenting his decision or feeling ashamed, the Adult knows that it was his own free will (and not blind obedience) that caused him to behave as such. Therefore, he learns from it, changes his subsequent behavior in similar situations, and grows into his "higher self."

Our "Whole" Self

Earlier in this book we explained the importance of not isolating a certain part of our personality to interact with somebody, but rather to be our authentic selves. This means being entirely who we are, with "entirely" being the key word. If we fragment ourselves to please somebody, we only break up our personality (ourselves) and enable the person to have power over what we are say or do. Some of us feel it necessary to fit the role of the rebel, the obedient, the goody-two-shoes, the nerd, the clown, the survivor, the tough one, etc. But as mentioned in a previous section, trying to fit ourselves into somebody's perceived image or stereotype of us only breaks us into pieces. It confines us and prevents us from being who we really are.

In the Adult role, we need to be consistent in our words and behaviors. If somebody wants us to act like a child, we must be mindful that whenever we conform to that person and change our behaviors to please them, we sacrifice a part of us. This inhibits our own personal development. The key is to accept both ourselves and other people as we/they are in order to create and maintain relationships based on authenticity, transparency and respect.

Never Too Early to Start Learning

This is a crucial lesson to start teaching our children in their formative years and to consistently give them the opportunity to develop their own consciousness and/or compass. The goal is for them not to be merely carbon copies of their parents or other people, but for them to evolve their unique and special character traits and personality the way God intended. Instead of imposing our own will and personas on them, we simply guide them in becoming the best version of themselves. We show them how to take responsibility in who they become and what they do. We enable them to make mistakes without judging or criticizing them, and teach them how to always look for the life lesson.

It is our main responsibility (and our privilege!) as parents, guardians, educators and coaches to continually guide and encourage this type of healthy development, no matter the age, and to accept them as they are (external appearance, personality, strengths, weaknesses, etc.)… always.

EVERY VOICE MATTERS: WHY WE SHOULD ALL SPEAK UP AND OFTEN

- I told you to shut up.
- But Daddy, it is…
- What do you want now? You just won't let me talk. I'm on the phone with your mother.
- I just need to know if she's going to pick me up after the end-of-course party tomorrow.

Anybody who has been around children for any period of time knows that they can be quite curious, excited or even just bored, which is often manifested in a lot of talking (questions, random talk, complaints, etc.). For some of us, our first instinct is to hush them up – especially when we are busy doing something that requires our focus, like working or talking on the phone. However, our more conscious self ("higher self") knows that it is very important to teach children that their voice matters and should be expressed. It is why instead of shutting them down, we should enable them to freely express themselves… without us getting in the way by hushing, judging, criticizing or ignoring them. When we tell them to be quiet, what lesson are we actually teaching?

A lot of discovery and learning can happen through the process of verbal communication. If children have questions, for example, we can answer them. If they have doubts about something, we can reassure them. If they feel bad about something, we can comfort them. Children are continually taking in external stimuli and trying to make sense of it. Through thoughtful dialogue and reasoning, as well as giving them the freedom of open and transparent expression, educators can guide children through that process and help them become more self-aware, more self-informed and more responsible for their own individual thoughts and actions.

As we grow up, we develop and learn skills of all kinds and in all different ways. Sometimes traditional education transfers information to children based on strict rules of behavior, which do not promote individual thoughts or freedom of expression. Some educators and parents who embrace this type of teaching believe their voice matters more than that of the child, and therefore are more prone to saying things like:

"Just do what I say."
"Because I said so."
"The discussion is over; go to bed."
"I don't want to hear your reason; you're punished."
"Don't argue with me. I don't want to hear you."

These types of phrases shut a child down. It is like we have cut off their wings so they cannot fly high to become who they were intended to be. Not allowing them the fundamental freedom to express themselves stifles them and prevents learning. How can they discover and leverage their power if we continually show through our words and our reprimands that what they think and feel do not matter?

Of course, there are times that warrant for a child to not be loud or to be polite, and we will need to provide guidance in those moments and teach them the optimal ways to voice their thoughts and feelings. In church, for example, it is not ideal for a child to yell out during the sermon or prayer. Each child, each situation is different, and if we are always conscious of how our responses can help or hurt them, we can be a lot more productive in our conversations with them instead of just instinctually telling them to shut up.

Same Action, Different Responses

We should also be mindful that not all children are affected equally by the same responses and forms of discipline. When scolded, some of them will become depressed while others will be apathetic or defensive. It depends on the child's personality and perception of rules and consequences. In general, those children who are more "rule-followers" will feel guilty or sad when they get in trouble for breaking them. On the other hand, those who are more independent thinkers and/or have a more rebellious nature, will either act like they don't care or will fight back when confronted. This may be because the latter group feels more confident in who they are and do not give somebody's disapproval of them power over how they see himself.

When we demand that children do things without explaining why and then expect absolute obedience, we are acting more in the role of a child who is unconscious ("lower self") than as an adult who is enlightened ("higher self"). Every time a dialogue between an adult and a child disappears, an opportunity to learn and evolve also disappears. Over time, this teaches children that they should only be seen but not heard, and consequently they learn that their voice does not matter. This can lead to them feeling oppressed, misunderstood or even unloved. As a result, anger, resentment, bitterness and/or rage begins to build, snuffing out opportunities to promote tranquility, peace, compassion and kindness.

Modeling Positive and Productive Communication

The freedom of expression does not mean that children are allowed to scream or curse at their parents, or communicate through disrespectful nonverbal cues, such as rolling their eyes, sticking out their tongue or making faces at them. It is quite the opposite, in fact. All communication – whether from the adult or the child – should be done with love. This means transparency, authenticity and respect. It is our words, tone and body language that can either help or hurt the dialogue. Everybody should view and approach somebody through the lens of love, which can then guide how one speaks and reacts. Just as parents and educators should remember that their responses can nurture a child's development, that child should keep in mind that his parents, coaches, etc. are trying to help him, teach him and care for him in the best ways they know how. For mutual respect to occur, each side needs to seek understanding of the other's intentions and motives.

Teaching children how to voice their opinions in a responsible, respectful and calm way will empower them with the skills of communication and the ability to speak honestly and openly from the heart. Instructing them properly requires us to consistently model that behavior, for children often pay attention to not just what we say but what we do in order to learn and model it. This means, when they express their objections, we adopt the Adult role, and calmly and carefully explain our reasons while looking them directly in the eye. We do not condescend with an "I am smarter than you" or "my voice matters more than yours" attitude but rather talk with them like how we would talk to a peer. Over time, we create healthy communication patterns that promote the freedom to express oneself in a positive and productive way.

Expression is Everybody's Basic Right – Regardless of Age

Having the right to speak is very important at any age. However, I did not learn this in early childhood. I remember one day when I was in kindergarten and I did not bring the reading book. My teacher reprimanded me by pulling my ears very hard. Of course, I never said anything to my parents for fear that they would be angry with me (even though they would not have been!). I remained silent because I had never experienced anything like that before and had no positive coping mechanisms (nor rules to follow). The only thing I knew at the time was that I should keep my mouth shut because I was told my action was wrong and that I must respect elders "because they were always right."

Throughout the years as I have interacted with or educated children, I have learned that many children are unaware of their human right to speak. Some have faced situations far worse than I had in kindergarten and have not spoken up because they thought it was the wrong thing to do or because they feared punishment. Being empowered with the knowledge, skills and freedom to express themselves is crucial to developing positive coping mechanisms as part of their ongoing healthy development. In many cases, if they do not speak up regarding how they feel or what they are experiencing (abuse, for example), they risk the chance of the bad experiences continuing – sometimes for years to come.

We as educators and influences in their lives should always be mindful not to discourage or prevent children (through scolding, disciplining, silencing) from expressing themselves. How else will they be able to learn and develop positive coping behaviors? How else will we learn what they are experiencing and feeling so that we can best help them? We cannot reprimand and/or silence them yet also expect them to grow at the same time. Remember the analogy that we cannot be cheese and butter at the same time, that is to say, that either we victimize them or we empower them. It is a conscious choice.

"HIGHER SELF" VS. "LOWER SELF"

- What do you want to do this summer?
- Go to the beach, drink a lot, connect with many girls and dance like crazy until dawn. Ah! And take a lot of photos of all my incredible experiences and friends to publish on social media. I will be the envy of all!

We can think and act using either our "higher self" or "lower self," depending on our level of consciousness and/or conscience at the time. The "higher self" thinks of others before himself, considers what is best for all, is connected with his environment, tends to be more generous and compassionate, promotes conversations to bridge conflicts, has an attitude of gratitude, and views people through a positive lens. A person who is using his "higher self" is typically self-aware, responsible and accountable for his actions, and thereby usually makes decisions based on insight and what is ethically correct, instead of operating off instinct or what seems fast or easy. He does not shy away from challenges or options he does not like, but chooses to face them, perseveres and makes tough or fair decisions.

The "lower self," however, only thinks of its own benefit through its own perspective. The person who is using his "lower self" tends to act based solely on instincts and desires in order to quickly satisfy specific needs. He has a more negative lens and therefore is prone to making snap judgments and criticisms without bothering to find out the facts or understand others. This "lower self" is on the bottom part of the pyramid, which means a state of unconsciousness (or very little consciousness), and prevents the person from evolving into his full potential.

Either/Or: Same Situation, Different Self

A simple way to understand the key difference between the "higher self" and "lower self" is with the following example. Imagine sitting in the subway, and at the next stop, an older lady enters. Seemingly tired and weak, she is searching for a seat, yet soon discovers that all seats are occupied. If we have our mind in the "higher self," we would happily give her our seat because we have recognized that she needs the rest a lot more than we do. However, if we are utilizing our "lower self," we will likely remain sitting and maybe look the other way to avoid the situation. Meanwhile we would think of excuses for our behavior. Our preferred justification: "We are tired and have the same right as her to sit here."

When we are thinking from our "higher self," the thoughts are integrated with those of the "lower self;" we are "whole" and are able to integrate and organize all of them. We can analyze each situation from all different viewpoints and sort out instincts from insights, which elevates our level of thinking (and responding). However, when we use only our "lower self" to think and act, we detach from critical thinking, relying solely on our primal instincts and behaving from a self-first (selfish) perspective. If the "higher self" is active or engaged (top part of the Pyramid of Consciousness), it becomes a kind of "mother hen," who welcomes all her chicks in her arms and gives them the best of herself. In this case, the "other" becomes more important than the "self."

We can often fluctuate between the "higher self" and "lower self" (bottom part of the pyramid). For example, assume you were up all night due to the neighbor's baby crying. Your "lower self" would become angrier and angrier as the night wore on due to lack of sleep. Paying attention only to your instincts and how tired your body felt, your primary objective would be to relieve your own misery as fast as possible while giving little or no thought to the neighbors (who were also up all night).

If you were using your "higher self," however, you would be more understanding that the parents have not been able to calm the baby and would also show compassion towards the family. Maybe the poor baby has a fever or is not feeling well, you might think. Perhaps you would empathize with the mother who is holding the crying baby (and could be crying herself!). Because you would have a higher level of consciousness, you would not allow your emotions to guide your decisions and behaviors but would first assess the situation, consider all the facts and weigh the factors, and try to understand the situation from all sides.

This "higher self" of you would be just as tired as your "lower self," but you would not rely solely on your instinctive feelings of exhaustion and anger to form your responses. Instead, you would view the experience in a calm and meditative state and move towards love (peace) and away from fear (anger). You would choose not to drown in negativity and resentment but instead act responsibly and decide not to let anger keep you from sleep.

Lens of Love

In order to evolve in positive, healthier ways and become more conscious individuals, it is important we continually monitor and reflect on our thoughts, feelings and actions/responses throughout the day or in specific situations. For example, are we viewing this particular moment or event from an optimistic or compassionate perspective? What are the benefits to that lens? Or, are we using a negative lens and becoming angry, critical or judgmental? If so, how are those feelings and responses making the situation worse? Let us always try to view people and situations through a lens of love and then respond from our hearts.

To delve deeper into this subject, it may help us to read the "Bhagavad Gita" where some of the ancient teachings of India are narrated, including the "higher self" or Krishna, and the "lower self."

THE TITANIUM SHIELD

> *- He told me he does not love me, but the truth is that I don't love him either.*
> *- Why do you say that? Up until two minutes ago, you did not want to leave his side.*
> *- Yeah, but the truth is that in the end I do not care. Nothing happens. It doesn't matter.*
> *- Do not start thinking that way. I do not really know how you do it. Suddenly you erase your boyfriends from your life without even thinking twice!*

Some of us have built a wall around us or have held up a titanium shield so that nothing can penetrate and affect (hurt!) us. We do this to not only protect ourselves but also avoid people or situations that can cause suffering. However, to truly learn and evolve, we must give ourselves the opportunities to live new experiences (even the most uncomfortable) and to make mistakes. Although we have good intentions, our metaphorical titanium shield actually can prevent us from connecting with people and challenges we need in order to learn and grow. It inhibits us from seeing the world as it is and therefore prevents us from fully understanding and responding to it through an enlightened, conscious perspective. It does not allow others to see in, just like it does not allow us to see out.

When we are in titanium mode, the ability to understand the reality of others can be very limited and thereby distorted. If we cannot fully see or understand them, it is difficult to develop empathy or sympathy, which prevents our relationships with others from becoming as honest and deep as they can be. This pseudo-perfect reality we create for ourselves can temporarily feel safe and comfortable as we "hide" from the world. It is easy to avoid challenges and only seek out what feels good to us.

What we do not realize, however, is that this is a false reality and at some point we need to "wake up" and leave the shadows to pursue the light. It is the only way we can truly evolve our consciousness and develop nurturing and deep relationships with others. Growing up, I never understood why people continually would ask me how I felt or if I was okay. I always felt the same from day to day, so I wondered why they would even ask. In my own little world I had created, I did not expose myself to new experiences – and so nothing much changed in my life. It was like my world was flat (static) without color or flavor. As a consequence, I did not evolve as much as I could have back then.

From Darkness to Light: It's a Journey

Transitioning from titanium mode into a more open, operational mode is not easy. It involves commitment, focus, great effort and our ability to give the best of ourselves. Consciousness is a journey, and we need to move beyond our shell or shield and bravely face the world. We need to view life more holistically, observe more carefully and analyze feelings and emotions more deeply. It is a process. Think of the sun, for example. If we exit a dark cave and look immediately at the sun, our first reaction will be to look away. However, if we gradually develop our sight in stages, such as focusing on the shadows, then looking at reflections, we will advance our way to the sun, as Plato tells us.

This titanium world where we may live distorts our perceptions and gives us the illusion of reality. But, it keeps us in limbo. We are not dead, of course, but we are not fully alive either. We have essentially blocked ourselves from external experiences and opportunities to become better people. In a sense, we have blocked our heart from showing or receiving love and gaining true knowledge. In this dimension of titanium, we keep life (smells, feelings, people) at a distance in order to manage our sensibilities, vulnerabilities and fears. It can be confining. Imagine if you literally all day, every day wore a huge plastic protector guard from head to foot, as if it were an immense condom. How would you feel? Weighted down? Constricted? Would life feel fun and rewarding? How would it alter your perception of reality and life? Would you even recognize you were wearing it?

If we are made out of titanium, important events and incidents might not have the value or meaning they have for others because we have not allowed ourselves to feel and experience them fully. Instead, we would isolate ourselves and live, to a large extent, in a material or shallow world that limited us. Life would not be as rewarding as it could be. If one day we wish to "awaken" to experience life to its fullest, we must be sure that everything (lens, approach, self-imposed barriers) changes. It will not be easy because it will require great determination, effort, time and perseverance, but the payoffs of enlightenment, fulfillment and enjoyment will be far greater. It's worth it!

Perhaps the most difficult challenge throughout this process of moving from dark to light will be to recognize the existence of a self-imposed shield or wall, for in most cases, we do not consciously create one. Some of us have lived with it so long, we are not even aware of it and therefore cannot imagine an alternative reality without it. We do not know we have suffered from it or that it has limited us because we take comfort in its perceived safety, solitude and protection. At some point, though, we need to acknowledge that it will eventually isolate us from the world and weaken us – emotionally, mentally and even spiritually.

THE CLOSED HEART AND SENSITIVITY

- She left me! We were getting along and we loved each other. I don't get it! It seems that she does not even care.
- I know. She is like that. Nothing affects her.

The individual with the closed heart is typically driven by fear and is rigid, although he is not often aware of it. He is fixated on his own point of view, and probably feels the need to rely on rules and obligations to guide him, even though it makes him feel more lost. Instead of being intrinsically motivated, he finds it difficult to be passionate about much of anything, for his heart is closed to new people and new experiences – all of which can potentially develop him in beneficial ways.

In the case of having a total blockage of the self, which includes the heart, some consequences and negative side effects are that the person likely enjoys life less than others. He is typically apathetic, insensitive and acts emotionally distant at times. Connecting with others is difficult, so he tends not to look others directly in the eye and avoids intimate conversations. He can quickly become frustrated or angry, or condescend and insult, when he cannot understand or relate to others. People and events that make him feel uncomfortable are generally avoided. In short, a closed heart is equivalent to not being connected to the world or universe, and the person separates himself from the rest. In a sense, he creates his own self silo.

Having spent much of my life with a closed heart has meant that I have lost many opportunities that could have led to great experiences, insight and personal development. I compare it to having one or more of our most important senses blocked or broken for a period of time. It limits the powerful experiences that can be gained. It is like going out to dinner but not being able to use your sense of taste. You can smell your favorite dish, but cannot taste it. Definitely not the ideal dining situation!

Opening the Windows of our Heart

As we become more openhearted and embrace new experiences and challenges, our ability to actively visualize, learn and understand (rather than only causally watching and passively memorizing) others and our environment will develop by itself. It is not something that can be forced, but that will organically develop as the heart continues to open and expand. This means we cannot become frustrated when we do not suddenly change overnight. It is a process, and it will require self-patience. First the window of the heart may open. Then another window will follow. Eventually the door will open wide.

There are techniques we can do to open our heart, such as performing heart meditation exercises, or volunteering our time and effort to support a charity in directly helping others. For me personally, a very effective technique that tremendously helped me (in only three days!) set a new milestone in my personal development process was when I completed an intensive Reiki Tummo course. I had spent an entire weekend in the class, which focused on connecting my exterior gestures and actions with my internal feelings and emotions. I had to smile for hours on end and continually exhibit feelings of love towards others there. In that short amount of time, something had transformed me, which increased my consciousness and elevated the way I lived my life. Now, I am happy to report that I smile and laugh very often.

Creating Balance

As referenced earlier in this book, Yin and Yang is a Taoist philosophy (originated in China), which says that although they are two opposing parts/forces in the universe, they have complementary energies. In each Yin there is a small part of Yang, and vice versa. Both come together and form a whole, which is necessary for true existence. This duality creates balance while ensuring that nothing is entirely good or entirely bad.

The same is true when it comes to viewing one's feelings. We will continually experience what we perceive as good and bad feelings; the key is knowing when to use them. If we recognize our feelings through a lens of consciousness and responsibility, we are able to better manifest those feelings in ways that help evolve us. Our feelings are in a continuous state of flux between love and fear polarities. Our goal is then to balance our energies so that we can live as our whole self in a constant state of peace.

Learning and Leveraging Sensitivity

Sensitivity (the ability to act to stimuli) can be learned, but first we have to rid ourselves of our self-imposed protective shields and accept the fact that the more vulnerable we are, the more in tuned to our feelings, the more flexible we are in changing situations, and the more we will be able to adapt to, experience and enjoy life. Increasing our level of sensitivity in the right way (fully absorbing and positively responding) gives us the ability to utilize all our senses in exploring our environment. Life will then become more enjoyable as we discover through our eyes, ears, nose, mouth and touch the incredible experiences life can bring. This enables us to eventually shorten the cycle of hurt feelings or bouts of suffering that can plague us, and even teach us how to avoid behavioral patterns that do not benefit us.

A great way to increase our ability to connect with the world around us to actively concentrate on seeing, on observing, on analyzing and on feeling. Instead of rushing through an experience without thinking, it is more ideal to stop, look and listen. But, be sure to keep an open mind and do not allow yourself to make snap judgments or baseless assumptions. As you move through an experience, you do not yet have the insight or the consciousness to be able to make correct judgments. Therefore, practice being in the moment and experiencing it with all your senses as best as you can without formulating opinions.

Of course, being sensitive is a very important and wonderful trait, but since the world is made up of Yin and Yang, we should be mindful of our level of sensitivity and the balance of our emotions and feelings. Just like we want to be personally connected to people and experiences, we do not want to be overly sensitive. In other words, we want to be perceptive, present and powerful, yet we also need to ensure that we are not emotionally weak or fragile or overwhelmed, or succumb to the power of a particular feeling. We will be able to create and maintain a balance of our sensitivities and feelings by increasing our consciousness and understanding who we are, who others are, and how we interact with each other.

Getting to truly know our full selves is something very few individuals achieve because many of us have grown up with restrictive and/or oppressive programs that rely on orders, rules and punishments to control our thinking, instead of enabling us to develop as free and independent thinkers through the lens of unconditional love and empowerment. From these types of negative programs, rebellion and anarchy are born. Anger, resentment, bitterness, rage and even violence increase. We can reverse a lot of this by putting focus on studying who we are and what we do in order to increase our consciousness and understanding. We can then teach others how to do the same.

Sometimes we will not notice change right away, or how something we are doing is affecting us. Imagine, for example, that you decided not to eat any food at all. Day after day of not eating would eventually cause you to lose weight, and you would likely notice the physical change. However, there would be other things that would happen in your body that you would not notice at first. As your body would start to enter starvation, for instance, it would begin to shut down your internal organs. Weakness and exhaustion would start to take over little by little and negatively impact your energy level or ability to think or reason clearly. At some point you will discover the bodily harm that lack of eating caused, although others might not be able to see those effects or changes. Meanwhile, you would be managing the best you can in the moment. This process is similar to those living metaphorically without food (love) and they manage their life as best as they can without noticing the negative or harmful effects of doing so.

Being sensitive, conscious and perceptive gives us inner strength through love. It allows us to receive more information, and it activates empathy, gratitude, transparency, truth, compassion – even joy and laughter. The more we experience and analyze our feelings, the more we will learn about ourselves.

EXPERIMENT, EXPERIMENT, EXPERIMENT

- I will not try that. I've been advised not to.
- Yes, I understand, but I'm going to try it.
- We've been told that they can be bad for our health because we
* have not acquired a taste for them yet, and we could be allergic.*
- I know it's not going to hurt my health and I'm going to eat a
* couple of them. I'll order for everyone. A plate of oysters from the*
* Cantabrian Sea gentleman, please.*

Throughout our life, new experiences arise that can bring new insight and new growth opportunities. Learning happens with experimentation because we have to leave our comfort zone and try different things, instead of hiding in our safe little world. If we do not seek out new people, events and situations, we tend to do the same thing over and over again. Why? Because it is easy or familiar or comfortable. Life is an experiment, however, and we should always be looking for the tests (challenges), the analysis and the lessons in and around us.

Fear tries to stop us from experimenting with life. It warns us of the likelihood of failure or mistakes or negative results. Society teaches us to avoid certain situations or people that have the potential to hurt us. It tries to guide us down the path of least resistance and always do what is safe. In the real world, though, we cannot shelter ourselves. Experimentation requires that we move through the experience – sometimes a difficult or painful process – and test our responses and make our own conclusions.

The Paradigm Shift

We cannot simply rely on other people's experiences to guide us; we need to endure them and persevere ourselves. Rather than fear or turn away from them, we should embrace the goal to "accept what life brings us" – without judging, victimizing or shaming. Sometimes life is not in black and white, and if we lead our life by limited thinking, such as "I'll only do things I like," or "I'm not doing that because I do not like it," we will never experience the freedom and benefits of life experimentation. It is therefore best to approach each situation with a lens that lets us see shades of gray, and adopt a "let life be manifested" attitude.

If we want to change our paradigms or just test them, it involves opening our minds and reflecting on what we have been taught thus far and what, if anything, has validity. We can then determine if there is a different and better way of seeing things (shaping our lens). In order to think reflectively and consider multiple viewpoints and perspectives, we need to shift from rigidity to fluidity. We should open our minds to develop a higher consciousness and more realist worldview, while restraining bias and judgment.

The most optimal school of consciousness, understanding and even spirituality is based on experimentation, testing and analysis. Again, just like conducting science experiments, the process to experiment with and learn from life follows a similar process: observe the experience, analyze what happened, reflect on the results, and learn from them.

Calculating Risk vs. Reward

Taking risks is part of life; the key is discerning between the large, small or manageable threats and weighing the costs versus the benefits of an action. The higher our level of consciousness, the more we will be able to manage risks in any given situation. Additionally, we should remember that everything that is presented to us in life has a reason – it has a "why"—although sometimes we will not identify the purpose initially.

It is important that we do not avoid too many risks when it comes to raising or educating children. Overprotecting children and avoiding challenges could delay their evolution and make them fearful of life and less equipped to overcome adversity and life's hardships. Over time, they can develop a negative predisposition or automatically conditioned response of always responding with a strong "no" whenever facing a challenge or decision before they even weigh the risk versus the reward. If we only inch through life in small steps, and never boldly try new adventures, our learning will be proportional… and very little.

Wait to React

When we are in the midst of a new experience, it is advisable not to judge or reach conclusions quickly. Instead, we should just try to be present in the moment and simply observe, experiment, practice discernment and "tentatively analyze" each situation. Remember that people process information and make decisions according to their perceived reality and past experiences. One of the underlying messages of this book is that we can improve how we assess situations and make decisions by increasing our ability to be more self-aware as well as wait to form conclusions until we have had time to collect the relevant information – discovery and investigation – and understand different perceptions. This prevents wrongly judging and instinctively reacting to certain emotions, while helping us to develop a more positive and conscious lens.

The decisions we make will be formed heavily on the basis of knowledge and experiences we have lived so far, because we tend to do what we know. However, as we all also know, the facts can be much different than our opinions or even our perceptions of the facts. Therefore, it is best to suspend these opinions and judgments until we have a clear and deep understanding of all factors (people, motives, events, etc.) involved.

According to the proverb of Heraclitus, a Greek philosopher: "You will never go exactly through the same river twice." This means that each time the water flows, it will change, implying that each new experience will yield different results. Moreover, if we look at that experience from another perspective along with acquiring new knowledge, it could be double the difference! The lens we use can change the view, just as our knowledge base can change it as well. Therefore, we need to be more conscious of how we see the world and how our internal biases shape our decisions and responses.

We should also be mindful that theories can differ from the actual reality. If we theorize something, we only have a part of the information we need to be discerning. It is only when we put it into practice that we will truly understand how it really feels and how it works. Consider the act of learning how to ride a bicycle, for example. We might have read a lot about how to learn the skill and might have watched a lot of people ride one, but until we physically get on the bike, pedal and maintain balance, we will not have actually learned how to ride it.

Arms Wide Open to Embrace Life

This is why it is most ideal to approach each experience and challenge with a high degree of consciousness. If we wait to collect the facts, understand the perspectives and, in some cases, metaphorically put ourselves on that bike so we can engage all our senses, we will be less likely to emotionally react in negative ways. This is a learning process in which we will need to consciously practice through trial-and-error the best ways to assess and respond to situations. As we continually practice and grow our skillset, we will open ourselves to numerous opportunities for learning and personal growth and be able to fully embrace and leverage what life can offer us – with arms wide open!

If we decide not to experiment with life and avoid anything that makes us feel fearful or uncomfortable, our world becomes smaller as opportunities pass us by. Change is necessary, but it is also difficult at times. If the thought of making big changes causes fear or anxiety, then try taking baby steps. Even one step forward is better than where we were. With each step comes more learning and more evolving – no matter how little that step might be. Deciding to put training (support) wheels on a bike might be best for the anxious person who is scared of falling. Those wheels might not enable him to speed down the street, but they at least allow him to move forward and start learning to become more confident and independent. With more practice and time, those wheels will be taken off, and he will be empowered and free to go as fast as he wants.

For those who want to take bigger steps, it is necessary to become a lot more conscious of oneself and one's environment. With bigger steps can come bigger risks, and we can better prepare for those challenges by learning how to develop into our "higher self" and avoid the emotional pitfalls of instinctive reactions. Jumping into a river, for example, requires awareness of one's swimming abilities, water temperature, rocks, etc. But once we have that knowledge about how to enhance our experience while reducing risks, we can make that jump – and have a joyful time! So, let us experience as much as we can in life without letting clouded judgments get in the way. Let us always assess and experiment with situations, weigh the risks and rewards, and practice a trial-and-error approach to learning.

Let Us Always Seek the Lesson

If we are acting in the Adult role, we can open ourselves and move into the world of conscious experimentation without letting judgments (our own and those of others) influence our behavior. Whenever a new adventure or challenge comes our way, a best practice is to analyze it from all angles: What are the risks? What are the benefits? What are the consequences? Who will it affect positively or negatively? To do this, you will need to continually touch, examine, test, probe, observe, reflect, rethink … experiment. What have we learned? What are causes and conclusions? Have we done this before, or is it a new experience? Life experimentation always requires analysis and introspection in order for valuable insight to be gained.

Life is what it is, and depending on the life lens you have, it can be perfect or imperfect. You can see it as beautiful or ugly, based on how you see the world and others… and how you see yourself. The key question we should also ask as we live new experiences, adventures and challenges is: What is the lesson that life is trying to teach right now? That particular situation or person or event might not be how you want it; it might make us uncomfortable or fearful or angry. Keep in mind, though, we cannot change that situation or that person – but we can change ourselves and our perceptions and responses.

So, let us accept everything that happens to us even if we do not like it or cannot change it. It is in our life for a reason, and we can use it as a learning opportunity to become a better version of ourselves. Therefore, let's always take risks and learn. Let's use introspection tools so that we can reflect along the way. The greater the analysis, the greater the learning. Let us accept the will of God and learn everything that life is trying to teach us. Let us give ourselves to the process with humility, responsibility, consciousness, faith and, most importantly, love.

SECOND PYRAMID LEVEL: OBEDIENCE

"Strengthen the female mind by enlarging it, and there will be an end to blind obedience."
Mary Wollstonecraft

HOW TO WAKE UP OUR MIND, AND KEEP IT VIBRANT AND ALIVE

- Mom, do you know that yesterday I got an 8 out of 10 on a French test? The teacher says that if I improve my orthography I can get a 10 in June. To add accents is hard for me, but I'm sure that with more practice I will get it. Mom? Mom, are you listening to me? Mom!

-Excuse me, son, what did you say? I was distracted and was thinking of something else.

-Ha! You always do that!

Sometimes life becomes a bit monotonous – so much, in fact, that many of us do not appreciate the day-to-day and tend to disconnect from the world. It is like our brain operates on autopilot and although it "drives" our mouth or body to move, we are not actually aware of what we are actually saying or doing. It is times like this when we are "not present" or living in the moment but are instead thinking about the past or the future.

Imagine that you are in a car stuck in traffic on the freeway, for example. Your mind is focused on what you will be doing that weekend or on what happened yesterday with your significant other. But then suddenly,

SHAKE BEFORE USE: A Basic Guide for How Life Works / PART 3

someone's car hits you from behind. In that moment, you are forced to focus your entire mind on the present moment so that you can recognize what just happened and react accordingly. In other words, your body automatically knew to tell your brain to focus on the here-and-now so you can problem-solve immediately.

Being able to focus your mind is a valuable skill. When you notice (or somebody tells you!) that while performing a boring task your mind has wondered and are therefore disconnected from the present moment, you can consciously switch up the routine by changing your physical activity. For example, brush your teeth with your other hand. Choose a different road route. Comb your hair an alternative way. If you are walking outside, instead of getting lost in your thoughts, deliberately focus your mind on elements in nature. Study the trees and figure out what type they are. Search for gardens. Consciously wake up your mind and keep it feeling active and alive by seeking new visual stimulations.

Imagine you were talking to a blind person and were trying to describe everything you perceived using all five of your senses. What would you be sure to observe and point out? Train your eyes and your brain to notice the colorful nuances of life.

THE POWER OF POSITIVE THINKING

- I'm sure I will pass the exam.
- With how much you've worked for it, I am sure you will.
- Yes, I am feeling good that my studying will pay off.

Seeing things from a positive point of view means that you are choosing love instead of fear. It is also essentially valuing and enjoying what we have, instead of focusing on what we lack. This appreciation of all that surrounds us is vital to continuing on the virtuous path towards consciousness. We should proactively develop a positive lens through which we see the world, despite any negativity that others throw our way. Their hurtful words can only affect us if we let it. Thinking and acting positively is a conscious choice, and over time if practiced consistently, it can turn into a healthy habit. So, choose to be happy and peaceful and do not allow others' criticisms to matter.

Neither should we take anything personally. At first it might be a bit difficult for us to learn to think differently – to give that person the benefit of the doubt that his words were not intended to make us feel bad. For example, we may think that this person has said something against us not to cause us pain but because he feels bad about himself and is taking his frustrations out in the wrong way. Or, maybe his negative emotions have been building up inside of him all day and they finally exploded when we just happened to be walking by at that exact moment.

Earlier in this book, I advised that we hold off on judgment until we had as much insight as possible and were conscious of all perspectives in order to more accurately assess the situation or person. At some point, however, we form opinions and conclusions, and those should be from a positive perspective. In fact, a good way to change a negative thinking habit is to create a positive thinking habit. For example, every time you catch yourself thinking something negative about somebody or an experience, add a positive thought. There has to be at least one positive or special thing, so your challenge is to find it and focus on it. Flip the lens.

The Shift from Wolfdog to Sheepdog

When we begin to shift our thinking from negative to positive, we not only become less critical about life but we also develop a broader and more balance mindset towards others. We discover more joy and a healthier outlook on life. Who would you rather be around: a positive person who builds people up, or a negative person who complains and criticizes? Become the person you would want to hang around. (I'm assuming you chose the positive person, by the way.)

In the end, the situation (or person) is the same, but it is our attitude that can change. And this attitude is a conscious choice in life. Positivity (love) or negativity (fear) does not merely "happen" to us, for the same experience can affect people in different ways. Our lens shapes our experiences which then shape our responses. When we have a positive attitude, we look for traits and details that fulfill us or excite us or that bring us joy. So, let us choose not to suffer and to be happy instead. Let us choose joy in every situation so that we can experience inner peace. Let us not get caught up with the haters, bullies or online trolls who annoy us or put us down. The challenge is then not to give into these people, for negativity is often contagious. Think of a negative person like a hunter who uses all kinds of lures so that we fall into their nets of despair and do not recognize it until it is too late. Learn how to spot them early – anywhere and everywhere.

Whenever I explain this concept to children, I use the analogy of a wolfdog versus a sheepdog and tell them to choose one for any given situation. The wolfdog (the aggressor) is the one who responds with a strong attack and has no control of himself because everything bothers him, as he has a negative view of life. On the lower part of the Pyramid of Consciousness, he gives into his animal instincts and becomes angry easily and even eats the sheep. On the contrary, the sheepdog (the peaceful pacifist) is calm and serene, is on the higher level of the pyramid and always responds through a positive lens once he has the right knowledge and consciousness to do so. Unlike the wolf, he does not eat the sheep and instead guides them. It is always my hope that children decide to be like the sheepdog.

LET'S ALWAYS SPEAK THE TRUTH

- Dad, why don't you eat the vegetables?
- They make me sick, son.
- But then why do you eat carrots at other times?

Whether we admit it or not, some of us have developed a habit of telling lies to make excuses for things we either did or do not want to do. Our intention is not to hurt anybody, of course, and so we think these "little white lies" are justified. However, these lies – no matter how seemingly small or big – undermine our integrity. They directly deter our personal growth development because to be fully consciousness of ourselves, we need to be as authentic and transparent as possible. Even the "littlest" lie hurts our ability to be completely "real" with both our self and others.

Consider the following example. Somebody phones our house and tries to sell us a product or service. Instead of blunting telling him the truth that we are not interested, some of us would say we already have that product and therefore do not need another. We justify that "lie" because it sounds a lot less rude than "we're not interested." It feels easier to just solve the problem with a lie so that the caller would go away without hurt feelings and we can get off the phone as fast as possible.

Although that lie did not seem to hurt anybody, it actually did – it hurt us. The "lower self" individual would likely not recognize the cause or impact of the lie, but the "higher self" individual would acknowledge that the act of lying disintegrates our system in that it utilizes only a part of a personality. It is the part of the self that wants to protect the individual from the fear of being judged or the fear of direct confrontation. Rather than acting with our entire true self, we isolate a part of our personality in order to please others and/or avoid situations. We can also lie to ourselves without even knowing. Those who frequently lie and justify it with excuses are typically on the lower part of the Pyramid of Consciousness (on the Obedience or Ignorance level). Their need to obey or avoid situations overshadows the need to be one's authentic self. As we move up the pyramid, however, we become more conscious of lying's negative effects on ourselves and on relationships, and learn how to integrate our whole self so we can live life more openly, honestly and fully.

Breaking the Habit of Lying

To break this habit, practice these useful (and honest!) responses as convenient substitutes for lies whenever it feels uncomfortable answering a question. These can be applied depending on the conversation topic and context.

- Option 1: *I cannot tell you.*
- Option 2: *It's something personal that I do not want to talk about right now or… Let's talk about this another time.*
- Option 3: *Why do you want to know about that?* (This question enables us to find out the intention or motivation for why this person needs the information, such as wants guidance or advice about something, or would like to provide assistance.)
- Option 4: *For ethical purposes, I cannot share what other people have told me, because they trust me and I cannot betray that trust.*
- Option 5: *I do not want to talk about that topic, as it is a personal and private issue, and is really nobody's business.*

POWER: OUR INFLUENCE OVER OTHERS

- *Boss, I think this time I can do it the right way on my own.*
- *If you feel sure, you can go ahead. Keep going, and I will finish other pending issues.*
- *Perfect, thanks for this opportunity.*

In the traditional educational system, rules and standards are enforced with strong discipline to deter students from acting out. Of course, educators typically have the best intentions of guiding students; however, this heavy focus on restricting behaviors and commanding absolute obedience can strip children of their power to freely and independently express themselves. It is not this way everywhere, as there are contemporary educational frameworks being used worldwide to empower and teach students and educators (parents, guardians, teachers, coaches, etc.) to guide learning in conscientious and responsible ways so that instead of restricting one's power, we can leverage it to learn and grow.

The first step to effectively guide a child's personal development (academic, mental, socio-emotional, spiritual) is to consistently provide a stable, secure and loving environment that can nurture him. Our goal is to equip him with the life tools and support to help him both recognize and harness his power, which is defined as the capacity to exert change. We also need to provide him with the right to speak openly and the freedom to communicate often and candidly with adults. It is the main way he will be able to understand all the environmental and social influences around him and gain the insight he needs to develop inner strength. The more power he has in life, the more he will be able to influence change.

With Great Power Comes Great Responsibility

However, with great power often comes great responsibility, and therefore we need to ensure that we always affect change in a positive way. The more power that is accumulated, as in the case of a high-profile and influential person or an authority figure, the more humility (defined as "the capacity to be taught") and responsibility are required. Without humility, power can easily shift into arrogance or illusions of grandeur that can negatively overpower or corrupt people. But, with a consistent focus on being self-aware, humble and loving, one's power (influence) can grow and change others in helpful, supportive and even inspirational ways.

My own personal experience with the educational system growing up was that it was too rigid and toxic for me to properly develop as a conscious and confident person. With its strict rules and need for blind obedience, it exerted way too much control over my behavior, my ability to learn and even my thoughts. This literally blocked any inner transformation that could have empowered me to be better and do better. I recognize that the idea of implementing a behavior regulation system in schools sounds appealing, but it is often distorted or abused to the point it infects everything it touches. It is like a Trojan virus where at first you do not see it, but then it spreads unknowingly until one day when you are blocked from the computer and discover the virus's poison.

There are many benefits to growing one's power in that it can help us deal with complicated situations and give us the confidence (and the belief factor!) to improve ourselves and respond to challenges in positive and productive ways. However, if we teach power-building techniques to children, but do not teach them responsibility or guide them to make better decisions, we are doing only half the work. If they develop the capacity to influence change, then that change should be used for good, not for bad. It is why children need to continually work towards their "higher self" so they can recognize and choose the best way to change the world around them.

RULES, RULES AND MORE RULES

- Daughter, you know I told you not to leave anything on the stove because it could burn. You always need to remember that!
- Mom, I'm not going to turn on the burner. Don't worry. I'll remove it in a minute. I have to finish washing the lettuce. Besides, there is no one else in the kitchen.
- No, I told you to take it off from there right now!

We generally have house rules that we expect family members to follow. The educational system also has its own rules for students to obey. Every day, children are reminded to follow rules or else suffer the consequences. These strict policies promote conformity, but they prevent self-discovery and the development of one's consciousness. Is this really the most ideal way to teach and guide children?

I have found that the rules that hurt children the most are those that restrict their rights and freedoms. The traditional educational system was developed on a type of military education where rules and orders defined how one should think and behave. Children are trained to ask permission for everything. For example, imagine a child is sitting in the home of a friend of the family. The friend offers the child a piece of candy from a dish on the table. In most cases, the child will first look to his parents for approval or permission. A slight nod or a "yes" then allows him to accept the candy offer, for the child has been taught that it could appear rude if he takes the candy without asking permission. His desire for the candy is overruled by his need and the pressure to follow the rules. It is in this way that being taught to make decisions solely based on rules and what is "right" and "wrong" limits our ability to think, speak and decide for ourselves. It takes away the opportunity to be responsible for our actions and makes us dependent on somebody else's needs and desires.

Applying responsibility assumes that educators have the ability to teach children to think for themselves. For this to happen, though, we as parents and teachers need the time, patience and knowledge to help them learn to discern (good and bad) and develop conscience along with consciousness from the moment they are born. Parents and the educational system need to be in sync throughout. Responsibility and consciousness (with conscience) do not happen overnight; it is through a gradual process (journey) over the span of years that enlightenment and full understanding of oneself and of others can be reached.

Reasoning skills will help us think more clearly and more holistically by enabling us to assess the benefits and consequences of our actions. Blind obedience removes the need for reasoning, however, and divides our world into what we should do and what we shouldn't do. It does not enable us to look around and assess all the "colors" of the situation. It does not engage our senses. Instead, it merely gives us only a black-and-white vision of our experiences. It is like we hold reality in one hand but an imaginary world in the other. But, what if we face a situation or experience that is not so clear cut and requires us to think outside of what we were told to do? What if there is no rule for that situation? If we were only taught to follow rules and not think for ourselves, we would lack the ability to problem-solve and see all the available options. Feeling helpless, we would then adopt the "poor little me" attitude and thus stay stuck not only in the situation, but also in life.

Why We Stay Stuck

We can stay stuck because we continue to use rules and obedience to navigate our internal compass. Why? Because accepting rules can be convenient – there is no need to think for oneself. There is no effort involved. Somebody tells us what to do, and we do it. That's it. We don't have to think or make hard decisions. We can blame others if something goes wrong. Also, at a very early age we learn the rewards and consequences of rules; if we follow them, we avoid discipline. If we don't follow them, we suffer the punishment. We grow up with this conditional thinking and behavior, and we are either 1) unaware (unconscious) that there is a better way to life, or 2) unknowledgeable of how to make decisions ourselves.

Some of us are stuck because we are not motivated to change as we do not know all the incredible benefits of thinking for oneself, expressing thoughts freely and creating our own life path. There are others who believe in the "I can have my cake and eat it too" philosophy and think that they can be obedient in the home and behave however they want outside of it. Unbeknownst to them, however, disintegrating their personality to fit the environment is another form of obedience.

It is important to note here that many people create rules to serve a good purpose. For example, young children need guidelines to avoid doing damage to themselves or causing others harm. But a central theme of this book is that we must also be mindful of how there are roadblocks to optimal consciousness development, and rules can be one of them. Too many of them, or too much focus on them, can remove individual thinking and expression, and demand that individuals function as mindless mechanical robots. Rules can remove the need to be responsible for one's actions. They can decrease somebody's power to affect change and keep them grounded on the bottom of the Pyramid of Consciousness (POC). By eliminating the special interests and individual passions of a human being, rules can force people over time to become apathetic. Why should we care about something if we cannot influence it, manage it or color it ourselves?

It is important to know that I am not advocating for a lawless society or the absence of rules; however, I am making a clear distinction between rules that restrict freedoms and individual expression, and rules that can guide and empower people to evolve. Rules are important for unconscious individuals (those on the bottom levels of the pyramid) because absence of rules and absence of consciousness can lead to unexpected, potentially dangerous actions as they are more likely to operate on animal instincts and negative emotions. As people move up the pyramid from the "lower self" to the "higher self," the need for rules will disappear as they are more enlightened, equipped and responsible to make positive decisions. Those using their "higher self" will not need somebody to tell them the right thing to do; they will already know. They will not be forced to act because they will be intrinsically motivated. They will not act out in negative ways but will instead embrace positivity through their lens of love.

The Consequences

Ironically, just as we are taught growing up that disobeying rules can lead to consequences, there are actually consequences for following them – although many of us do not notice them until after they have occurred. A simple example of this is to imagine that you have programmed a water sprinkler to automatically water your lawn for 10 minutes in the morning and then 10 minutes at night. But what if one day it happens to unexpectedly rain? Obviously, the lawn would not need to be watered that day, but the sprinkler does not know that, and so it would "obey" its programming and water the lawn. The consequence: You just wasted a valuable resource. Now, apply this to people obeying rules regardless of the circumstance. If we are programmed to follow rules at all costs, and not use our environmental and social cues as determining factors to influence our decisions and behaviors, what are some of the possible consequences?

When we are stagnant on the first two levels of the pyramid, we continue to let authorities control our lives and restrict our thoughts and actions. Unless we decide to move up the pyramid and become more conscious individuals, we will not change. The consequence of those who continue to act on instinct and emotional impulses is that they can eventually develop counterproductive thought patterns and/or abusive behaviors. Because they trust others' orders to guide them rather than trusting their own insight and experience, they can feel a general sense of helplessness or confusion when faced with new experiences, relationships or challenges. Without feeling empowered to make their own decisions, they blindly submit to authority.

In Full Bloom

Those of us who seek love but are not nurtured throughout life will never feel completely fulfilled. It is a like a flower that wants to grow, but if it is not watered, it begins to wither. One of the underlying themes of this book, however, is that there is much hope and we can plant many seeds. In fact, there is a definitive way to empower and nurture both ourselves and others (children) to develop into the amazing people we are designed to be. And just like a flower, if we find water and are supplied with nutrients, and also have the freedom to grow the way we need, we will surely bloom for all the world to see.

SEMANTICS: WHY WE NEED TO DISCERN "IMPORTANT" FROM "URGENT"

> - *CHARLES: Doctor, you need to take care of my mother right now, for she is very ill and is feeling dizzy. Listen to me, please, it's very urgent!*
> - *ANGELA: No! My husband has lost consciousness and is bleeding through the ears. This is more important.*
> - *DOCTOR: I will inform the nurse to admit the most serious case first.*
> - *CHARLES: But, sir, I arrived earlier.*
> - *NURSE: Sorry, kid, your mom will have to wait. Angela, please enter.*

As discussed earlier in this book, to be in our "higher self" is to be able to carefully observe and analyze a situation or experience from the love approach (good faith, good intentions). As we use our senses to interpret experiences, it can often lead to much input that we will need to decipher and discern. This will help us to prioritize and organize. As part of our lens through which we view the world and to understand our role in it is to differentiate between what is "important" and what is "urgent." They sound the same, but they are in fact quite different. "Urgent" implies there is an impending deadline – something that needs to be attended immediately –, but is it real? Or is it just associated to someone's wishes in order to accomplish things faster that probably could be delayed after analyzing the real circumstances? Furthermore, "important" pertains more to people and tasks that contribute to our long-term missions and goals. It also means that we cannot postpone something and it needs to be on our top priorities.

The following is a simple example. When the sick or injured arrive to the emergency room, doctors or nurses usually catalog each patient according to the standardized procedure that factors in the level of severity. After performing the initial checkup, they organize the final admittance list, which then identifies the most serious patients who are able to proceed to consultation before any others. Initially, this sense of urgency is conveyed solely by the patients' expressed desire to see a doctor. However, the doctor or nurse then assesses the patient and the situation based on a number of factors (passed out, bleeding, difficulty breathing, chest pains, etc.), and adjusts their preliminary analysis of situational severity and urgency.

Some issues in life might be "important," but they might not be "urgent." Conversely, some issues might be "urgent" but that does not mean they are "important." A patient might enter the ER with a broken hand and urgently need a cast, while another patient also needs urgent help as he is bleeding out. Which case is more "important" to the person's overall health and well-being? Doctors and nurses have been trained to assess situations and make informed decisions, and so they would likely choose to treat the latter first.

In life, there will be times when "urgent" and "important" will coincide when it comes to decisions, actions and experiences, but our "higher self" should be able to discern which should be focused on and addressed first. It is up to us to evaluate whether what is presented to us as urgent really has an important condition, since the confusion between the two terms is common. If we cannot recognize what is important in life, we will become overwhelmed as we focus on "treating" everything that seems urgent and important. Being able to discern between the two will help us better focus on what matters in our life.

HOW TO GET OUT OF THE HOLE

- *Jeff, I need you to stay tonight to help a customer who is going to call from Australia. His name is Mr. Gibson and you need to help him with a problem that has come up with a contract.*
- *EMPLOYEE'S PERSPECTIVE: "The nerve of that guy! My boss is always asking me to work long hours, instead of asking the newest or youngest hires to stick around. I'm tired! I'll talk to him tomorrow. Why should I donate more of my time towards this job? The more I give, the worse he treats me!*
- *BOSS' PERSPECTIVE: "I am confident that we will resolve this client contract because Jeff will be managing the Gibson account, which is so important. I know Jeff will do a great job because he likes challenges and he has the expertise and experience to overcome this contract problem. He is the type of person the company needs. Once he solves this challenge, I will make sure to promote him to Department Supervisor.*

Clearly, there is a perception issue and misinterpretation of feelings and motives. Jeff is giving into his "lower self" and is reacting to feelings; his boss, however, looks favorably on Jeff's perceived "higher self." Of course, conflict will naturally occur and result in a breakdown in communication. As this section will explain, there are ways that we can better interpret and manage emotions.

When we are feeling sad, angry, desolate, depressed or overwhelmed because something has happened to us or someone has said/done to us, we often take it personally, feel deflated and battle negative, demoralizing feelings. We find ourselves in an emotional pit of despair and we wonder if or how we will ever get out. But good news! There is a way to get out of the hole (sometimes referred to as "a funk") – and it is simple, practical and empowering. To learn this technique, continue reading.

As we already know, emotions are temporary; that is, they pass and do not stay with us forever. But that does not mean we should disregard or reject emotions. Instead, we should observe and monitor them and see how they manifest within us so that we can learn from them and improve the way we manage them in the future. It is especially important to recognize one's feelings and emotions while they are in their self-designed hole. Being in the hole or even digging it means that we are currently in a state of helplessness, which causes us to cling to "poor little me" feelings. This dysfunctional type of attitude can cause individuals to become addicted to suffering (masochism). The feelings associated with pain and feeling like a victim gratify them. It is like they find comfort deep in the hole.

Examples of "Poor Little Me"

In the following examples, the "poor little me" syndrome is alive and well:

- You went to class and the teacher punished the entire class for cheating on a test; however, you did not do it! You were just answering the exam questions as best as you could. But because others were cheating, the teacher punished all of you with a low grade. You become depressed and it ruins your entire day. "Poor little me," you think.
- Your boss at work has not behaved in a professional manner and has also said that your work has not been good enough within the commercial department. However, you know that you have worked very hard and have made great progress – and he hasn't even noticed! This causes you to feel overwhelmed by all the frustration and disappointment you feel after all the work you put in, and now you are very angry. "Poor little me," you think.

To calm down and eliminate the negative feelings or anger that arise within us, we can focus on assessing and learning about what we are experiencing. In these situations, we should try to return our mind to a state of calmness so that we can see things more objectively and make better decisions. If we are responding just based on the "poor little me" feelings, we are more likely to act out in negative ways. To calm ourselves, consider the facts from a different perspective instead of focusing on a particular emotion. This way, we reorient our mind and shift it away from feelings of anger or rage.

The Technique is as Simple as 1-2-3

The following three steps that focus our feeling, thoughts and imagination (creativity) will enable us to shift our mindset to positive thinking and responses. Once you have learned how to implement these steps in this order, feel free to use this technique to guide others.

After proceeding through the following, which will help organize our inner state, we will later learn how to develop the ability of compassion so that we can move from negativity to positivity, thus stabilizing our energy and improving how we respond to any situation.

1. Recognize Feelings

In the moment, focus on all the feelings that arise within. Distinguish each one and observe whether it is negative and is manifested by fear, confusion, anger, resentment, etc. Find the positive feelings as well. Typically, when we are upset or bothered, the feelings we are experiencing at that moment are predominantly negative.

2. Recognize Thoughts

Recognize whether these negative feelings are directly linked to our negative thoughts. For example, I am experiencing anger (feeling) and I am thinking that my boss has deliberately not paid me the bonus, even though I have worked so hard for it (thoughts). Our thoughts might then build on negativity as we justify why we are right to think this way. However, the more we focus our mind on the negative, the more negative feelings it will produce.

To guide our ability to focus inward and recognize which thoughts are leading to specific feelings, we can ask ourselves questions like:

- *What happened specifically that caused me to feel this way?*
- *Am I angry because of this one incident alone, or have I been accumulating feelings of resentment and bitterness for a while that is making me extra sensitive now?*
- *Are my past experiences affecting my current experience?*

The answers will enable us to link present feelings with either present or past thoughts. When we pay more attention to the direct link between what we think and what we feel, we can redirect our brain to more positive thoughts and therefore create more positive feelings. Looking at a person or an experience from another perspective while seeking understanding will enable us to better identify and interpret motives. For example, maybe our boss did something to us we did not like, but we realize he did not do it on purpose and did not think through the consequences. Or, maybe our boss suffers from low self-esteem or anger management problems, which causes him to make poor decisions. Maybe he had had a bad night and was not able to sleep due to sick children. By taking a moment to just breathe and access our experience or interaction with others, we can collect the insight needed to respond with integrity, positivity and love. We can then be more compassionate in our approach towards him instead of unleashing our rage, and potentially resolve the situation a lot easier and faster.

3. Use our Imagination

If we cannot think of anything compassionate to neutralize those negative thoughts, we can use our imagination and be creative in terms of our problem-solving responses. Let's return to the example of the boss upsetting the employee. We might have to get creative in terms of understanding the boss's perspective. Maybe we could ask questions like: What other things have happened that I do not know? Could his car be damaged? Could he have any family or medical problems? Could he be afraid of or threatened by something and so his fear is causing him to respond this way?

Sometimes we won't know the answers; if that's the case, focus on instead seeing the experience as a challenge for self-improvement and personal development. Seek out the lesson. Look for ways to learn and grow. Be creative in terms of how you problem-solve, with the end goal being to recognize your thoughts and feelings and then to redirect them towards the light.

It's the Climb

Once the process is completed (we have identified our thoughts and feelings and were able to shift them from negative to positive), we can start crawling (or jumping!) out of the hole. There will be times, however, when we will not succeed at first – it will depend on how entrenched those thoughts and feelings are, and on the depth of our hole. So, practice patience, focus forward and persevere. Exiting a particular hole might take us having to repeat the 3-step process a few times before we can finally climb our way out.

Using this technique does not mean that the problem has been completely and forever solved, but at least it can help us calm the mind to develop a more intelligent, balanced and analytical approach towards any problem or situation. Once harmony is restored, we can calmly talk to the person with whom we have had the conflict so we can really understand his perspective and all the dynamics of the situation that influenced his behavior.

Resolving the situation with a direct conversation should happen as soon as possible, but only when both sides are in a calm and collected state. During that time, focus on restraining assumptions, judgments and accusations, and instead ask discovery questions and take the time and effort to hear and understand each other's side.

In summary, the following figure visualizes the three steps to examine one's self in any experience that causes undesired feelings or actions. As we learn to better recognize what we think and how we feel, and then create new positive options in terms of our responses, we benefit from using our "higher self" and can leverage our power to climb out of any hole of despair.

The three steps to examine one's self: How to Get Out of the Hole

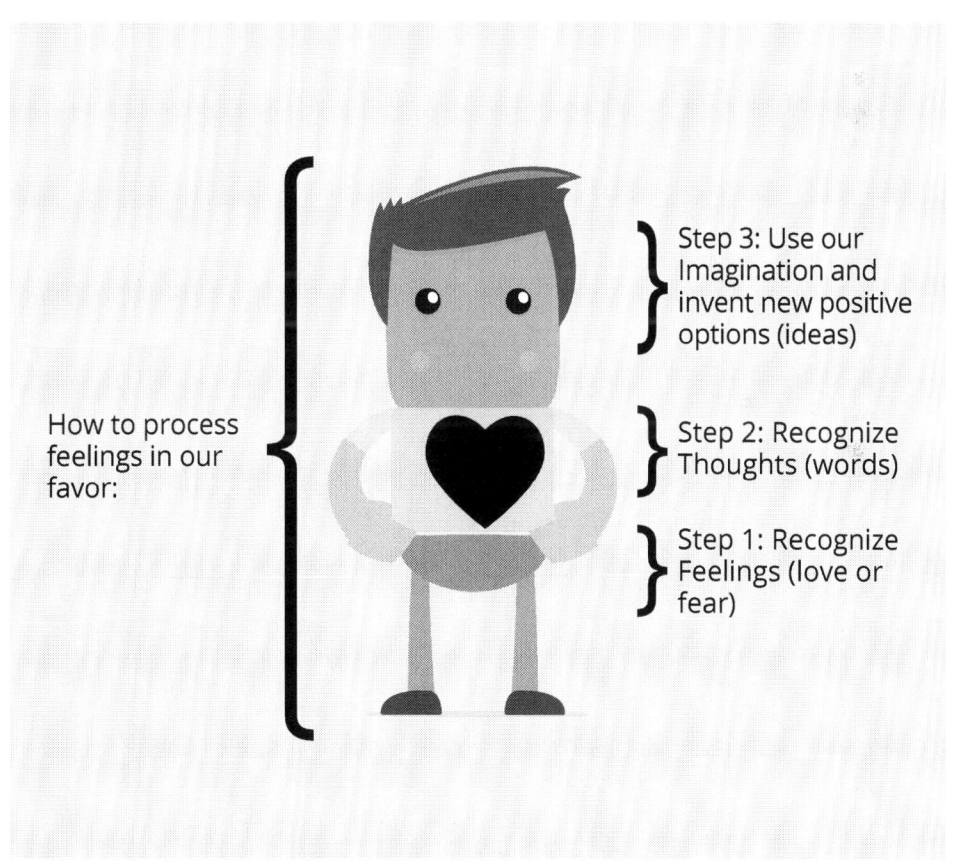

How to process feelings in our favor:

Step 3: Use our Imagination and invent new positive options (ideas)

Step 2: Recognize Thoughts (words)

Step 1: Recognize Feelings (love or fear)

QUESTIONING OUR VERSION OF THE TRUTH

> *- Give me back my candy. I know you have them.*
> *- What candy? I do not have them.*
> *- Liar! I saw you taking the bag. Surely you have them in your*
>   *backpack. Let me see it… Oh wait, it's true, they are not here.*
>   *What have you done with them?*
> *- If you mean Juan's bag of candy, he told me to pick them up from*
>   *the table and hand them over to him. I thought they were his.*
>   *Sorry, let me talk to him so he can give it back to you. I think it*
>   *was a misunderstanding.*

Having an opinion about something means we have formed a subjective conclusion based on the information we know about a particular person or thing. On certain occasions, we generate opinions that have little foundational basis and are instead gleaned from something we skimmed through, rumors we heard or stories we saw on the Internet – without relying on reliable sources or verifying the information.

With personal relationships we tend to follow the same behavior or pattern in jumping to conclusions based only on what we think we know. Sometimes relational miscommunication problems are due to incorrect perceptions, assumptions and opinions, which can frustrate and upset us. Whenever there appears to be tension or conflict in a relationship, until we have the opportunity to talk to that person and find out what happened or what made him act in a certain way, we should not form an opinion. It is better to hold off on formulating any conclusive thoughts until we have collected all the necessary facts and insight. If we hear a rumor for example, that our best friend has criticized us, it is wise to hold off on blaming him or becoming upset until we talk to him and find out the story. Maybe the rumor is untrue. Maybe we heard it wrong. Maybe our friend is upset with us. We will not know until we dig deeper to find out the truth before we become defensive and responsive.

Distorted Reality

If we decide not to gather such information, then we are essentially creating "our own truth," whose version might be completely different from the actual truth. In my case, whenever I find myself wanting to draw conclusions based on incomplete information, I consciously repeat to myself that "things may not be as I think" and this helps me to process the experience, collect as much insight as I can, learn from it and then formulate conclusions that are not clouded with self-serving opinions, emotions or judgments.

Also, keep in mind that there are individuals who tend to express themselves in certain ways that could lead to misunderstandings. Passive aggressive comments, back-handed compliments and half-truths can often cause confusion and frustration. What they say contradicts how they really feel, which only complicates the communication process and deters us from accurately reading the situation or relationship.

Imagine, for example, that someone says he will give us a luxury car if we jump without a parachute from any plane. We all know how dangerous it is to jump from a plane while it is in the air, and so we refuse the challenge since we conclude it will likely get us killed. However, this person then tells us later that we missed a great opportunity because he was referring to a plane that was on the ground. Did he confuse us on purpose? Did he try to set us up to fail the challenge? Or, did he simply forget to tell us? Some of us might automatically judge him as a mean guy and assume he had purposely tried to deceive or prank us. Others might give him the benefit of the doubt.

If we restrain from judgment and instead ask him the right questions, we might learn he did not mean to manipulate us and that it was an honest mistake. There are individuals, though, who play the "not being specific" game to intentionally create confusion. Later, I will present a strategy that will enable you to get a more complete idea of what they really say or mean.

ASSIGNING BLAME

- DEBBIE: Why is this book broken?
- MARY: (Points to Sara) They did it.
- SARA: No, that's not true. We did not do it. We left it on the table
without any scratches.
- MARY: Okay. No problem. Let me see how I can fix it. I'll use this
transparent lining, paper and glue.

One of the first lessons I learned when I started my instructional journey on the spiritual path was the meaning of pointing at someone and assigning blame to him or making the pistol sign with my hand. Blaming others shifts responsibility onto them as a way to not be personally accountable. I learned that the only person who has the ability to actively intervene and influence immediate change is ourselves – while other people's parts become secondary or passive.

I remember one occasion when I continued complaining about something that someone else had said. I insisted that it was all his fault regarding the behavior. At that time, I was asked if I really believed it was 100% his fault and if there was any chance I could share even a 1% responsibility in it. After some introspection, my answer was "yes." I could have intervened in a more compassionate way, and so I had to share the responsibility, however small.

The Symbolic Hand

When we assign blame to someone, we sometimes point our index finger at the culprit, which reminds us that assigning blame means putting a finger in the direction that is causing us or provoking undesired words or actions. The index finger always points forward (away from ourselves), and refers to the others involved (the allegedly guilty ones). We can also make the symbol of the hand (pointing) in the form of a pistol, where in this case the thumb will point upward towards God or "higher beings" and is essentially blaming Him too.

Taking the above into consideration, the other three fingers involved in the gesture are the heart, ring and pinky fingers that symbolize most of the blame, 60%, and that are bent towards the inside of the hand. These point directly at our own body, as if to remind us that our responsibility is always greater than the rest. It means that it is in our hands to change our thoughts and behaviors so we can change the situation. We cannot force anyone to transform or do something that we think is right or just, especially if he adamantly disagrees. We may not be able to change him at that moment – but we can change ourselves. In my personal example I had referenced, I was looking at the others (outward) and not looking inward at my own behaviors or motivations. As a consequence, I blamed him rather than deciding to accept responsibility and change myself… and potentially influence the outcome.

Leader vs. Victim Example

The difference between a Leader and a Victim lies in their ability to manage the problem. The Victim typically increases the difficulties in resolving conflict by letting emotions, words and behaviors get out of control. However, the Leader has already learned through experience and practice how to diminish the flame of conflict and create a contingency plan. He knows how to prevent and mitigate risks. When a Leader returns home, he removes his muddy boots and places them on the porch so he does not drag mud into the home. He then proactively uses a hose to wash the boots and lets them dry. The Victim, on the other hand, struggles to remove his muddy boots, so he instead wears them directly into the house and announces there is now mud all over the floor. Instead of problem-solving, he leverages the "poor little me" attitude to get attention and excuse his behavior. In this case, the Leader is more conscious and responsible and proactively minimizes the problem of muddy boots while the Victim only exacerbates it by blaming his boots instead of himself.

Independence comes from a state of inner peace and never from conflict or blaming others, for we are all responsible for our own thoughts and actions. Nobody can make us feel something we do not want to feel. When we say, "You made me angry," we are blaming them for our anger. Instead, we should be saying, "I allowed myself to become angry by your actions" or "I am angry because I permitted you to have control over my feelings." The good news is that once we accept blame and responsibility for our actions, we are empowered with the thought that we can then create our own change and our own circumstances.

COMPENSATORY ANSWERS

- CHRISTINA: I'm tired that I am never allowed to do anything. I've decided to go to the party. What about you?
- SARA: I am not going. It's for seniors and alcohol will be served.
- CHRISTINA: Even better! I will say that I am going to sleep over at your house. My parents will not know, they'll think I'm studying, as always.

We use compensatory behaviors – positive or negative – to offset or counterbalance situations that oppress us. They are our defense mechanisms. Sometimes the behaviors are manifested in acts of rebellion that can temporarily release us from the confines of absolute obedience or control. I mentioned earlier the example of the old type of pressure cooker that releases pressure through the valve, which prevents it from bursting (a compensatory response). These behaviors are carried out differently, depending on whether the person is based in love or fear.

Some compensatory behaviors may be spending time at sea or on the mountain or where there is abundance in nature. It could be performing an intense sport, such as running or boxing, having sex, eating heavily or indulging in any type of addiction like drinking alcohol, smoking or gambling, or even causing harm to others. Perverse practices are a type of negative compensatory responses in that they are performed in order to compensate for wicked or unfilled desires. They can result in twisted and harmful actions. Sometimes individuals will engage in them to counteract what is being done to them. If somebody grows up having been abused as a child, he might repeat that behavior by abusing his own child, for example. These behaviors are often performed without thinking, and even while they might provide a temporary feeling of relief or "fix," the person feels just as confused and unstable after it disappears.

I remember years ago when I was living life at the bottom of the pyramid (ignorance and obedience) and allowed fear to guide me. It was very difficult to process the world as I see it today. It felt like having a nail in my shoe that was pricking my skin all the time and prevented me from enjoying life or experiencing inner peace. I was confused and preoccupied with things that shouldn't matter in life. I acted out accordingly because I tried to compensate for my inner turmoil. It wasn't until I became more self-aware and had more self-control over my thoughts, feelings and emotions that I could redirect my behaviors in more positive and productive ways.

SELF-REPRESSION AND DEPRESSION

I love eating chocolate, but I cannot – otherwise, I will lose my great figure. Well… okay, I will only buy a small tablet and I will eat a piece right now and make sure nobody sees me. Yeah, I'll do that – just a few bites – and then I'll throw away the rest.

Self-repression is keeping one's self in the background, as though hiding certain desires or needs from the world. In self-repression, we can often become uncomfortable or overwhelmed because we do not want to engage in certain behaviors, but we feel we need to. These behaviors are considered negative or incorrect (morally, personally or socially), but we still like and enjoy them. For this reason, the internal struggle exists. On the one hand are our desire and instincts (I want…), and on the other is our will (…but I should not). What typically happens is that desire appears when we want something, and then in that moment or day we allow ourselves to give in to enjoy it.

Often times we will not acknowledge those desires until it becomes absolutely necessary to indulge in them – even if it is only for a few hours. Later on, after the enjoyment wears off, we return to ignoring or hiding that desire. We think we have done a good job controlling our desires, but we are actually irresponsibly managing them. Allowing them to surface for a short bit, and then burying them along with guilt or shame disintegrates us. We only accept a part of our personality in some cases, and it is difficult to feel "whole" and live our lives in its entirety, if we have to continually pick and choose which parts of us are acceptable in any given situation. It is like programming the old-style pressure cooker to release pressure temporarily but not completely. There is always a constant pressure to hide parts of ourselves and not accept who we are – flaws, weaknesses, desires and all.

For example, let's imagine that we repressed our desire to eat sweets for a long time, but then one day we pass by a bakery and cannot help but to walk inside and purchase two large pieces of chocolate cake. Already feeling guilty but can no longer deny our craving, we eat them both without letting anyone see us. Then we put the entire experience out of our mind. We return home and act as though nothing happened. We tell nobody what we did and try not to think about the shame we feel.

This example can be applied to situations where we like something but we do not allow ourselves to do it normally, like watching a certain television program, having a night-stand with a stranger, etc. Another example, suppose that we want to leave the house and go have fun, but then we tell ourselves to stay as long as possible because we feel we need to take care of the family. At some point, though, desire overwhelms us and causes us to escape the house so we can do what we want.

It may also happen when one day we decide not to repress ourselves anymore and that we will eat chocolate whenever and wherever we want. We no longer want to oppress ourselves; instead we want to learn how to better manage our desires so that we can balance our behaviors and not feeling guilty about them. Of course, eating chocolate all day, every day is unhealthy so if we decide to free ourselves from the confines of our desires, we must progress up the Pyramid of Consciousness (POC) so that we can become more self-aware of ourselves and more responsible in managing our desires and their resulting actions.

From Lack of Desire to Depression

Many times we have heard how people can fall into depression; in fact, we likely know people who have suffered with it. Depression is the general loss of will, that is, of desire. It includes the absence of hope. It affects the mind as well as can affect the emotional self and physical body. When one begins to fall into a depression, his preservation instinct kicks in and warns the body physically, such as weight changes, sleeping problems, or fatigue. Over time, the manifestations of depression can worsen and one's desires disappear.

For example, imagine that a girl has deeply fallen in love with a guy who she is strongly attracted to but has discovered that they can never be together, for they want very different things in life. The thought of never being with her perceived soulmate has caused her to become very depressed. She is miserable and has lost hope. If she continues to drown in her sorrow, she risks the chance of spiraling down to the point where she can lose her desire to live. Her strongest desire was to be with this guy, and now without him, life has lost meaning.

SEX

- Jim, do you know what sex is?
- Of course, I am a boy and you are a girl, and what adults do is bad.

We are all born with sexual instincts and desires. Sex is natural and is, of course, required for reproduction; however, we often are discouraged to think or talk about it at home until we are at least teenagers – and only because we have to protect ourselves from the risks of pregnancy and sexual transmitted diseases. Meanwhile, children are often kept in the dark when it comes to education about our sexual nature. As adults, we can sometimes pay attention to only the pleasure side of sex and forget its role in reproduction. The key point: We as a society have a distorted lens of the subject of sex, both in how we view it and in how we teach it.

There are some individuals who do not integrate their sexual self or acknowledge their instincts and desires, even though they are an important part of the whole self. It is no wonder that we can have a skewed perception of sex, for many of us have been taught growing up to adhere to a strict ethical and moral code of when to have sex, when not to have sex, how to have sex safely, what is considered "appropriate" or not, etc. This just complicates the whole subject of sex even more! As we begin to increase our consciousness and become more self-aware of who we are (sexual instincts and all!), we begin to accept our "whole" selves and better recognize and balance our instincts, needs and desires. This creates harmony – inner peace. Think of the Monkey Mind we discussed in an earlier chapter. When you learn to calm conflicting thoughts, you will experience more serenity and peace, which improve your thinking and analysis skills.

Sexual Taboos and Moral Codes

Each generation and social group has its own sexual taboos and views on the topic. Some are more open about having or talking about sex, and therefore promote sexual freedom and expression. Others are quieter (or silent!) about the topic and teach that it is "bad" or "inappropriate" to have it or discuss it before a given age or relationship status. However, the reality is that sex is a big part of our lives (biologically and socially), and it is my view that we should introduce and accept it as a fundamental part of life, while learning how to integrate it into our complete self-image. This is why children should learn from a very young age how to develop a healthy perspective about sex as a natural and integral part of their self-identity. This approach is much more ideal than simply avoiding the subject altogether or trying to make children feel bad or wrong for being curious about it.

There are times when culture, moral codes or religion impose rules about sex that society either accepts or rejects, which influences our behaviors. If our religion teaches us to wait until we are married before having sex, we will either obey that religious code, or we will break it and perhaps feel ashamed. For centuries, some religions have tried to control sexual practices with rules and mandates, and have associated sex with being a sinful act if it was outside the confines of marriage. Or, the church has criticized those who seek pleasure rather than reproduction as its purpose.

Signs of the Changing Times

One thing is clear: Sexual stereotypes and practices are definitely changing as society continues to evolve. The trend seems to be that we are expanding our mind and becoming more conscious in terms of our view and approach to it. What is now considered "normal" in some social circles was prohibited or scandalous back in the day. For example, there are many couples today living together without being married, which used to be very much frowned on decades ago. What older generations tried to restrict or repress, younger generations are starting to embrace. This will likely affect future generations as we typically teach what we were taught.

The key is to view and accept sex as an important component of who we are, and to integrate it into or whole being. Our sexual partner and relationship play an important role in shaping our views and experiences. If there is a healthy sexual relationship, it can help us become more conscious and more integrated, as the sexual experiences can nurture and fulfill us. However, if it is a dysfunctional sexual relationship, it can disintegrate our self in various ways.

When it comes to sex, the greater consciousness and evolution we have, the more responsible and careful we usually are with whom we have sex. Being well educated and experienced in terms of our sexual nature and the role relationships play in it will help us better recognize and pursue healthy relationships that promote emotional stability, inner peace and personal growth.

LET'S CHANGE IT UP: RISK, TRIAL AND ERROR, AND PERSEVERANCE

- Hello Dad.
- Hello son. How did it go?
- We had a good time. We danced and then we took an Uber and left.
- Did you kiss her?
- No, I could not. It was impossible. We were with friends.
- But did you not dance together?
- Yes, of course, but not in the old style like you did in your parties. Now everyone dances on their own, separated and without touching.

If we do things in the same way over and over again, but it does not work for us, maybe it's time to change our strategy. Failing repeatedly can sometimes be a sign that we need to modify some variables or attempt something different. Otherwise, how will things ever change or improve? If we can never convince friends to join us at the cinema, maybe instead of asking those who prefer outdoor activities, we ask people who love movies. Our strategies in life should be directly aligned with our goals. If the ones we had initially created do not seem to produce the results we want, then it is time to change it up.

The following steps will guide us in situations whenever we are stuck in repeated failures due to utilizing the same strategy or repeating the same process. Use these steps to change (redirect) relationships or situations, as long as the ego (self) allows it. The problem is that the ego sometimes makes us falsely believe that we know everything, and so we can often ignore or overlook life strategies that need a major shift.

We can use the steps in any occasion in which we want to change the result of something. Some examples of when we would likely want to implement a new strategy are when we want to start a conversation with a guy we like but who does not seem to want to talk to us; or if we want to improve our academic performance at school; or we decided to change jobs or positions in the company. These steps can be repeated as many times as needed to achieve our goals:

1. Calculate our Risk: Assess the situation or person and the associated risks of proceeding with your goal. Then proceed slowly and cautiously, taking "baby steps." For example, if you wanted to pet a wild dog, you know that the risk could be that it might bite you. So, you would likely approach it very slowly and calmly while observing its reactions. Eventually you would reach out your hand so he can sniff it, and then carefully extend your hand to pet it.

2. Practice Trial and Error: The best way to learn in a hands-on way is through trial and error. Test something, and if it does not work out, test something else. A two-year-old baby who was trying to discover the world typically touches or licks or sucks on everything that catches his attention. This enables him to perceive, interpret and learn from different sensations, tastes, and above all, how things work in life. If something does not taste or feel good, he tries again. If he touches something hot, he will feel the pain and learn that fire is hot – and it hurts! If every time we try to use the freeway to visit our parent and the entry pass is blocked, we identify the pattern and then use side streets instead. The more times we try different options, the more likely we will succeed in reaching our goal.

3. Use Perseverance: It is crucial that we not only do our best in terms of achieving goals, but that we persistently pursue them, even if we fail the first few times. The important thing is to keep trying and to not give up. Perfection will come along with practice, as per the popular saying, "Practice makes perfect." Similarly, we can pursue the search for the "DO", which is a Japanese verb that means the path to perfection through practice. Or even through the Chinese TAO which also mentions practice as "The Way" to follow. Consequently, if we were tennis players and we wanted to improve our serve, the more repetitions we make, the more likely we will improve. Similarly, a child who is trying to ride a bicycle will only succeed if he picks himself up every time

he falls. If he falls 11 times, he will need to get back up 12 times to be able to ride the bike. To achieve this, the boy will not only need to focus on his strategy for riding a bike, but he will need to persevere in order to finally do so.

By developing a strategy that focuses on calculating risks, practicing through trial and error, and persevering, it is likely that one can achieve his goals. Sometimes that strategy will take time and practice for it to work, and so the person will need to continue applying the steps in order to test new options and find new alternatives. But, insight and knowledge will definitely come.

DISCERNING BETWEEN DIVINE WILL, HUMAN WILL AND FREE WILL

> *- Cameron, I do not know what we're going to do with this very serious problem we have. We are not making enough money. Not even to eat. We have not been able to continue paying the mortgage. I cannot find a job, and the eviction will be in a week.*
> *- Do not worry, Andrew. Whatever has to be, it will be. Tomorrow I will talk to the bank, maybe they will give us more time, but above all we will continue doing our best, look for work, ask for help from our friends and family, and the rest we will leave in God's hands. We have to trust that something good will come out.*

Whenever we have a problem and do not know how to solve it, we often need light or spiritual support to move forward and choose our best option. Problems bring much stress and chaos to our lives. Praying or meditating can help us stabilize our emotions, calm our thoughts, and align ourselves with our intuition to transition into a peaceful state of mind and experience serenity. "Serenity" is the ability to accept what is. Once we accept what life hands us, we can experience a calm and peaceful state. As just mentioned, prayer and meditation can help us shift focus from life's difficulties and challenges, and focus our mind on spiritual matters or inner thoughts that restore inner peace.

Every time you are feeling a lot of pressure and need a mental break, it can be very helpful if you say a specific prayer or write your own affirmations. Try reciting the following:

> *God, I receive and respect your divine will, accepting*
> *everything you wish to bring to me. With human will,*
> *I sculpt the life I want by means of my effort, and*
> *along with free will, I decide among the options I have.*
> *However, on this occasion, please, free me from my*
> *resistance and allow me to fulfill your divine will. Amen.*

If we think again what the objective of suffering is, we will remember that it presents an opportunity to learn and grow. Everything has a reason – even if we cannot see it right now. With increased consciousness, insight and experience, our "higher self" will be able to eventually join the dots of our present to those from our past. We will then be able to see more clearly our life plan, benefit from spiritual guidance, and face and overcome challenges.

The "Wills"

There are three forces – Divine Will, Human Will, and Free Will – that interact with each other throughout our lives.

- Divine Will: Everything that happens to us but of which we have no control. For example, circumstantial things that occur, like the rain
- Human Will: All that we think, imagine, plan, do or execute; we have the ability to change the facts, influences and circumstances in our lives and shape them according to our goals and desires. For example, do what we want to do, like eating a pear
- Free Will: The power to choose according to our goals and desires. Ideally it should be aligned with the common good and focus from the higher self.

There are times when life takes us down a road where it seems that nothing is going to go well; however, suddenly when we least expect it, and when we thought everything was lost after having changed course, life suddenly gets better. This is when the "wills" (divine, human and free) can intersect and throw us off our planned path so that we can walk on a better one. For example, there are some well-known individuals who left the university, and against all odds, they founded very successful companies and used their wealth to help change the world. Dropping out of school was actually the best thing they did in their lives. There are also those with the exact opposite experience: their studies at the university provided them with knowledge that has given them the ability to take charge of their life and be financially independent.

None of us can predict the future, and so we will not know with absolute certainty where life will take us – until we get there. We may have a plan, but life may have a different one for us. We might think we have control over something with our free will, but then divine intervention occurs. It is why we should always seek consciousness and keep our eyes open to new experiences. Sometimes people and experiences will come in our lives for a reason. In these cases, let's try to listen to our intuition and figure out how all the pieces of life's puzzle can fit together. Let's focus on our education so that we obtain the knowledge we need to expand our minds. The more prepared and the more we learn how life works, the more opportunities we will have to catch and ride any wave that comes to us. What is most important is to be able to see the wave coming and then leverage the insight and experience we have to surf it all the way to the shore.

HOW TO AVOID TAKING THE BAIT

- Hello Paula. Look, your daughter's dress has a stain.
- You're always complaining. I do what I can. You are always criticizing me. You say that I do not do this as well as your mother. You always point out what is not clean or ironed. Hearing your criticism every day is exhausting for me.
- I have to get out of the car right now. We will continue talking later.

Many people seek conflict without realizing it. In other words, they are "unconscious" of how they tend to either start conflicts or participate in them – and get others to join in too. They are very good at making it look like they are not trying to cause conflict, for they might not directly attack or insult us, but they do it more subtly through passive aggressiveness (indirectly communicating hostility) and backhanded compliments (insincere niceties). We do not realize that they throw hooks with tasty baits at us so that we will take hold of the bait, unknowingly engage in the conflict, and then discover that they are exercising their power over us.

If we use the example of a fish that is in the river, it would first have to be caught. This means that the fish bites the hook, we reel it in, and then we have the power and the choice to either eat the fish or do whatever we want with it. We have essentially deceived the fish with our hook, and when it took the bait, we used the hook to pull it in and overpower it. The fish is in our hands and is powerless.

Power of the Hook

In life, the person who threw the hook has power (sexual, emotional, etc.) over the other (the one who bit) and can either abuse or leverage that power. In this case, the hook is the tool in the "power game" and entices many of us to engage in the confrontation or conflict. The person with the hook typically has an agenda or goal to achieve and is using us as "pawns" to serve his own purpose. He is manipulating and controlling the situation, and he likes that position of power.

For example, let's say your friend, Frank approaches you and expresses his anger that Paul has not called him to go to the movies with the rest of the group. Frank begins to say negative (and mean!) things about Paul. You know them both, and you feel like you are now in the middle of them. You have choices. You can:

- Bite the hook and engage in the negative conversation with Frank, affirming his views and even expressing your own
- Listen to Frank but not comment on it
- Remove the hook from the conversation by changing the subject

When they throw us a hook, we can leverage our own power and cut it off, metaphorically speaking, in a polite way. For example, if somebody calls me and throws me a hook I do not want to bite, I can say, "Sorry, but I have to keep working, but let's talk some other time." Or, "I can't talk right now, but I'll call you back later." Postponing the conversation until a later time is a good technique to change the subject or the tone.

Be on the Lookout

It is important that we are able to recognize these hooks as they come, which can be difficult because a hook is sometimes disguised as a victim, anger, etc. Phrases like the following can be clues about the tone of the conversation about to transpire: "You told me that ...", "I cannot ...", "Do not call me today to go out ...", or "I've had very bad luck in life lately ..." They may also come in the form of an attack or a complaint, as when the person tells us that we have not done something right, and now we have this or that problem.

In these cases, the individual seeks our response to either begin a dispute or conflict, or validate his negative feelings. A hook can appear in any type of situation – even the times we least expect. For example, somebody throws a hook at us while we are in the middle of another important conversation. His strategy is to distract us from some other sub-ject he does not want to talk about, and therefore flips the subject to one that he can leverage and control.

DIFFERENCES BETWEEN RESPONSIBILITY AND OBEDIENCE

- I do not want to go.

- Then why are you going? Didn't you talk to him?

- No, I didn't have time. I am going because my father wants me to go.

- Ahhhh!! I understand. And you're going to stay in that role as a child your whole life? You know what it entails, but I will not force you to do anything. It is your responsibility. You are going to feel terrible and you are going to disintegrate when you lose power, but it is your decision. Obviously, you need to go through your experience again to finish learning it once and for all.

Responsibility

We often confuse *responsibility* (responding with ability), with *obligation*, and use the terms interchangeably and incorrectly. If something is obligatory (mandatory), you cannot be responsible. *Mandatory* means being required to do something – you do not have the freedom of choice. Responsibility means being able to be free to make the best decision at any given time without constraints. As mentioned earlier, responsibility must be taught little by little to children as they grow up. The journey of raising consciousness begins at birth, and our personal compass (conscience) is nurtured through proactive conversations that include questions, persuasion and thoughtful explanations. In the beginning our compass is immature and must be expanded and fine-tuned through practice and the process of discernment (better/worse).

If we are irresponsible, we succumb to obligations (imposed obedience) that we must meet and are typically not able to respond adequately in any given situation. For example, last minute we may have to do the homework we did not want to finish during the week, and now that it's the end of the week, we are obligated to do it, which bothers us. If we had been more responsible, we would have known it was better to do the homework each day throughout the week so that we could have more free time during the weekend. If, on the other hand, we left all the homework for Saturday, we should not be angry since it was our decision to procrastinate until the last day.

Responsibility means managing ourselves without rules or obligations forcing us. It also means not creating inner conflict but instead having a conscious dialogue with ourselves. Responsibility includes freedom and negotiation. During a negotiation, the individual should make the final decision about what to do. Obedience, on the other hand, gives the allusion of free will, but it does the opposite by making the person dependent on the demand, decision or acceptance of another person.

Obedience

Obedience means being in a kind of prison where we occasionally allow ourselves to indulge in certain desires (e.g., eating ice cream, watching television or going out to a sports game), however, we do it all from within our prison. They tell us what to do and what not to do, and we follow their orders. We do not have free will, even if it seems so.

They teach us to behave and to obey, but not to *be*. To be able to truly be we must go through a different kind of educational process – a process that can teach us right from wrong, but also give us the freedom and opportunity to create our own experiences, make mistakes and learn from them. The number of mistakes does not matter, for those present learning opportunities that enable us to become more responsible. Therefore, the most ideal learning process is through the supportive guidance of our parents, the ability to make our own choices, and the insight gained from our past experiences. The sooner we start making mistakes, the sooner we will learn.

Many of us continue to rely on obedience to guide us. This dependence on being obedient could be due to various reasons. For example, some were raised in households and school systems that strictly enforced obedience through rules and punishments, and as a result, their actions became conditioned responses. Some have not been taught how to develop their own consciousness, and therefore continue to operate in the "child" or "father" role. Or, others just do not know what to do with their internal navigational compass without the rules to guide them. There are others who simply do not know how to become conscious adults.

Obedience can cause people to take on the role of victims. Often when orders and rules are not followed, reprimand (scolding) and even punishment soon follow, causing the "rule breaker" to think "poor little me." If a responsible person in the "adult role" receives the same criticism, however, he will have the awareness and insight to learn from his mistakes. He attitude will be one of empowerment in evolving himself and increasing responsibility while learning how to change his circumstances and create his own destiny.

Some people have been educated in a freer society that supports individual growth, where they can develop their own identity and be who they *want* to be, not who they are *told* to be. In order to create an even freer society that does not use obedience to guide others, it is our responsibility to teach future generations how to recognize and harness their own power and connect with their spirit. There are some countries and cultures that currently support this way of thinking, while there are others who discourage or prohibit it.

Speaking a specific language can influence how somebody uses his energy. In my opinion, languages can be complex and originate from various elements. For example, they reflect a country's culture. Some languages focus on the beauty of their sounds, on the inherent grammar, structure, syntax or structure (rules) and are maybe more rigid. Equally, other language systems focus on the verbal expression and how they're used in conversations, (direct to the point), so they achieve more in less time. Following this idea It may seem paradoxical, but in order to express myself more clearly, I communicate in my limited English, where I require much less mental energy to speak freely (with less judgment or conflicted thoughts) than when I have to reason and analyze in Spanish. Hence, following the same path at other times, when outside of work, if I want to feel empowered I revert back to American English to have more clarity, which helps me communicate and understand intuitively from my "higher self" in difficult or complex situations.

ROMANCE

- "And they lived happily ever after."
- Mom, so when will I meet my prince?
- Someday, dear, someday.
Then the girl tucked herself and closed her eyes with the image of the perfect prince in her head.

From a very early age, many of us read and watched fiction and fantasy stories in which the characters experienced adventures with happy (and perfect!) endings. After all, who does not remember *Cinderella* or *Snow White*? The classic storybooks always featured a prince who fell in love with the maiden and then "lived happily ever after."

Of course, then we grew up and learned that "real life" was much different than the fantasy life we had idolized throughout childhood. At some point we unhappily realized that life is not as perfect as what we were told to believe it could be. Our ideal expectations clashed with our real-life experiences, and this caused disappointment and discontent. We were left with inner turmoil, as we knew we were "supposed to" be perfectly happy in life, but we weren't.

Growing up, we eventually realize that "live happily ever after" is not as we were told. Life can be difficult. It gives us challenges when we least expect it. It involves moments of pain and heartache. But we will never see these moments as learning opportunities if we are always clinging to the dream of the perfect life. At some point, we need to toss aside our romanticized notions of a perfect relationship or marriage, and instead focus on evolving with our significant other.

As we become more responsible adults, we will discover that one of the greatest challenges in life is to let our partner be who he wants to be, without imposing ourselves on him. At the same time, we need to be who we are, without giving up our freedom or sense of self to the other. Each person in the relationship needs to own their own responsibility and autonomy to continue developing into the person he/she was designed to be; otherwise, imposing our will on the other (or vice versa) will create a self-contained prison. Sacrificing our own rights, our personal independence or a part of our personality to appease the other will only lead to resentment and bitterness.

If we are with someone and have consummated the relationship, the pleasure of the physical body (sex) can lose its intensity over time. It is why the mental, emotional and spiritual connections should continue to be nurtured so they can grow. People evolve at their own pace and in their own way, with some partners evolving together, and some evolving apart. Meaningful and intimate long-term coexistence requires each partner to give one another the freedom and support to individually grow. Sometimes, couples marry and nurture a fulfilling and long-lasting relationship. Some individuals close chapters of their lives with a person so they can open up a new chapter with others. Some couples temporarily separate, while others divorce. Evolving oneself while having the freedom and support to do so can play an important role in the vitality and duration of relationships.

GLAMORIZE VS. DEGRADE

- I'm in love with this boy. He is perfect.
- Well, Alex, I'm sure you do, but you're just getting acquainted. It has not even been three weeks since you first met.
- Yes, but I know he's my Prince Charming. He is the most handsome and intelligent man I've ever met.
- But, a prince? Really? He is just an average boy. He's my neighbor and I've known him since we were kids. Okay, okay, we'll see you in a couple of months when you've come down from the cloud.

People often love to imbue themselves with personal drama and illusions. Some individuals, when they do not like something about their life, prefer to indulge in the life of others. Focusing on another person instead of ourselves can be a welcomed distraction from our own reality. It can be tempting to focus on those who seemingly have lives we either envy or frown on, as it takes our mind off our own problems and circumstances. It lets us mentally escape life as we know it to temporarily observe life as we would like it to be.

To "glamorize" something is to idealize it or glorify (romanticize) it so that it appears better than before so that we like or appreciate it even more. In today's society, for example, we tend to "show off" certain parts of our body depending on our goal. If we are going out to a nightclub and want to be noticed by the opposite sex, we might want to call attention to our chest or our butt with a shirt that shows cleavage or a tight pants outfit. We are accentuating (glorifying) those body parts for a particular purpose – to attract and impress.

Usually when we glamorize something, we want something in return. If a car salesman wants to sell a standard car to a person who would rather have a state-of-the-art sports car, he will need to glamorize the basic car in order to make it seem more attractive. The salesman therefore does not focus on the transportation functionality of the car but likely emphasizes its unique sleekness and the beautiful roar of the engine. He glamorizes certain aspects of the car in order to make it look more special and more appealing to the prospective buyers, as his goal is to sell it. Equally, in order to sell products, such as luxury fragrances, fast sport cars, or impressive watches, we glamorize just about everything related to it by turning simple things into "special" things, like fancy packaging, expensive materials and even eye-catching advertising campaigns.

We tend to glamorize (beautify) life and make it more exciting during times we are bored with life or feel bad about something or need to make ourselves feel better. We can be attracted to activities like crime, sex or beauty treatments because they make us feel more alive. There are things we do to mentally or emotionally escape a current feeling or situation we are facing. For example, some people will go on a shopping binge ("retail therapy"), or spend a relaxing day at a spa, or have casual sex when they need moments away from the realities of life.

To degrade or debase something is to do the opposite of glamorizing it, and leads to people, events or things appearing meaner, uglier, worse, etc. For example, imaging your dog dies in an accident, but instead of burying him, you decide to dissect and display him in the front entrance of the house. This is so dismal – but sometimes we like drama. How depressing!

THIRD PYRAMID LEVEL: UNDERSTANDING AND COMPREHENSION

"I think, therefore I am."
René Descartes.

"A man has free choice insofar as he is rational."
Saint Thomas Aquinas.

Note to the reader: If we were brought up in a traditional and restricted education, it could limit our inner strength and development. Therefore, in other more favorable conditions and with a different educational system, we should very quickly reach the third pyramid level of understanding and comprehension.

DATA, INFORMATION AND LIGHT

- *Hi, Rosanna, how much electricity have we spent in the office monthly? I need to do the detailed budget for next year, and they say that power costs will increase again. Do you know how much we paid each month?*
- *I don't know; all I have is the total expenses of the company.*
- *That does not help me much.*

The existence of information (facts, figures, details, statistics) is called *data*. This data does not serve us much until we can organize and turn it into a clear and meaningful analysis of information. With high quality data comes information that both enlightens and enables us to make informed decisions. This process involves using raw data (a collection of facts) to create an analysis based on valuable information, and means we move from a confused or un-informed state of mind to one of enlightenment and clarity, thus moving us closer to the light and improving our decision-making skills.

Data is about *quantity*, and refined information is about *quality*. From here we can jump to what is *excellent quality*. Let's apply this concept to the culinary arts. Assume you are making a cake: the "data" is a standard large and thick cake; "information" is a medium round cake covered with vanilla cream made with the highest quality of ingredients; and "light" is the exquisite gourmet cake made of the finest organic ingredients and creatively decorated with all the trimmings. The "light" cake is of the best quality and superior to the "data" and "information" cakes. It is not just about quality over quantity, but also about the highest level of quality that matters.

As your senses take in sights, sounds and smells from the environment in various situations, you will need to be discerning in which facts will help you collect the right information to make the most informed decisions. In other words, what will help you make the best cake?

THE BENEFIT OF MEDITATION

- Margaret, the baby is crying a LOT. I'm getting very nervous about it. What should I do? Is he hungry?

- Relax. He just woke up. You can hold him if you want. He is upset and needs comfort. Try rocking him gently while you sing a lullaby. He needs to relax a bit and feel soothed by your touch and voice. It's times like this when he simply needs attention and wants to know that you are there.

- How can you be so calm? I do not know how you do it.

Meditation is the practice of calming one's mind through mental exercises focused on establishing a state of inner peace and stillness. A key benefit is that it can reduce or eliminate suffering in that it helps us find peace, balance and enlightenment. Consistent meditation can also enable us to reduce stress, change our perspective, deepen our compassion, increase self-awareness, improve concentration and contribute to our overall health and happiness.

To meditate, we only need to have a quiet physical space that allows us to be with ourselves, alone, and to remain in that state as long as we need, without interruptions. One usually meditates while sitting cross-legged (Indian style) and with a straight back. Each person creates an ambience that best helps him easily and comfortably enter that state of concentration, like dimming the light or burning some incense. It is advisable to make meditation part of one's daily routine and practiced at the same time. Ideally, between 4 am and 5 am before the day has officially begun and schedules fill up.

Clearing the Mind

One of the challenges of meditation is clearing our mind of all the thoughts, fears, ideas and worries that can keep us up at night or distract us. If we find it difficult to have a blank mind, we can perform other meditative practices, such as breathing, that help with focusing our brain on one specific task. Try this: Sit and close your eyes, and then begin to count your breaths. Focus only on your breathing. Inhale deeply through your nose and then begin to count each breath. It is similar to counting sheep before bed, but in this case, you want to stay awake while heavily focusing on every inhale and exhale.

During meditation, various thoughts might come to us, which can serve to distract us. Some of them might ignite certain emotions or upset us. In these moments, we should consider spending a few minutes to discern and understand what is happening within, and then resume our meditation. Or, we can also put those thoughts aside and continue focusing on calming the mind. The constant goal should be on clearing the mind, relaxing our bodies and focusing on our breathing. Ideally, the meditation exercise is about 20 to 30 minutes, but the duration really depends on the individual person.

Finding What Works

Meditation is a beneficial exercise to incorporate into our daily routine. We can either use the same technique or change it up with different exercises, like reciting mantras, within different environments on an individual or group basis. Some religions, such as Buddhism, have a methodology-oriented approach for faster personal and spiritual development. These meditative activities have been part of the cornerstone of my spiritual development and have helped me immensely along the way.

I have found through my experience that making meditation a daily priority is very beneficial to improving oneself, regardless of background, culture or religion. I have observed how people from other religions often come to Buddhist centers to increase their inner knowledge and practice. I am not insinuating that we change our religion, but we can still try different spiritual techniques and practices to support our spiritual growth.

On this personal journey of consciousness and light, I realized that an important component of meditation is not just having a focused mind but also an open heart. Unless our base or motivation is love, we cannot open ourselves fully to the benefits of meditation. It is like wanting to read a book without being able to open it; that is, we must open our hearts to work within ourselves.

Visualization Practices

Another way to meditate is through the process of visualization, which helps us cleanse our body and mind of negative thoughts and feelings. Visualization exercises are most effective when we are in a dark and quiet room. This physical environment connotes the feeling of being in a hole and releasing negativity in order to get out of the hole and seek the light. This practice helps hardened thoughts and feelings to dissolve over time.

The visualizations that I personally like to use involve being in a meditative state where, with closed eyes, I create images that help me develop empathy and compassion, as well as positive feelings and thoughts towards someone in particular. This could be a person who has done or said something negative to me in the past, which led to me holding onto resentment. I have found that visualizing this person in a positive way and consistently doing so, I can turn those feelings around. It just takes practice and perseverance.

Sometimes it can be difficult to positively visualize people we do not like or who have hurt us, and therefore struggle to pursue feelings of sincere compassion. In this case, start with visualizing somebody whom you very much appreciate. Think of all the qualities you like about him or her or favorite moments spent with that person. Then focus on the feelings that come with those thoughts, such as love or respect or gratitude. The next step is to redirect those thoughts and feelings towards the other person for whom you dislike or resent. You may find that by repeating this visualization process over time, and little by little, you will condition your mind to view and experience this person in a more positive, loving light.

Another tip is to simply use your imagination and make up the character or personality traits you would want this person to have. The main point is that you will likely need to try out visualization techniques to help you cleanse yourself of the negative and toxic feelings you have towards somebody or something.

THE RIGHT TO SPEAK

- *But I do not want to go to German classes. I do not learn anything there. I do not like anything about it.*
- *I told you that you're going, period. Do not contradict me!*
- *It's just that we only learn words, and I get bored.*
- *What did I tell you about arguing with me?! You are punished with no television!*

As mentioned earlier in this book, previous generations' educational system was typically much stricter than those of today. Back then, it was expected to always behave "correctly" both in the home and outside of it. Broadly speaking, behaving "well" meant that we had to proceed down a specific path in a specific way, and rely on praise, reprimands and punishments to guide us.

Meanwhile, we were taught that to be "good" meant to be quiet about what we truly thought or how we felt. We learned there were rewards and consequences that lined up with being good or being bad. Good behavior said you would be successful. Bad behavior stereotyped you as a loser. Of course, reality often said different. I remember back in school some of my classmates were always considered rude or obnoxious. At home, they sometimes disrespected their parents and verbally acted out. Fast forward to now, and they are very successful – personally and professionally.

Growing up, I was discouraged to speak my mind. I remember in preschool I had accidentally cut my finger and ended up in a hospital room with a few kids who were also waiting to be examined. Like the others, I remained standing in the emergency room, but I stared at the empty chair I wanted to sit on because I was very tired (and in pain!). I knew better, though. Nobody offered me that chair, and so I did not sit in it. After a while, my legs started to buckle because I had been shaking for some time due to loss of blood. Then one of the doctors noticed my condition and told me that I could sit on the chair. So, I finally sat.

I have since realized that I had stood so long (although I was tired) because I had learned as a child not to ask for things I wanted. I was taught that it was "rude" to request something without it first being offered by an adult. Expressing my own views and desires to authority figures was discouraged. This was so engrained in me as a young child that in this situation I chose politeness and obedience over my own needs and well-being. This is how having a focus towards fear and obedience affected me back then. As a consequence, even as an adult, those conditioned thoughts and behaviors still affect me, although they might not be noticed by others.

Children Should Be Seen ... AND Heard

I have learned that many of my friends who were cut from the same cloth (raised to value "good education and obedience") have also struggled with what they were taught throughout childhood compared to what they believe today. One day, we discussed how certain situations or challenges were difficult for us – even at work – despite having positions of responsibility. We struggled with expressing contradictory views or concerns about something. Sometimes, we felt uncomfortable defending ourselves and voicing what we thought or believed during an argument. When somebody aggressively confronted us, we would shut down due to being overwhelmed by fear or guilt.

My friends and I learned that we approached and responded to situations in the same way we were taught growing up, which was to shut our voice down and retreat. We had not been given the right or freedom to speak our mind as children and had therefore not learned how to respond to uncomfortable situations in a responsible (response with ability) way. Instead, we reverted to what we were trained to do as children: to be quiet.

A few years ago, we discovered similarities in terms of our upbringing and views on life, for we were "domesticated." We were at the bottom of the Pyramid of Consciousness, although some were higher than others. Even though we had similar educational experiences, the manifestations differed from person to person. For example, my sister, who had her base in love but was a natural rebel growing up, was not affected at all when she became an adult. As a teenager, she used to argue to anybody about everything that seemed unfair to her, which in my view, did not make her life easy in a society that enforced obedience and discouraged freedom of expression. However, she continued to fight against a restrictive society by always speaking her mind. Today, she is happy and content with life, as she had learned at a very early age how to recognize her abilities and develop them to the fullest.

Always Speak Up

We must always practice our right to speak, which is so important for our development, and not avoid changing the subject when something is difficult or uncomfortable. Even when something is painful or "secretive," do not hide it. We tend to do so because we think that others might think badly of us or judge us and/or our families. But hiding goes against our freedom and right to speak and to be. So, talk to someone you trust, even though it is hard.

Remember, we are all imperfect beings, and there is nothing that we have done that has not happened to somebody else. We all need to go through certain experiences in order to learn. Therefore, let us not limit or hide ourselves. Let us instead be open to experimenting with life while gaining consciousness and insight so we can develop into better versions of ourselves.

THE FIVE BODIES

- I don't know what comes over me whenever I am with your friend; he understands me so well! When we are together we understand each other very easily, and also, he is so handsome and attentive. Not to mention that he knows how to get out of trouble easily. I think I like him because I can connect with him on several levels. Nothing like that has ever happened to me. I'm going to ask him for a date.

Human beings have five bodies in one. These bodies are organic, inorganic and energetic, and are organized interdependently with other bodies made up of self-determination or will.

In broad terms, the bodies could be composed as follows:

1. Physical and Animal: The physical body is our avatar, which is the hair, hands, legs or bones, and survival instincts, such as eating or reproducing.

2. Emotional: The emotional body, or astral body, is composed of the emotions (ephemeral or of short duration), which come from both the physical and emotional body. The part of the physical body is programmed by the instincts. The emotional part of the body is mainly the heart and the fascia (tissue that is wrapped around different parts of the body like muscles). The emotional or astral body are the emotions (dreams and illusions). It is a world that we create ourselves according to what we want, as a kind of cyberlife.

3. Mental: The mental body is the part situated between the spirit and the brain. If we use the analogy of a computer, it could be something like this: the brain is the hardware, and the software comes from somewhere else (perhaps the spirit). The soul is the part that connects the human being with the spirit, installs the

mind and through this, develops knowledge in the brain. The soul could be the router, since it brings information, passes it and connects with the spirit (Internet). It is the connection between matter and non-matter. The world has two components: 1) matter, where energy is trapped in the form of atoms (cloth or table), and 2) spirit, refers to energy.

4. Spiritual: If we follow the same analogy, it is the interface that connects with the world; it is like the Internet or the World Wide Web.

5. Aura: The aura is a kind of organism or complete entity. It is our energetic manifestation in life. It represents our footprint, and depending on our aura, people and things will react in one way or another. It is something like the sum of the previous ones.

Individuals can connect with peers at different levels, and this connection could be achieved partially or totally, depending on how many bodies are active. This will also depend on the connection that is achieved with each person. Broadly speaking, the connection can occur in four ways, and not all of them have to be active at the same time. The fifth one is the sum of all the above.

All bodies create a specific energetic manifestation, and when they are integrated, they give off a more complete and strong signal, which is different for each person. It is what we call our "personality" or "ego." Therefore, the manifestation of the five bodies coexist together as we relate with the world around us. Our personality is the image (interface) we project and use to relate with people and the environment. Some of us have learned to leverage this personality in beneficial ways. For example, there are people who naturally attract others and therefore find it easier to get support. Some are lucky with money, while others can get along with anyone in just about any social or professional setting.

Usually, at any given point of time, one of the bodies is the leader while the rest of them are lined up behind and following the leader. Alignment of these bodies is key to functioning as an integrated and "whole" person, and can only happen if we are conscious and responsible. Integration takes into account the higher and the "lower self," and ensures that all five bodies are interconnected. Disintegration focuses only on the "lower self." The deeper the knowledge of life, the greater integration of all the bodies, and the more whole we become. This means less inner conflict.

SHAKE BEFORE USE: A Basic Guide for How Life Works / PART 3

WHAT WE WANT VS. WHAT WE NEED

- Dad, I like that watch. Can you buy it for me?
- Yes, it's very nice. But why do you need another one?
- This model is the new one of the season.
- I do not understand. You already have a cell phone that you carry
  everywhere and you have a good watch. What do you need it for?
- Because I want to look cool, Dad. All my classmates will be
  envious that I have the latest model!

Have you ever wished for the ultimate convertible car, or a big penthouse in a city like New York? Or, dreamed of a closet full of expensive clothes? Have a goal of becoming so wealthy you never have to work again? We all desire things. But, would having them really make us truly happy? I have found that sometimes those who have the most in life are the least happy. For example, there has been several media reports about people winning the lottery, but after a while, when the novelty wears off and life returns to normal, they are actually no happier than they were before. Maybe life is a bit easier because financial burdens have been lifted, but other problems may arise now that they have all this money to spend.

Consumerism is rampant in today's society, and people are generally taught that buying things can validate us and increase our happiness. However, it is a myth: more things do not mean more happiness. External things do not improve us on the inside, and materialism just leaves us feeling empty and discontent. As we climb the Pyramid of Consciousness, we learn that it is who we are and how we feel that matter most. We realize that we actually need less things to fulfill us and be happy.

Of course, having money can be beneficial if it enables us to take our next step in our evolution process. Sometimes the goal of wealth can provide the extrinsic motivation we need to achieve our goals, expand our mind or create new experiences. For example, an individual can be motivated to work hard in class if she knows that getting a good grade will earn her a summer trip to Greece with friends. Monetary rewards can act as effective incentives to experience more and live more. But they should not be the end goal; rather, they should be a resource to support a life development goal.

Getting What We Want, But Not What We Need

There is an old Chinese proverb that sums up this important life lesson: "Be careful what you wish for, lest it come true." You might want something you believe to be good, but it can also bring with it something bad; therefore, be mindful of what you need versus what you want. Even if we are fortunate to have things we need or desire (money, house, material things, etc.), we should never give them control over our life or distract us from our focus in life, which is to better ourselves and help others do the same.

If our primary purpose in life is to develop ourselves to the best of our abilities, our mission then should be to become more conscious and more responsible individuals who seek out new experiences and opportunities in order to learn and grow. If we focus only on increasing our wealth or buying a bigger home, but do not work on ourselves from a mental, emotional and spiritual standpoint, we are left only with material objects in the short-term and no personal development in the long-term.

There are times when we work really hard towards something but do not get what we expected in return. Rather than being disappointed and not accepting the results/consequences, seek the lessons in what comes to you. Life often does not give us what we expect or think we deserve. If we go through life always focused on what we did not get, or complaining about what we did receive, we will continually experience inner conflict and discontent. It will make it harder for the universe to give us what we need.

Thus, let your desires and goals be manifested through your efforts, and then just accept what life brings you – even if it is not what you wanted – in a purely loving and humble way … because maybe you *needed* those things or those lessons and just did not know it. Be curious and openminded. Whenever you distrust or resent results that do not align with your efforts, focus on calming your mind and listening or looking for the lessons and experiences the divine has gifted you.

Keep in mind that sometimes there are reasons why something we want may not happen due to circumstances beyond our control, which can cause inner turmoil and relationship conflicts. For example, a parent has promised to give his son an expensive electronic device as a birthday gift for getting good marks in school, but is conflicted because the family is currently struggling with financial hardships. The father faces this dilemma internally but also externally with his son, as the boy has worked all year long to earn this device and is now angry that his father has not followed through with his promise of a reward. The man then calmly explains the situation that although he wants to reward his son, the family's financial situation will not allow him to sacrifice the money. However, if the boy operates in his "higher self" and can see the situation through an informed, holistic lens, he will better understand and accept the situation – without anger, but with compassion. And if he really thinks about it, does he really need the expensive device to be happy? Probably not.

SUFFERING

- Hi, son, are you crying? There are times when it is good to cry and let off steam. I do it frequently when I get emotional; there's nothing wrong with that.

- Dad, I'm so sad! A kid at school insulted me today and told me I'm not worth anything.

- Well, do you believe it? Why do you take it personally? Why are you giving so much power and control over your feelings to somebody else? If they tell you these things they are probably suffering themselves and have many insecurities. They are projecting their lack of self-esteem onto everybody except themselves. It looks like today was your turn.

- You're right! I let myself get carried away and let him control my feelings. I lost my power. Dad, thank you for helping me to see that. I feel better now. I do not know why I am so sensitive today.

- Of course, happy to help! But, remember that you do not need me; you can do this analysis by yourself. Use this experience as a lesson to empower yourself in future situations. Whenever you feel somebody has wronged you, always take the time to reflect and figure out their motives so that you can understand why they acted as such. Then do your own introspection about why you are so bothered and have given them control over your thoughts and emotions. This will be an important response tool for you to remember and use on your own.

When we suffer, there is usually something we do not yet know or have not learned in order to resolve the pain. In this way, suffering means ignorance, as life can use pain to teach us valuable lessons that bring forth transformation. In reality, people suffer all the time, at every step up the Pyramid of Consciousness, until one day we empower ourselves to reduce suffering or prevent it altogether. To do this, we must learn how to most effectively anticipate and quickly respond to people and experiences with the potential to cause us pain. If we are able to recognize the source or cause of pain, we can appropriately respond – ideally before suffering finds us. It is like anticipating a difficult academic exam and so we make sure to study hard to avoid failing. The quicker we can respond to pain triggers, the more we can avoid unexpected consequences and negative reactions.

Every time we move up the pyramid, the tests and their corresponding spiritual learning become more demanding to challenge us so we can continue growing. Without upward mobility, we cease learning and stay stuck where we are at – and even risk the possibility of actually regressing at some point.

Suffering is part of the evolutionary process of human beings, and the lesser resistance, the lesser suffering. However, each of us is different in terms of how we think and respond, which affects the degree of difficulty and types of challenges we will face. Just as there are very stubborn and closeminded people who resist change, there are also those who are openminded and welcome change. Some are so adaptable to life's experiences and just "go with the flow" that they might not even recognize their suffering or problems. Although that might seem ideal, it can be to their detriment as they might not notice the lessons that life is trying to teach them and, consequently, not grow.

Treat the Problem, not the Symptoms

Understanding why we suffer relieves bitterness and helps us rectify the behavior. Metaphorically, we might see it as a person who has a rash on the skin because of an allergy, but does not know how to heal it. He can treat the symptoms, but until the root problem is discovered, the rash will continue to cause anxiety and pain. Once the person realizes that allergies are the culprit, he will be able to a create solution plan, remove certain foods from his diet, and eventually cause the rash to disappear. And, because he solved the problem (and just did not treat the symptoms), he can prevent the rash in the future.

While trying to respond to an experience or solve a problem, it is common to make mistakes. In fact, mistakes can help us learn. They let us see the direct consequences of a specific action, which enable us to gain the experience and insight to look for an alternative option. There-fore, we should hold ourselves responsible for learning from any expe-rience. Sometimes you will have to proactively look for the lesson, as it may not initially be visible. Practice some of the techniques and tips discussed throughout this book to increase your level of consciousness.

Seeking Spiritual Solutions

When experiencing deep suffering, some people will turn to religion or spiritual practices for guidance and relief. The key is for them to inte-grate their systems by seeking spiritual balance. Instead of merely per-forming religious exercises on an unconscious level to only alleviate suffering, it is most helpful for them approach spirituality using their "higher self" (enlightenment) so they can learn and evolve. Devotion (religious worship) means loyally following certain rules. Therefore, following one's faith, without consciousness or responsibility, is "obe-dience" since we are only doing what we were taught or told. Religious practice provides relief, but it can also provide little learning and there-fore little evolution. A large number of religious people and parishio-ners could be trapped and stuck in the routine of religion, rather than enlightened because of it.

Religious people who are highly evolved are those who grow, have high standards for their personal development, and are normally at the top of the pyramid while empowering and equipping those below them. They usually leverage the "doing and learning" approach to life, which is very similar to the learning process of experimenting, analyzing and re-flecting discussed earlier in this book. To better understand this concept, let's use an analogy. Those who are blindly devoted to religion just for the sake of going through the emotions are essentially treating their pain symptoms with a "quick fix" (temporary) drug. However, they are not recognizing the real source of the problem and therefore are not treating it. How can we fix something we cannot see?

There is no "quick fix" to alleviating suffering; it is a journey of self-discovery that involves working first on ourselves from within (thoughts, feelings, desires), and then with that understanding, moving outside our body and gradually interpreting what is happening to us and why we feel the way we do.

Spirituality, instead of blind religious devotion, awakens the mind and helps in moving us to our "higher self." Through spiritual practices, we approach God directly and engage in an intimate dialogue with Him about our daily lives. In doing so, we create a strong connection with Him. It is important to always be mindful that as human beings we are interconnected with each other and with the divine. This can be a great source of strength as we look pain in the face and learn how to not only manage it, but also leverage it.

Sources of Pain

As mentioned earlier, the system of human learning about life expects a great amount of suffering, such as sadness, depression or anxiety. First, we typically go through a moment of confusion (turbulence) that prompts our dismay or distress at the unexpected experience. There is a period of time in which we can lose ourselves and experience a period of suffering (emptiness, pain, hunger, depression, sadness). At some point we need to realize that remaining in this state of mind is detrimental to our development, and therefore we should look for its meaning and life lesson so we can resolve and move forward.

Life often just happens to us, and some of us feel emotionally weighed down because of it. There are verbal cues and expressions that communicate the desolation that individuals feel. For example:

> "I studied a lot, but I still failed the exam!"
> "How could you treat me this way?!"
> "I lost my job and cannot find work. What am I going to do now?"
> "It's just one bad thing after another. I can't seem to catch a break!"

These moments or experiences can overwhelm us with uncertainty because we are not enlightened to effectively manage them. Instead, we magnify them and obsess about them. Hopefully, this book will empower you with the awareness that although you might not be able to change your external factors, you have the power and the freedom to change your internal self. You can develop the tools (consciousness, responsibility, etc.) to simply accept what life hands you, learn from it, and turn anything perceived as a negative into a positive.

On other occasions suffering comes through a series of circumstances in which the individual is without consciousness, has become irresponsible in life, and is addicted to distractions and behavior patterns that threaten his well-being, such as consuming too much alcohol, gambling, or increasing debt by buying more things than he needs or can afford. The good news is that in these cases, the person can change his external circumstances, which can aid him in eventually changing his outlook on life.

Making Life Lemonade

Always welcome everything that happens to us in life, as it brings opportunities for enlightenment, empowerment and evolution. Just because we might not like or know how to do something, we should not feel lost, fearful or anxious. Remember that when we do not understand something, it means we have not learned it yet. We can view it as difficult or challenging, but nothing more. Insight and experience will help us overcome life's challenges, but we must proactively face them, not passively dismiss them.

Each person can view, experience and enjoy life experiences through his own self-made lens – ideally a lens of consciousness, responsibility and positivity. Rather than complaining what we cannot do, let's be grateful for all those things we can do. It is like that popular adage: "If life gives us lemons, let's make lemonade." So, let's always look for the positive side, take it, celebrate it and enjoy it.

LEVELS OF CONSCIOUSNESS AND CONSCIENCE

- I really like the language teacher we have. He knows all of us perfectly and blends language instruction with cultural history. He makes everything much more enjoyable and easy for us. It is the first year that I can actually enjoy this subject.
- Lucky you!

Facts or actions can be processed through our spiritual, mental, sexual and emotional bodies. The type and depth of information collected will depend on our level of consciousness and what we individually observe and assess at that time. Consciousness ability will vary depending on the situation and on the external and internal factors involved.

Likewise, having a developed conscience typically means to make better decisions. The grown conscience becomes immediately attached to our own will. This way we can feel and perceive which path in life is right or wrong when making decisions. In general, pleasures are in the wrong way, especially when we exceed the limits. That's why the best way – usually – is the middle way. For example, if we have not developed our conscience, we are hungry and we decide to eat whatever we have on hand – or what our instinct ask us for – our conscience and/or consciousness will be at a lower level than if we decide to eat something healthy, like fruit, because we know it will nourish us with vitamins and fiber. In the latter case, we are more "present" in the experience and are not instinctively relying on merely satisfying our hunger pains (pleasures). We are operating on a more conscious level as we think about the nutrition the orange provides and how our body will be healthier because of it.

For example, if we are hungry and decide to eat whatever we have on hand, our consciousness (and conscience) will be at a lower level than if we decide to eat something healthy, like fruit, because we know it will nourish us with vitamins and fiber. In the latter case, we are more "present" in the experience and are not instinctively relying on merely satisfy-

SHAKE BEFORE USE: A Basic Guide for How Life Works / PART 3

ing our hunger pains. We are operating on a more conscious level as we think about the nutrition the orange provides and how our body will be healthier because of it.

Let's use an additional example. Assume that a girl discovers that she is physically and sexually attracted to a boy, but feels nothing for him beyond that. She is not interested in his mind or personality – only in her chemical attraction to him. However, another girl might like the same boy because she loves his mind, has been able to have very interesting conversations with him, and knows he will be a good influence in terms of her own personal development. The second girl is operating in more of her "higher self" and leveraging a higher level of consciousness. Of course, the first girl could eventually elevate her opinion and deepen her attraction for the boy as she gets to know him more. Our lens, our sense and our ability to be self-aware shape our experiences and behaviors, which ultimately shape others' actions and consequences.

INTEGRATION VS. DISINTEGRATION

- Charlotte, I'm going to drive the car today.
- But aren't you afraid?
- Yeah, but I have to. I cannot go on like this all my life. I need to get around, and public transportation does not work very well in this city. This is my challenge, here I go!

Disintegration or fragmentation is the consequence of splitting ourselves into two or more personalities or parts at the same time, using the one that best suits us in each circumstance. This is what was previously referred to as "broken in pieces," which allows us to play "the smart," "the brave," "the flirt," etc. role to achieve something we want (admiration, praise, desired behaviors). Disintegration is meant to teach us. Remember that to learn about life we have to go through a self-discovery process that takes us from darkness to light; that darkness, in some cases, may disintegrate our system first so that we can eventually learn how to integrate ourselves as "whole" beings. Think of it this way: If it does not challenge, it will not change you.

Disintegration causes us to behave one way in front of people, and then behave a different way with another group of people. For example, we might act like the "good" son/daughter in front of our parents; or, we might appear naïve and innocent when trying to avoid discipline or punishments. But then, when we are around our friends, we adopt a different persona that is typically more free-spirited, does what it wants and embraces risks.

Parts Do Not Equal a Whole

If we disintegrate ourselves and use different parts of our personality to please or influence others, we are not consistently behaving as our authentic "whole" selves. We are instead sacrificing certain traits to leverage other traits, which causes inner conflict about who we really are and who we want to be. Thus, behaving as different people in different situations actually weakens our ability to approach life as a complete person. How can one truly understand himself if he can only see parts of it at a time? How can others really get to know us if we only show them one side of our personality?

As mentioned earlier, disintegration leads to inner conflict as parts of our ego compete with each other. As a result, we can become frustrated, confused, angry or resentful as our internal battle rages on. To resolve this problem of disintegration, we usually must go through a type of negotiation process in which the five parts of our body (physical, emotional, mental, spiritual and aura) become aligned towards a common goal. Once all parts accept each other and start communicating, our mind can then expand and integrate all bodies. This helps move us towards our "higher self," which is more conscious and unified.

The more integrated we are and the more our mind expands, then the more learning opportunities will open for us. The following example illustrates this concept. Assume you first lived in a room, then in an apartment or flat, then in a chalet or house, etc. The physical space around you would likely increase, giving you more options and opportunities to experiment with furniture placement, lighting, floor materials, etc. However, there would also be more opportunities for elements to get out of control, such as breaking, cracking, fading or getting stolen. As we continually expand our mind (increase consciousness and responsibility) and gain more knowledge, we will create more space to experiment with life. This means we will face more challenges and make more mistakes, so that we can learn from them and grow.

Integration is infinite, which enables us to always learn how to integrate more and to be more consistent in remaining integrated. Even those who have a high degree of self-integration will experience times when they are not as integrated as they should be. Life brings many different adventures and challenges at different times, and therefore our thoughts, feelings and behaviors also fluctuate. So, even the most integrated person still has a lot to learn.

Life Teaching: Dividing Yourself Will Not Manifest Your Whole Strength

Since disintegration can teach us important lessons about ourselves, we need to be able to recognize and manage it whenever we experience conflicted feelings. We can unconsciously have an agenda behind what we say and do. We then strategize and plan to achieve a specific and temporary goal. In order to obtain a state of peace or control in a situation, we tend to strategically put a part of ourselves aside so that we can leverage another side of us. That side might be able to achieve the goal (desired feeling or action) for a moment, but we will not be able to fully engage our entire self and reach our full potential in that situation. Our core strength is weakened because we have sacrificed a part of us for another part. At the same time, we often hide or ignore the other parts of ourselves that do not agree with the part we chose to leverage in the moment.

Imagine that we are afraid to speak in public, but we know it is a good thing to move up in our career. In this case, we can experience disintegration and unconsciously create a strategy to deal with this inner duality. So, although we force ourselves to give a speech, the rest of our bodies do not agree. For example, maybe the mental body says "I should do it!", but the physical and instinctive bodies scream, "No, I am afraid!"

To better understand this concept, imagine two brothers who are always hitting each other. One day, the frustrated parents decide to separate them temporarily for the weekend; they leave the older one at home and send the younger one to stay with the grandparents. Of course, since the boys are now physically separated, no fighting occurs. The parents enjoy peace in the house and can hang out with the older son and spend quality time with him, without worrying about brotherly fighting. But when the other boy returns home on Monday, the fighting resumes. So, the strategy was temporal and did not solve the problem – it was just not visual for a while. Hence, parents and kids (similar to what happens with our five bodies) should mediate and persuade each other to not pick fights in order to avoid conflicts and keep a peaceful home for the good of the family. The solution: understanding, not fractioning.

Moving Beyond the Walls

Whenever there exists conflict within us (duality), we sometimes fear the uncertainty and vulnerability we feel, and we therefore act out in ways to try to protect or shield ourselves from anybody or anything hurting us. For example, let's say I am the King during the Middle Ages. Because I have enemies in surrounding lands, I always wear protective armor and make sure my knights are with me every time I exit the castle. I fear that an enemy will try to kill me if I appear to be in a vulnerable state, and so I arm and protect myself. It is only when I return to the castle that I can once again feel safe, remove my armor and relax.

Rather than shielding (hiding) oneself from potential confrontations or uncomfortable feelings/situations, it is much better to face fear or uncertainty through communication and negotiation. Perhaps, the king could come to an understanding with his enemies through compromise. Instead of hiding behind the walls of his castle, he can open a door to creating a pact with those he fears.

...And Again, Find Unity in Strength

The primary goal of recognizing the duality that can exist within all of us is to learn from it. Fractioning our personality only diminishes our power. It weakens us, and we cannot fully pursue enlightenment and personal development. It is like trying to run a race with only one leg and no vision. When we are divided within, conflict grows while responsibility wanes, and the result is that we have silenced a lot of our "Self" in order to sacrifice one part of the body for temporary gain. In the long-run, however, we have not moved forward in life.

As discussed earlier, when our bodies are integrated, we are more self-aware, informed, responsible, and can make better decisions. There can be no peace within us if there is no unity between our bodies. A popular and profound proverb is "Unity is Strength," which means that interconnection is a source of strength. When we have aligned our mind and body with our soul, we can view and approach life as a "whole" person.

Intentional Consciousness

It is important to note that integration does not just happen to us on its own. In fact, integration requires intention. It depends on the will of a person to want to do it, with the desired end result being harmony. In other words, it is a conscious choice to integrate oneself and seek harmony… and then stabilize and maintain it.

There are times when we are forced to face or experience something, and we instinctually rely on a part of our self to help us adapt. This is when disintegration comes into play, and we are forced to impose one part over the others. As noted earlier, this strategy can serve a short-term (temporary) purpose, but it does not help us develop and grow in the long-term. If we are integrated and responsible, we would be able to respond to these types of forced, and often difficult, situations in ways that can strengthen us.

Here's an example: Imagine that we are very afraid of driving a car for the first time but were forced to do so. If we do it from a point of disintegration, we could drive it temporarily, but this experience would have no impact on our future self-development. However, if we are integrated and conscious, we would likely view this experience as a challenge to not only overcome a goal, but to also make us stronger and more courageous. Although others in this same situation might try to use a tip or trick to push through their fear of driving, the most ideal and long-lasting solution is to increase our consciousness.

Because the integration process is infinite, we can (and should!) always continue to focus on trying to integrate our systems more and not fall into a specific role/part to achieve a temporary goal. With integration, we increase the capacity to perceive, discern and manifest. We live better because we become better – mind, body and soul. It is how health comes from the whole of our self, not from the division of its parts.

Integration depends on the level of consciousness, so it is not what you do but how you do it that matters most. For example, assume you felt a sexual desire and wanted to satisfy it. At that point, you have a choice:

You can either focus on physically satisfying that desire (without involving the mental or emotional aspects of it), or you can integrate that desire with the rest of your bodies and engage in sex in a way that not only satisfies your physical need but enables you to seek pleasure and enjoyment, without feeling judged, guilty or ashamed. In the latter situation, you have made a conscious choice to experience something with your whole self, rather than sacrificing a part of you.

SHAKE BEFORE USE: A Basic Guide for How Life Works / PART 3

PASSIVE-AGGRESSIVE BEHAVIOR

Esther was about to serve dinner at home. John had not yet arrived,
but it was already nine o'clock when the telephone rang.
- Esther, I'm not going to eat dinner at home tonight. I will stay
* with my friends at the bar. We are going to celebrate Julio's*
* birthday. I'll be there until about eleven.*
- OK. No problem. Bye.
* …At eleven o'clock John arrived.*
- Hi, Esther, I'm here.
- Hi, John, I hope you had a good time at the birthday.
- Oh, yes, sorry to leave you with dinner.
- Never mind, John. I'll save it for another day. It seems the
* birthday party was more important to you than our family dinner.*
* But that's fine.*

Although Esther made sure not to show any emotions or expressions
on her face, she was seething inside. "How dare John choose his
friends over our family – and after I spent the entire afternoon
making dinner," she thinks. Of course, she does not show her anger
at that moment, but she has made sure to hint at it with a lightly
sarcastic (passive aggressive) remark. Meanwhile, she is boiling
inside. Poor John might face her wrath someday soon.

As you continue your journey towards enlightenment and consciousness, while migrating from fear to love, you will likely face or experience
a form of passive-aggressive behavior. *Passive aggressiveness* is a negative
behavior pattern that is often used as a self-defense mechanism to avoid
direct confrontation. It is difficult to predict or immediately recognize as
it is often an indirect resistance that is invisible to both the person who
exhibits it and the person who is at the receiving end of it.

The passive-aggressive person is a product of the "lower self." In many cases, passive-aggressive behaviors are learned in the home, where it
is used by at least one other family member, and the child unconsciously

learns to copy the pattern. Sometimes passive-aggressive behaviors are acted out on a completely unconscious level and offer no external decodable responses. It is like a person who has been diagnosed with a disease but shows no visible signs that he is ill; in fact, he looks and acts normal. Other times, phrases like "It doesn't matter" or "I don't care" can provide clues that he does in fact care but is acting like he does not so that he can avoid confrontation or obtain something in return.

Two Types

There are basically two types of passive-aggressive behaviors: the first one is the pseudo-passive-aggressive (or non-genuine) type that is typically used to solve a problem or solicit an intended behavior, while the second type is true passive-aggressiveness and deals more with emotional coping mechanisms.

Those who are pseudo-passive-aggressive pretend to be passive-aggressive, but in reality, they are not. They do, however, tend to use the same strategy to get what they want, without asking directly for it. They can cleverly manipulate a person to get what they need or desire. They make it appear that they genuinely need help so that their request or behavior "seems real," when really all they are doing is slyly controlling others – with them not even knowing they are being used or controlled. There is no internal conflict they experience because they intentionally know what they are doing to get what they want.

Imagine that a person wants to become a member of a specific social club, but he cannot afford its high annual fees. So, he schemes to befriend somebody who is already a club member, with the intent of using that member to gain access to the club, without having to pay. Therefore, he uses niceties and compliments to win over the club member and to inspire many social invites. Once he is then inside the club, he will befriend other members in order to get them to invite him to future club events. Not only does he now get to be part of the club, he did not have to pay a dime. Problem solved!

Passive Aggressive Inner Wars

Regarding the second type, people are genuinely passive-aggressive, but are mostly unaware of it. Passive-aggressive individuals generally put up resistance to doing what others ask or demand. They do not want to obey, and instead of expressing that, they bottle up their emotions and create resentment as a coping mechanism. Meanwhile, by engaging in this behavior of acting one way while feeling another way, they create their own internal conflict.

In some cases, these people might temporarily diminish their power by giving up (sacrificing) certain personal rights in exchange for something else (tangible benefits, attention, desired actions from others, etc.). We see this a lot in relationships. One partner might reduce his/her individual power to avoid confrontations or conflicts with the other person. Instead of facing the problem head on with direct communication, the person does not leverage his/her right to speak and instead bottles up the upsetting thoughts and feelings.

In other cases, there are those who "silently and softly rebel" in a passive-aggressive way. These individuals do not express or show opposition, but they still do what they want. It might seem like they are happily agreeing to follow specific rules, but they then intentionally break them. This type of rebellion can occur even in children, where they look like they are living according to society's rules and standards, but then "escape" reality and revel in their own fantasy world, which can be as addictive to live in as drugs.

Imagine that we want to live similarly to how we did when we were young – when we had loving family that nurtured us and gave us everything we needed. We now want that exact same thing and so we look for it in our current relationships. In fact, we might want to recreate that environment so bad, that we actually put up with things in the relationship that we should never allow. For example, if our partner abuses us but provides us with a nice home with and everything material we need, we might silently suffer with the abuse and build up resentment in exchange for the type of lifestyle we have dreamed about. This strategic agreement when have made with ourselves (and our partner) can trigger passive-aggressive behavior.

Unintended Consequences

Holding upsetting feelings inside while acting as though nothing is wrong can have detrimental effects. The passive-aggressive may be easily angered by something he believes others have done to him (assigning blame) and so he feels he is neither to blame nor responsible. He can even play the role of victim and feel sorry for himself. Remember "poor little me" syndrome?

Passive-aggressive individuals may possibly indirectly punish those they feel have wronged them. This can manifest in behaviors like intentionally NOT following through with requests or obeying rules or saying sarcastic remarks. But, when they are then asked if anything is wrong, they pretend that it is and say things like, "I'm fine." They might even invite the person to the movies or to do something that they mutually like, but then use excuses (resistance) to delay or cancel the event, or they attend and then purposely make sure the person has a miserable time. Their goal: to cause trouble and attract attention while making it seem like they are a good person who only has the best intentions. This is how they have chosen to indirectly communicate their inner frustration, anger or resentment without actually verbally expressing it.

INTROSPECTION

- Why are you crying? What happened to you?
- You know, the usual.
- But how come?
- He pushed me past my breaking points, and I just couldn't handle it.

Supporting our daily meditation work with other practices that will shift us from a negative mindset to a positive one will help us pursue more fulfilling personal and spiritual development. With introspection, strong will, tenacity as well as commitment to evolve, we can learn from present and past experiences to create positive change in the future. This is not very difficult to do, but it does require focus, effort and perseverance.

Throughout this process of self-discovery, we may likely notice times when we feel impatient or restless in terms of our progress. However, if we focus on facing uncertainty, learning to understand ourselves and becoming more responsible adults, we can continue to move forward. Our biggest challenge will be our self-created limits and fears. Our attitude and focus – and above all else, our level of consciousness – will be key to us finding peace and joy. This journey requires a calm mind and a positive attitude.

Introspection is the observation and analysis of our mental and emotional state. Whenever something happens to us, introspection can include examining our thoughts, feelings, desires, motives and reactions, and reflecting on how it all affects our lives at any given moment. A best practice is to perform a daily introspection, where every night before bed (and ideally first thing in the morning as well) we do a mental review of the day's happenings and analyze how they affected us mentally, emotionally, physically, etc. Setting some time aside every day "to look inside" and recognize how we experience life and interact with others will increase our level of consciousness and empower us to live more responsibly.

Ask the Right Questions

The main thing about introspection is to consciously examine our situations in detail. To help with this, we can ask ourselves questions like: *How did it happen, or how did we feel about it? How did we respond? What thoughts and feelings went through our head? Did we act without thinking, or was it difficult to control our actions? Do we behave this way with everybody or with only certain people? How could we improve our responses in similar situations in the future?* Those who do not routinely practice introspection will miss out on the incredible learning opportunities that can develop self-awareness.

Other self-examination questions to consider: *Why did this happen to us? Were there any previous indicators or signs that we ignored? What can life teach us on this occasion? How can we understand something that happened to us years ago, and tie it to what we know today? What could this situation look like with a new perspective and with more knowledge? Does what happened to us have any meanings that we do not yet understand? What links can we make between our present experiences and those that have happened in the past?*

By answering these questions in depth, and figuring out the who, what, when, where, and why of our experiences or situations, we will be able to expand our perspective and gain valuable insight into who we are, how we live, and why we act/behave the way we do.

Create a Routine

In addition to doing a personal introspection at night, it is advisable to do so in the mornings. Right after you wake up, ask yourself: *How do I feel? What do I need?* If you feel emotionally upset or particularly sensitive that day, think about what could improve the morning and then, if feasible, do it. It might be as simple as eating a healthy breakfast, styling your hair a different way, taking a hot bath, etc. The important thing is that if you wake up feeling like it is already a bad day, you can plan how to create a good one. Since this will set the tone for the rest of the day, you will want to create positive experiences as soon as possible.

To really benefit the most from personal introspection, it is best to spend an hour of daily spiritual practice to clear our mind, open our heart and cleanse our soul. It is also ideal to devote at least an hour a day to light exercises like stretching, Pilates or Yoga in order to improve our physical strength, flexibility and posture, and also enhance our mental awareness.

PEOPLE DO NOT CONTROL OUR EMOTIONS – UNLESS WE LET THEM

- You're a fool; I told you that you cannot play with us. Besides, you do not have nice doll dresses. You only have a cloth with two holes to put the arms in and a belt loop.
- Well, my parents cannot buy me the nice ones you have.
- Get out of here; we do not want to play with you!

Verbal aggression is everywhere, including on television. It is common when someone verbally insults somebody else, that person will return the insult. When the aggression is shared between two people, the argument can become even more heated while each of them try to yell louder and deliver a worse insult. But, we would all likely agree that this is not the best approach to expressing oneself.

Responding calmly from the heart, with kindness and respect, is not easy, especially if we think they are criticizing or verbally assaulting us. Not allowing other people and external factors to affect our thoughts and behaviors enables us to express ourselves responsibility, which is key to inner peace and personal growth. Two cannot get angry if one does not want to, for as the popular saying goes: *It takes two to tango.* When you remove yourself from the equation, there can be no interplay of anger.

In these types of situations, it is important for us to set clear boundaries for how we allow ourselves to treat others – and how we allow them to treat us. These limits might change according to the circumstance, but if we do not at least set them, it will be more difficult to recognize and gauge certain behaviors. This will help us respond in more responsible and productive ways. The more responsible and serene we are in each situation, the more easily we can face each circumstance.

Remember that no one should decide how we feel and, if they do, it is because we have given them permission to. In other words, we have allowed them to control our own feelings and emotions. This insight should empower us, as although we cannot change people, we can change ourselves. We would never give a thief the key to our house; we would keep it safe, right? So why do we allow another person to make us feel bad or annoyed? Let's try not to care about what others think of us or tell us, and instead seek understanding. We should not allow them to provoke us. We own the key and our house, and no one can take it from us – unless we let them.

When we get angry with someone we are also giving that someone power over us. We are basically indirectly (and automatically) communicating to him that we care about his opinions more than we care about our own, which backfires on us and shifts our power over to him. We must not forget that he is belittling us and trying to make us suffer, because it is actually he who is already suffering. If we take the time and effort to look for the source of why he is acting out, we can little by little be able to act with greater responsibility. We will learn not to take it personally. Meanwhile, we will empower ourselves and gain self-confidence instead of giving away our power and getting stuck in somebody's trap of despair.

This search for inner peace is extremely important for our overall well-being and happiness. Unfortunately, we are usually not taught in the home or at school how to achieve it. Regardless of what happens around us, we should maintain serenity and manage our feelings and emotions. It is our responsibility to control our own selves. This will come in time through mental training and practice, for our mind can be either our best friend or our enemy. It is why increasing our consciousness is so beneficial in that it gives us control over our thoughts and emotions, instead of them controlling us. This is a proven strategy to enlighten our mind and empower our bodies. In fact, even professional athletes use mental exercises to prepare for tournaments and competitions. The key is to consistent focus, commitment and perseverance.

POSSESSION AND DETACHMENT

- Mario, what are you going to do with your birthday money?
- Spend it. But I do not know how. I have to look at what I can buy.
- But why don't you save it in case you need it for something else?
- No. I need to spend it and buy something today. Oh, I know now!
  I'm going to buy this video game that just came out.

We live in a world of consumerism and materialism, and our society is obsessed with owning things and accumulating more and more, even if they are not needed or used. We tend to look to material objects to make us feel content, safe and happy. We even go as far as to assign possessive pronouns to the things. For example, when referring to a car, a man might say, "Her engine is so smooth… my girl rides very fast." Some of us subtly refer to our friends in a way that implies ownership. For example, "This guy is my brother" or "She's my sister from another mister."

However, no friend or person "belongs" to anyone, not even the child to a mother. When we assign labels to people or things, and experience feelings of attachment, jealousy or dependence can ensue. Our need to own or control them is a losing game, for it sets in motion our instinctive "lower self," which dismisses logic and reasoning in favor of satisfying needs and desires.

Conscious Detachment

When we attach ourselves to others, we tend to take on their emotional burdens. If, for example, somebody close to you continually vents about their frustrations, it can be difficult not to internalize it. However, when we allow others' emotions and behaviors to influence our own, we are essentially giving them permission to control our state of mind. It is why the ability to detach is so important to one's own evolutionary process. The concept of detachment is easy to understand, but it must be done from love and not from avoidance, anger or apathy.

To continue ascending the Pyramid of Consciousness, we should learn how to distance ourselves from feelings, thoughts or ideas that someone or something triggers in us and, in turn, affects our behavior. The process of learning initial detachment is not easy, but through the Buddhist meditative practices and visualization exercises, it can be a much simpler process than others might think. It just requires effort, persistence, love and higher consciousness. Over time, the negative energy associated with strong attachment to (and dependence on) people and things can be changed to positive energy and redirected to creating a more positive and spiritual path forward.

From Dependent Children to Independent Adults

We are all born with survival instincts and the need for attachment and dependency. We initially require these dependencies in childhood because we have not yet know learned how to care for ourselves and navigate the world around us. As children we depend on our parents to fulfill our basic needs for food, shelter, safety and comfort. We operate from a base of fear, in that we know we will not survive without these basics. But as we age and become more mature, that dependency can become malignant if it prevents us from developing our own individual identity and responsibility.

The journey into adulthood should therefore equip and encourage us to develop our own sense of independence so that we are no longer dependent on somebody or something to provide for us, nourish us or validate us. As a child grows and stabilizes, he does not need to worry about basic survival. Instead, he should focus on becoming more independent in all aspects of his life, while reducing his dependence on others. In doing so, he will move towards his "higher self."

Once we have no more desires or feelings that support attachment, we can begin to separate ourselves – mentally and emotionally – from others and not rely on them for our own fulfillment and happiness. Detachment needs freedom, responsibility and consciousness in order to help us evolve; it needs a strong awareness of the self. Detaching from others means the opportunity to live life freely with peace of mind and an internal source of power that nobody can take away. It means not turning to things or people to fulfill us but instead relying on our self to create our own happiness.

The practice of meditation, visualization or reciting mantras can help teach and guide us on how to reduce our unhealthy attachment to people or things. The concept of "I miss you because I need you" fades because we can be happy independent of our family and friends. Regardless of whether they are physically next to us, or on the other side of the world, our connections to them still stay strong while giving us the space to be who we are.

ENERGY FOLLOWS THOUGHT: THE POWER OF VISUALIZATION

- *Hello, Peter, come back to Earth. It's your turn to roll the dice! What are you thinking about?*
- *I'm wondering how when I'm older I'd like to change the huge garden at the back of my house.*
- *And ... how would you like your garden to be?*
- *I'd have a little sandbox so my kids could play. I would also plant fruit trees and vegetables that we could eat throughout the year.*
- *I get it. I have an idea. Peter, why don't you draw out your vision, and then we can create an action plan to build it little by little? I would love to have freshly picked oranges from the tree every morning. But it will take you quite a lot of time and effort. Are you willing to put in the effort to do it?*
- *Yes, I am. I'm going to start right now. Thanks, Mom.*

The visualization technique or "energy follows thought" is very popular. There are some well-known authority figures who have used this technique to make their dreams come true and have talked about their experiences publicly. You can see examples on social networks, television or radio. This method starts by leveraging one's imagination.

The first stage of the visualization process begins with a simple exercise that everybody loves to do: to focus the mind on a specific goal and then imagine achieving it. The more real we make that vision, the better. So, we need to think of our exact plan and then imagine in detail how we will carry out that plan for success. The better we imagine it, the more real it seems, and then more we believe it.

In the case of an Olympic runner who is in the middle of his training regimen, he would visualize his actual race and literally see himself winning it. He would imagine exactly his environment, the people around him, the feeling of adrenaline, and when he would accelerate throughout the race, for example. Then, once he reached the finish line, he would visualize the race again and again, in slow motion, like a movie on re-play. Every stride, every second he would recreate so that his mind could clearly imagine what his senses would feel like. Was there wind, and how would that affect him? Did the sun feel very hot that day? If he was like typical serious athletes, the runner would devote time every day to this visualization exercise, with the goal of continually seeing himself win the race. Each time would bring about more details that would engage more senses. The more real the mental experience, the better.

Think it, Do it Mentality

In the second stage, now that we have a clear vision in mind of what suc-cess looks like and how we want to get there, we need to put in the actu-al work (studying, researching, training, practicing, etc.) to support our mind in reaching our goal. Depending on what we want to achieve, this can take days, weeks, maybe even years of work and can involve great per-sonal sacrifices on time, health, finances, family and social life. A strong mind with a strong vision is not enough to accomplish our dreams; we need to physically put in the work to materialize those dreams. If we can align our mind with our bodies and a determined attitude, we can mul-tiply results.

Finally, in the last stage, we need to make sure we have a concrete plan – and then follow it. We can have a vision and a strong work ethic, but if we are not continually moving forward on a predetermined path, we can get off course. Would you ever go on a scavenger hunt without a map? You might know what treasure is waiting for you, but if you do not know how to get to it via a map, you will waste hours and effort travel-ing in circles. A plan helps you quickly recognize when you are stuck or when you are moving towards your goals. It helps us to not lose sight of our vision and objectives, and then redirect ourselves earlier in the pro-cess rather than later.

CONNECTING THE DOTS AND DISCOVERING OUR LIFE'S PURPOSE

- Sarah, what do you want to be when you grow up?

- A hairdresser or a teacher.

- Why?

- I love to comb people's hair, but I also like to teach others and to learn.

- What about you, Jeff?

- I will be a policeman or a fireman.

- What for?

- To save people from the bad guys and rescue them from the fires.

Our life's plan is composed of adventures, challenges, opportunities and resources so that we are exposed to experiences from which we can learn and grow. If we regularly engage in introspection, we will increase our knowledge and be able to become more conscious and responsible adults as we follow our plan.

As mentioned earlier in this book, there are various "wills" at play in our day-to-day lives. Sometimes our human will can diverge from the divine will, which creates inner conflict and can lead to suffering. Fortunately, however, we also have free will, which is the power of choice that can mitigate the disparity between the human will and the divine will. It is God's will that governs the world. This insight is empowering in that through free will, we are able to decide our path forward, which presents different learning opportunities. Life might place us in certain situations, but we can make our own choices in terms of our lens/perspective, attitude, responses and actions in those moments. We are responsible for charting our course in life.

So, regardless of the life events that may come our way and the decisions we make, the important thing is to keep learning and evolving so we can access new knowledge about how life works and make informed and wise decisions. However, sometimes we do not recognize or learn from those opportunities, which stunts our personal development. It is why we should remember that every decision we make will either add to or subtract from our life and shape our future path. Consciousness and responsibility can guide us on this path, but we need to discover our purpose and create our life plan – our mission – so we can connect the dots and know we are headed in the right direction.

Discovering our Purpose

Some of us are so focused on the day-to-day that we lose sight of our overall purpose in life. Our typical day may be structured according to tasks we should do and objectives we want to achieve, but when it comes to our life's direction, we might feel like we are a boat lost at sea. This could be due to our lack of understanding about who we truly are and what we want to become and to not knowing our life's purpose. Whatever our mission is in life, let's try to find a way to always make sure that part of our mission is to help other people. Maybe it's inspiring them to become better people, or equipping them with resources or offering support to achieve their goals. Helping others is one of the most noble and rewarding acts we can do in life.

Purpose can guide our life decisions, influence our behavior, shape goals, provide a sense of direction, and create meaning for our existence. There are those who find their purpose by chance, while others have known it all along, ever since they were very young. Some search for it for years before they discover it, and some never discover it at all. Purpose is important in that it can inspire us, guide us and motivate us. Sometimes we think we know our purpose and we try hard to fulfill it, but we feel we are fighting against a stone wall. In those moments, it is important to take a moment, recognize, analyze and reflect. Is this really what we should be doing with our life? Or, is life trying to point us towards a different direction so we can pursue a different path?

Learning to Connect the Dots

Purpose can be overwhelming for some of us, especially if we do not know exactly how to fulfill our purpose. In that case, build an action plan that outlines all the steps that will take you there, and then track your progress. If the plan is clearly laid out, it will only be a matter of time before you complete it. Expect missteps along the way and embrace them. Through daily introspection, we can learn from our mistakes since they are often the best teachers. However, the question is: Are we good disciples? Mistakes can only teach us if we are conscious enough to let them.

A true disciple is a committed person who seeks to learn from a teacher, leader, mentor or prophet. As we already know, life offers us lessons in the pain, and we tend to hide or dismiss people and experiences that make us feel uncomfortable. Additionally, the tension between the various wills at play (divine, human and free wills) can lead to great resistance to collecting insight. However, being a good discipline means not resisting the lessons and instead being open-minded, observant and self-aware. The experienced disciple begins to understand better how the world of cause-and-effect works, and is able to connect the dots of life together so he can move towards fulfilling his purpose in life.

I remember when I was young that I had been given some connect-the-dot puzzle notebooks that provided pictures outlined in a specific arrangement of numbers of dots that I would need to trace and connect in order to complete a picture. My fellow students and I were learning the number system at the time and focused on tracing the sequential numbers with our pencil, starting at one. At first, the picture was a mystery to us. But then, as we connected more numbers, the visual became clearer. We could never know for sure the exact picture (animal, scenic location, cartoon character, etc.) until we had finished stitching together all the points.

Think of the visual of our life purpose in a similar way. As we join more points together in life, we start to gain a clearer vision of what our purpose is or could be. The dots or the numbers are often our life events or experiences that help navigate us. Once we have connected all of them, we see the planned picture for our life – our mission, our purpose.

Pursuing our Mission

We should never give up once we discover our mission in this world. Sometimes, when we are aligned and connected with the world, we can through meditation access valuable information that comes to us through intuition (spirit or energy). This helps guide our steps and decisions towards fulfilling our destiny. Being aligned also assumes the balance of the three parts of our life, or, as Buddhism notes, to take refuge in the "Three Jewels" to reach enlightenment: Buddha, *Dharma* (teachings) and *Sangha* (the community that practices Dharma).

Discovering our mission will open new opportunities to challenge and grow us. However, God is the one who knows and decides what is best for us. He will guide us little by little through "the writing on the wall," which are subliminal signs of small things that we perceive and that guide us all the time. These signs can change throughout our life and give us navigational markers, but we must pay extra attention when a message is repeated. Looking for patterns in life can provide useful clues for knowing when and where to go in life.

Signs can point us in the right direction and help us to evolve, but often we do not like to follow them because it can involve us having to go beyond our comfort zone. The key is to do what we *need* to do – instead of always what we *want* to do – with a positive can-do attitude, and to find the joy in the journey and not just the destination. Let us strive to achieve this; otherwise, we might lose our way. Life will then reward us by providing what we need. We may not always receive tangible rewards for our efforts, but steadily do and give what life requires from us, as the counterpart will balance itself.

Let us not forget that our soul knows our purpose, and when we listen to our intuition, it can prove to be an effective life guide. The universe constantly moves the pieces (dots) according to what we contribute to our development, in order to expose us to what we need to learn so we can fulfill our purpose in life. Let us broaden our knowledge as much as we are able.

Guiding Principles

The following are some guiding principles that can help us pursue our mission towards our life's purpose.

1. Let us always keep ourselves pure; that is, let us have good thoughts, act in good faith, always think the best of others, and try to do what the universe is proposing to us through the signs. Do not try to escape or avoid what we think is not for us, since it can hinder our evolution.

2. Always think in terms of our own personal development. Choosing the easiest or simplest options do not mean they are the right ones, which will make our path to evolution more difficult. Ask yourself: *What does the universe really want from us? What does it want us to do?* And let's carry it out as good "servants." If we do everything right, the world will treat us well so that we can feel fulfilled. If we show love to others, they will show love to us. Likewise, if we show hate, we will receive hate.

3. Trust that the universe is here to support us on our journey.

4. Everyone has to do what is right for them and to go through certain experiences so they can continue learning and evolving to their maximum potential. Let's develop our capabilities and help others with theirs. The world needs us.

5. Put your plan of action in writing so that it works as a guide and keeps you on track until you have completed it. Mark and monitor commitments, timelines and objectives, while beginning and ending each day with introspection.

THE QUALITIES OF HUMAN BEINGS AND THE SOUL

- Rita, are you going to quit now? You have hardly tried.
- I have tried.
- Yes, but you have not persevered.

There are four levels that make up the qualities of the human being and the soul. In ascending order, they are the physical, the emotional, the mental and the spiritual levels. They can be divided into two categories: the first three correspond to man, and the last, the spiritual, to the soul. Those of man belong to a lower level and can be expressed with words such as emotion, will and persistence. However, those of the soul, which come from God, and sometimes from the spirit, are aspiration and perseverance. Although they are all very similar, their nature is different.

Although we have already addressed this topic earlier, I wanted to reiterate very briefly the example I learned about the qualities of the human being and the soul. Imagine that the physical body was a binary system, with zeros and ones; the emotional body was an analog system; the mind was a computer; the soul was the router; and finally, the spirit was the Internet. They all work together, and each one has its assigned function. If they are not properly configured or lack a wire or cable, the connection between them fails. If there is no planned design about how they should all interconnect, the system will break. The process is therefore not completed.

Let's apply this example to understanding how life works. If we are trying to achieve something important, we need to know the necessary steps to complete it. Everything needs to be aligned in order to create a functional system. So, let's make sure to align our mind, body soul without gaps or broken wires. If we were all together and trying to move a boat from the sand to the sea, we would all need to pull the strings in the same direction at the same time. This makes the process a lot more effective, which enables us to reach our goal a lot faster.

FOURTH PYRAMID LEVEL: RESPONSIBILITY

"You cannot escape the responsibility of tomorrow by evading it today."
Abraham Lincoln

LEARNING TO BE RESPONSIBLE

- Well, have you thought about it yet?
- Why don't you choose it for me instead?
- But which university would you like to study at? Have you researched any of this?
- No, not yet. I don't care.

We come into this world with a series of abilities and gifts to be developed throughout our lives that will allow us to be competent and independent. Although we all have gifts, sometimes we do not want to spend the time and effort to perfect them. It can be easier at times to play the helpless role and get others to take care of us, do things for us. What we do not realize, though, is that in the long run, depending on other people will take a heavy toll on us. The more we allow them to make our decisions and do our work, the more unfulfilled we will feel. When we are unconscious, we choose to blindly accept rules so we can avoid challenges and pain. Of course, not having to do things we do not want to do, or not thinking for ourselves, seems nice and comfortable at first, but it sets us up for overall discontent with our lives.

Independent Housekeeping

Responsibility is defined as responding with action to anything that comes our way. It is essential to healthy development. Taking life's reins as a responsible adult means that we need to have at least a minimal "housekeeping" of our life, which means taking responsibility for basic things that sustain us. Think of having a car, for example. A responsible car owner would make sure to put gas in it, occasionally clean the exterior and interior, take it in for regular maintenance checks, repair any broken components, change the oil and wheels, pay the auto insurance, etc.

Therefore, in order to take control of our lives, we need to be financially independent when becoming adults. This will give us freedom and, above all else, enable us to feel very proud of ourselves. We will feel empowered with strength and a sense of independence. We can stand on our own, which helps boost our confidence. Meanwhile, our jobs will continue to challenge us in ways that can grow our knowledge and skillset.

As mentioned earlier, when we are irresponsible we are likely operating on the bottom of the Pyramid of Consciousness, in the areas of obedience or unconsciousness. This prevents us from developing our gifts or abilities and realizing our potential. It may even stop us from discovering new gifts. The higher we climb the Pyramid, the higher we become in terms of being able to clearly see both inside us and around us, and visualize our true potential. Consciousness allows us to realize what is happening around us. We first need to develop our consciousness and also conscience before responsibility.

Understanding our Decision-Making Process

Being responsible does not mean to blindly obey somebody, but rather to do a benefit-cost analysis, which involves weighing the pros (benefits) against the cons (risks) before making a decision. This way, we are able to see each choice from different angles and can select the wisest one. Of course, we will not always make the right decisions at the right times, but with practice we will learn to discern better. It is just like any other skill or sport that when you practice it, you improve; it is the same way with informed decision-making.

Many of us make decisions based on prejudices or a moral code we were taught in adolescence; however, have we ever asked why we think the way we do? Has our transition to adulthood altered our views and decision process at all? Throughout my own journey of self-discovery and enlightenment, I have realized that my knowledge base is full of information and a belief system that others taught me was good and valid, but as I move forward towards my personal growth, I try to continually revaluate what I know and what I believe, and then update it accordingly.

When we decide to lead our own lives, it does not mean that we will always make the decision that benefits us the most; however, whatever we do we will need to accept the consequences in an adult role and seek the lessons. Negotiation will be part of responsible learning. Sometimes we will need to give a little, to get a little. Other times we will need to do what is hard in the short-term so that it will be easier in the long-term. Making the right decisions is a process, and the more we practice, the better we will become. Meanwhile, life will serve as a guide to helps us make the best decisions. Without the ability or the freedom to make our decisions, society and its laws will make them for us and control what we do.

Building our Responsibility Toolbox

In addition to taking control of our life and becoming responsible for what we do, we need to also be competent (i.e., people who know how to do things) and to use all the tools at our fingertips to build our knowledge base and support our development. This "toolbox" should include the internal traits, insight, skills, resources and support we will need to become responsible adults. Let's always have these tools ready to use when whenever we need them. For example, to continually be able to use our favorite printer, we should always make sure it is running smoothly, and also learn how to solve typical printing problems or issues.

If we are going to be responsible for something or someone (like ourselves!), we will need to make sure we have all the functioning tools we require so that we can immediately fix or adjust things (attitude, motivation, goal, responses, etc.). Whatever we do "let's do it once and do it well." Meanwhile, as we become more responsible, toxic feelings like guilt, shame, bitterness and regret cease to exist. As we continue to learn from our experiences and empower ourselves, the "poor little me" attitude also disappears, along with the role of child and father (discussed earlier in this book). The ethical precept of "Let's do what is right for the right reason" prevails, and our actions are aligned with our inner motivations. We will also become more respectful of both ourselves and of other people.

Taking Control over Life's Reigns

Part of the road to responsibility is treating ourselves with respect and using introspection to help guide and teach us all the time. We will have the last word in negotiations about what we can do and what we cannot; this will be the difference between obeying obligations and using our free will. We will not learn by merely doing what we are told to do, but by observing, discerning and reflecting.

Over time, we will add to our knowledge base through experimentation and analysis. Consciousness will develop throughout life, and is infinite – we can always learn more and grow more. As a result, we will be able to effectively manage ourselves, including our thoughts, emotions and actions, through a conscience lens. Therefore, let us empower ourselves to reach our maximum potential, and then help others do the same.

We are powerful, and we alone can really change our circumstances in life – it is nobody else's responsibility. We cannot rely on orders, rules and opinions of others to guide us and create our sense of worth; we need to make our own observations and draw our own conclusions. To live consciously and responsibly we will have to take the reins of our lives, define a positive path towards enlightenment, and a journey forward.

DIFFERENCES BETWEEN EFFORT
AND DIFFICULTY

> - *I can't keep climbing. This climb is a lot more difficult than I thought. I do not feel safe and I'm exhausted.*
> - *Me neither. I feel like I'm going to fall at any moment. I've lost concentration. I need some sugar. My whole body is shaking and I feel weak.*

We can often confuse *difficulty* and *effort* because both words imply exerting force; however, they are different in terms of meaning. They are each a part of the same learning process, but they appear at different levels of knowledge. For example, if we were learning a new language, like French or Chinese, initially we would require much effort to acquire knowledge about basic words, grammar and pronunciation. As we become more absorbed into the language-learning process, we will likely experience higher levels of difficulty, moving from basic texts to advanced studies and poetry, with nuances in inflection and syntax. Finally, with a lot of hard work, we would reach a point where we understand, speak, write (and even dream!) in French. If we continued increasing the difficulty, we would advance from being a proficient to an expert in the language.

Let's illustrate this concept a bit more: In school we learn subjects like Mathematics and Language, and each year the level of difficulty increases. But, if we started learning something completely new, like Latin, it would require a greater amount of effort. Consequently, as part of the natural progression of the learning development process, the sequence of minor (beginning) to major (advanced) would be: effort (force), difficulty (subtlety) and, lastly, the sublime (orator). If we compare this last concept with an earlier one that we have already addressed in this book, we could say that the effort is the data, the difficulty is the information and, finally, the sublime is the light.

To become more conscious individuals, it is important for us to always recognize when things are difficult and when they require effort, so we can adjust our perspectives and behaviors accordingly. This is how we will be able to know ourselves better and learn how to grow.

WE SHOULD ALWAYS MEASURE OUR EFFORT IN TERMS OF EVOLUTION

- I need to figure out what else I'm going to do. I have to pay the bills for the second building I bought to rent out and receive more monthly income.

- How did you save so much money to buy another apartment if you earn as much as I do?

As discussed in earlier lessons, moving beyond our comfort zone (or body consciousness) is not easy due to homeostasis. Our animal part seeks comfort and does the least possible to survive once our basic survival instincts are met. Some of us operate this way in our day-to-day life, where our animalistic needs and desires unconsciously drive our thoughts and behaviors. Mental processing and reasoning combat this instinctual need for comfort, and is key for continued learning and evolving. But this evolution requires effort on our part, which is led by our "higher self." This effort involves voluntary sacrifice (without victimization) and our constant focus on proactively looking for the most learning opportunities. It also means avoiding the easy thing so we can pursue experiences that will challenge and make us stronger.

Effort has value in and of itself. If we are doing something to expand our mind or skillset, such as playing sports or learning to play a new instrument or cooking, it means that we are helping to improve ourselves and can thereby learn from those experiences. Measuring one's level of effort is both about how good we can play or cook, and how we are physically or mentally working towards something. Therefore, we should not measure our effort in terms of the goals (limit) we want to achieve but rather on the actual labor put forth. Otherwise, if we achieve our goals, we will inevitably stop working because we are comfortable in the fact we reached our targets. However, this can trap us into thinking we did as much as we actually could, instead of striving for the maximum that our capacities allow us. This is the difference between doing the minimum versus reaching our maximum potential in life.

Additionally, always be mindful of thoughts that reprimand you as a failure because you did not reach a goal. This type of thinking can prevent you from progressing towards consciousness and personal growth. An ideal measurement of success is always evaluating our effort against our evolution. We might not have achieved a specific goal, but all our hard work might have created many experiences from which we learned more about ourselves and others. In order to benefit from our efforts, it is important to create a strategy or plan that guides our actions.

For example, imagine that a company hires us. Working for others can be much easier than working for oneself as it has fewer responsibilities and can involve less effort. There is a certain comfort in being paid salary and receiving a monthly paycheck, regardless of how the company performed. But, what would happen if that company decided to fire us? We would then need to decide the next chapter in our professional story. To do so, we should reflect on our past experiences working for this company and weigh the pros and cons. Should we find another job with a company in which we work for somebody else? Or, should we avoid this dependency and create our own livelihood? If we decided to start a company, what type would it be? Or, maybe we join the family business. What will provide the best economic structure for our family in the future? Whatever we decide, the important thing is to always be aware of what we are doing and what can happen to us. If we are going to put effort towards something, let's define the best strategy to evolve us in empowering and productive ways.

Good effort requires a good attitude; in fact, attitude is more important than aptitude. If we believe that we can do it, we are more likely to persevere and succeed. In life it really does not matter what we do; what should matter is how we are going to do it. Attitude becomes especially important whenever we are tempted to stay in our comfort zones and only do the minimum (working at half power). Having a positive and determined can-do attitude can help us overcome these moments and work towards becoming better versions of ourselves.

It does not matter if we work for others, or for us, because that's not the important thing. The key to our evolution is the attitude, the enthusiasm and the effort we put into everything we do. This effort should not be forced because we are obeying orders. Remember doing what others demand from us (obedience or forced work), and putting effort towards something (because we want to), are different things. There will be some jobs that will inspire us to work hard, just like there are others that will not. Regardless of the job, company or situation, let us always remember that our evolution depends exclusively on our attitude and level of commitment we put forth. In the end, if your effort made you a better person, then it was worth it.

FACING OUR FEAR

- Why did you get out? What happened?
- I was scared at sea. I thought the ocean current was dragging me
* and something bad was going to happen to me, and so I panicked.*
- But there is no current. Perhaps, you were scared of the darkness,
* and then your mind played on that fear? You are safe here.*
* Nothing can happen to you. Face your fear by trying to enter the*
* ocean again. I will watch you from outside.*

Spending most of our lives in fear exposes us to constant challenges. If we do not have the necessary insight and consciousness to interpret and navigate life, we can spend our whole lives without evolving while lost in a world we do not understand and that we may not even like. Once we discover how life works and believe that we can be empowered to change it, we will be ready to take control of life's reigns. The journey towards enlightenment and empowerment will require our commitment and effort. It is reassuring to know that no matter what we have done or what we have been through, what matters most is what we do with our life from this moment forward.

Throughout this journey of self-discovery, we will face challenges and fears. If any past experience has generated an irrational fear, it is advisable to go through it again as soon as possible. Once we learn that fear has no meaning unless we assign it meaning, we can repeat the experience and view it from a different perspective and a source of strength. As discussed in the lesson of integration versus disintegration, fear can be confronted in two ways: through fragmentation or integration. In the first case, it can be confronted with a child or father role that fragments and uses one of many personalities (the strong one, the brave one, the intelligent one, the fighter, the flirt) to face it. This strategy of fragmenting oneself in order to obtain a desired result might work for a certain period of time, but can lead to internal conflicts in the long-term caused by separation and disintegration.

However, when we use the second form, integration, we approach the situation from an adult role that is more conscious, empowered and responsible, and that unites all previous roles within a single "whole" individual, with each part interplaying with the other parts to fully support him. Because his system is integrated through understanding and comprehension, he can control the situation and make more informed and responsible decisions.

Therefore, in the first case we use the "divide and conquer" strategy against us, where we leverage only one part of us, and the rest we silence, conceal or ignore. Remember the example of holding something heavy with a single finger – that finger might be strong, but a hand is much stronger. In the second case we use the tactic of "union makes strength," where we unite all the parts to achieve something. This second approach of intentional integration is important for children because if we give them a chance to negotiate, rather than imposing our will on them, they can feel empowered and encouraged to overcome their fears in life through understanding and not because of forced obedience.

Brute force power is disintegrating. It happens when we force something to happen. This force generally accomplishes its purpose but has consequences that come from the disintegration that we will have to eventually manage. If we are afraid to do something that we have not been exposed to before, the best thing is to overcome it through integration, without internal conflicts. Otherwise, the consequences on the person may be negative. It is like the difference between memorizing without reason (unconsciousness) and learning while acquiring knowledge (consciousness). If such learning is done through obedience or fragmentation, its use is usually temporary, rather than long-lasting.

In order to face our fears, we will have to experiment and find out what works and what does not. It is different for everybody. What might work well for somebody, might actually make things worse for you. The only way you can truly know is to go through the actual experience, analyze the results or consequences, and then learn from them. Let's say, for example, that one man was in a bar and was hesitant to drink a glass of wine. But after drinking it, he realized his social awkwardness had disappeared and he suddenly was not scared to talk to the girl across the room he had been eyeing all evening.

In this situation, he discovered what worked for him in terms of reducing his fear. If he realizes it was only a temporary fix and uses the experience to learn more about managing his social anxiety so that in the future he does not have to rely on alcohol, then he would have increased his consciousness. Acting responsibly will always help us face and overcome our fears. When something does not work, try something different. Experimenting is the key to our evolution.

LEARNING AND FORGIVING

> - *ADAM: Lucy, you've broken my Star Wars action figure. It was the one I liked the most. Why did you do it?*
> - *LUCY: I'm sorry, Adam, I had not noticed.*
> - *ADAM: That's not true. I know you did it on purpose.*
> - *LUCY: Well, forgive me then. I did it without wanting to. I guess I fell and stepped on it.*
> - *FATHER: Adam, please forgive your sister. She did not notice it.*
> - *ADAM: Well okay, I forgive you.*
> *Later…*
> - *LUCY: Has someone seen my Barbie doll? I can't find it anywhere. Aggghhh!!!! I found her, but without the head.*

Usually when we forgive, we are accepting the apologies of someone for harm or damage committed against us. It may be about something they have intentionally or unintentionally done or said to us; for example, somebody betrayed us, insulted us or physically hit us. Accepting this apology typically only clears the surface, like the tip of an iceberg, and is usually related to good manners and artificial niceties. But what about everything that is not spoken, or that is hidden or pending? Even though we verbally acknowledged their apology, we can still feel hurt or angry. There might be a temporary band-aid on the relationships, but what about the emotional aftermath that plagues us?

In order to sustain personal relationships, whenever we forgive the other person, it should be authentic. And even though we might think we are truly accepting their apology, there are times when we hold onto negative thoughts and feelings that do not automatically disappear. In fact, sometimes these feelings involve the need to seek revenge and retaliation. However, this is toxic to us and prevent us from moving on and evolving. Even though it can be hard, we need to cleanse our heart and not hold any grudges in the form of anger, hatred or jealousy against the person who has caused us the offense. Otherwise, similar situations in the future will trigger those feelings and cause us to act out.

Talking to the individual we forgive can help to clarify some issues we did not previously understand. Learning their perspectives and motives can help us reassess the situation and reflect on the experience through a lens of compassion and humility. There are many meditations and techniques we can use to facilitate this and to let go of the residual feelings that burden us. However, before we move on, we must first find the lesson from the experience so that we can add to our knowledge base.

By doing this, we can forgive by being responsible, that is, by becoming more conscious adults without feeling guilty or resentful. Let us examine what comes to us and be open to what it is teaching us (not cling to what only makes us feel good), and then hold onto the knowledge gained while letting go of the negative feelings. Those feelings can dissolve when we cleanse our heart and continue to evolve through our spiritual path.

If we consciously and objectively review the wrongful act somebody has done to another person (or to ourselves), we can usually avoid feelings of shame or regret, expect if there is significant damage. If, however, we fall into guilt – a learned pattern of feelings that make us feel bad – then we cannot grow. Guilt can be a powerful force over us and distract us from learning and responsibility, and therefore not let us evolve. Remember that in these situations, you have a choice: to learn or to feel guilty. You cannot do both at the same time.

Using the 3-Step Approach to Forgiveness

There are many ways in which forgiveness can be realized, but one of the most sincere and complete ways is to follow the three steps already explained earlier in this book: examination of conscience, act of contrition and commitment to change. After examining and reflecting on the experience, the individual begins his repentance with a genuine desire to positively change his past actions and repent for his transgressions at all levels. Then, this same person will talk to the affected one to ask for forgiveness from his heart. Finally, the individual who asks for forgiveness will know that it is now up to the other person to either accept or reject the apology – but it will be on that person now.

No matter whether or not his apology is accepted, the person can cleanse his heart and seek balance and inner peace. His inner conflict will settle. To forgive, taking responsibility is the only thing that can make us clean karma. It has been said: "If we haven't forgiven, we keep creating an identity around our pain, and that is what is reborn."

The fundamental thing is that we carry out a deep analysis and re-pentance through the aforementioned three steps, and that we show empathy and compassion towards the aggrieved person, with the goal of not repeating it again. To do this, we must always see the experience as a learning opportunity. Also, we can try to do something that can improve the situation in which damage was done.

SUPPORTING VS. ENABLING BEHAVIOR

- Dad, can you give me money?
- And what have you done with all the money you received from your salary this month? Since you live at home, you don't have to pay for anything – so where has all your money gone?
- I spent it. But I want to go to a very interesting seminar.
- Alright, here you go.

When we receive support (emotional, social, financial), we usually feel more inspired to achieve our goals, which means we will likely contribute more effort. If we decide to go to college to study, for example, some of our parents will contribute to the education expenses, especially if they recognize our hard work and dedication to doing well in school and setting ourselves up for professional success. In this case, the money we receive will be put to good use. On the other hand, if we only think about having fun in college and do not care if we fail our classes, their money will not be help us, since its intended purpose was to empower us to build a strong educational foundation so we can pursue our future career. If we do not fulfill that, then their money was wasted.

Support from one person to another is often a facilitator or motivator for us to reach our goal. In a sense, they reward us with something "Y" in exchange for us to make or achieve an "X" objective, which should be clear, specific and tangible. A Supporter can both help us and motivate us to pursue our purpose and fulfill our destiny.

Enabling is not Supportive

On the contrary, an Enabler is one who encourages (enables) negative or self-destructive behavior in somebody else. For example, if a parent continues to give an irresponsible teenager money, yet he has no specific objectives to best use that money and continually wastes it. Enabling another person might seem like it is supporting them, but it is actually pouring more gas on the fire for no reason and just letting it get out of control. Enabling behaviors do not help us; instead they distract us from evolving by encouraging us down a destructive path.

Other examples of enabling are when parents allow their grown children (who have already finished their studies and have jobs) to live comfortably at home for free and without any responsibilities. Of course, if there are special circumstances, such as that the son has lost his job, or has had a personal problem and has returned to the parents' family home, the individual could temporarily stay there while finding a new job until his life stabilizes and he regains independence. In this case, this would be "supportive" rather than "enabling" behavior in that the parents are helping their son in the short-term so he can become independent again in the long-term. A responsible son would then reimburse his parents for their expenses once he has the financial means.

Other factors, such as an economic crisis or social issues, can compound the problem of enabling behavior. Additionally, there are occasions in which people find great pleasure in either enabling others or feeling they are benefiting from being enabled, which is a key reason why enabling behaviors can persist for long periods of time. For example, some who enjoyed having their parents take care of all their needs and pamper them growing up might look for others (spouse, friend, etc.) in their adult life who can do the same for them. They have in a sense become addicted to the comforts of not having to do things for themselves. Meanwhile, the person (the enabler) caring for them loves the power and influence he now has and the satisfaction from feeling "needed." However, as adults, this dependency on others can be dangerous to one's own personal growth and evolution. Enabling is not responsible behavior, nor is it supportive.

CREATING GENUINE RELATIONSHIPS

- Daughter, what did you eat at school today?
- Soup and fried steak with potatoes.
- Do you have much homework today?
- Not much, but I have to study for an exam.

There are many people who are used to talking to their closest friends and even to their family about unimportant issues. This is often referred to as "small talk." Most of these conversations revolve around what they have done or have been told during the day, without significant context or meaning. Without having deep or meaningful conversations with others, it is difficult to create a bond of trust with them – even if they are family.

We can, however, proactively engage in thoughtful discussions with others and thereby build stronger, more meaningful connections with them. For example, if we return home from school and our father encourages us to share our point of view, and there is an authentic dialogue back and forth that expresses each other's opinions and feelings. When there is a sincere and respectful exchange of personal information, in an environment that promotes openness and acceptance, we feel free to say what we think … and trust begins to build.

Freedom to Speak our Mind

The most authentic relationships, such as true friendships, are based on absolute honesty and openness. We are free to be who we are and can openly admit our fears or desires without others judging us. Rather than restraining our thoughts or words because they may not endorse societal moral codes or social rules, we do not need to filter our expressions since the person loves us – unconditionally so – regardless of what we say or do not say. Being able to discern people with whom we can have open and honest relationships is key to our evolution. Therefore, the sooner we find them and open up, the better.

When those opportunities to engage in meaningful conversations occur, we can start an open dialogue by asking questions like: *Are you feeling overwhelmed by all the changes that have come to you after that challenge or experience? If so, tell me more about what you are thinking and how you are feeling. Do you want to talk about what happened with your boyfriend, since you no longer go out together? How do you feel today? Is there something you want to share or are worried about?*

In principle, we should have the freedom to talk to our parents about anything as equals, rather than hiding it and talking about it with everybody except them. In a society that is guided by rules and uses obedience and discipline to control others, it is difficult to feel we can speak our mind. As parents and educators, we should always encourage children to talk about their problems without us reprimanding, criticizing or dismissing. If they do not feel comfortable confiding in us, they will likely talk to other people. Wouldn't you prefer they talk to you instead so that you can guide them?

Sometimes we engage in "small talk" with people instead of expressing our true feelings and opinions because we fear judgment or retribution. We talk superficially and act a certain way in order to "fit in" and be accepted by others. For example, we join the basketball team not because we want to play the sport but because of the perceived social status we think it brings and the star athletes we can associate ourselves with. None of this brings about genuine relationships, however, since we are either acting a part or not allowing people to get to know the real us.

Trying to be someone who appeals to everyone is practically impossible; there will always be someone with whom we do not get along, and there will also be situations in which we cannot please everyone. However, we can still find ways to relate to other individuals and speak without aggression, judgments, etc.

Turning on the Light

Personally, I have become more accepting of myself in terms of what I do not like about my traits or mannerisms and what I have tried to conceal or reject in the past. Through my self-discovery journey, I have become more integrated since I know that I can only be "whole" if I accept all parts of me – my strengths, my weaknesses, my challenges – because I know that collectively they have made me the person I am today. Understanding more about how my system works has given me the knowledge I needed to recognize and comprehend what was happening within and around me. This process has made me more conscious and more responsible, and a lot more fulfilled. I am better able to recognize and manage experiences that make me feel uncomfortable, learn from them and continue to evolve.

My life is now very different since I stopped spending energy on trying to hide or ignore things I did not accept about myself. I no longer need to break myself into pieces, and instead can consciously be who I really am. Throughout my personal journey, I found that my subconscious made conscious those things that I initially did not like about myself. When they surfaced and I was able to acknowledge them, they lost strength and started to disappear. I compare this to the fear of monsters that small children have at night that suddenly disappears when we turn on the light.

The Value of Authentic Relationships

As mentioned earlier, true friends will need to accept us fully before we can have open and honest conversations with them. Transparency, respect and direct feedback are crucial. If somebody says or does something that bothers us, it is ideal to communicate quickly and directly how we feel about it before that action is repeated. On principle, people should always express what causes them discomfort, because holding it in runs the risk of turning into hate and resentment. Likewise, just because we express what makes us uncomfortable, it does not mean that the other person needs to stop doing something we do not like. It is wiser to use this awareness to begin a constructive dialogue that encourages interactions and leads to experiences that both parties can learn from and grow.

Having honest and open relationships with others help us verbalize our thoughts and feelings, which raises our consciousness and enables us to better understand and integrate ourselves. So, let us accept all the emotions that we experience, and not ignore or reject them. Recognize them, feel them and take the time to process and reflect on them. Although these feelings and emotions might make us feel uncomfortable, they are an integral part of who we are and can teach us valuable life lessons.

DO NOT STUMBLE WITH THE SAME STONE TWICE: RECOGNIZING THE SYMPTOMS

(Alfred's thought): Ummmm, that boy is staring and smiling at my girlfriend. He surely wants something with her. He's not more handsome than me, but ... what is he doing? He's greeting her affectionately. I do not understand what's going on. Why is he laughing with her that way? I'm sure he wants to take her away from me. Yes, I can see that those are his intentions - and I am sure of it! Okay, I am getting very angry. When I'm alone with my girlfriend, I'm going to speak my mind and find out what's going on.

- Alfred, come over here! Look, I want to introduce you to somebody very special to me. It's Ricardo, my cousin who lives in Holland and is visiting us. Tonight we are having dinner with the family. Do you want to come with us?
- Errrrrr, of course. Nice to meet you, I am Alfred. Sandra has told me a lot about you – it's great to finally meet you!

Jealousy blinded Alfred to the reality of the situation. Instead of finding out the story about why this other man was talking to his girlfriend, he automatically listened to his instinctive feelings and formed his own conclusions based on false perceptions and assumptions.

Do you get carried away by your feelings and thoughts, and make instant judgments instead of trying to understand what is really happening? To change this behavior, before going to bed be sure to review the day's events and the corresponding behavioral responses. Daily introspection will help to bring to the surface thoughts and feelings that manifested in one's actions. This awareness can inspire changes in both the mind and heart in terms of how we view, approach and respond to similar events in the future, and ideally minimize negative patterns and consequences.

Symptoms of a cold are easy to detect: nasal congestion, watery eyes, tiredness or headache, and we usually reduce them immediately by getting warm or having hot chicken soup to help us recover. However, when it happens to us with feelings and thoughts, we generally behave just the opposite: we magnify everything that is negative, which only causes us to feel much worse. It's like stepping out onto the street when it is raining and very cold but without an umbrella and without enough warm clothing.

In fact, most individuals do not routinely do daily introspection or a detailed analysis of what has happened to them during the day. They do not observe in detail what they have felt, what they thought and how they reacted, and therefore are not able to reflect on and learn from their experiences. We should, however, instruct ourselves through observation and inductive reasoning so as to absorb greater teachings in our database (brain), with respect to past events throughout our life, including childhood. This will help liberate ourselves and understand why we behave in one way or another.

Introspection and subsequent learning techniques resemble the same process we go through when we take an academic exam. After the test, we are assigned a grade that indicates our performance so that we can thoroughly review the exam and see what we did wrong – and learn how to improve. It is the same as in life. When we go through a challenge or an experience, it is important we look back and review our responses and behaviors with the goal of learning from them. This is the life lesson. Suppose, for example, we make a decision for our work team without consulting them. When we then notice their frustration about not being a part of the decision-making process, which negatively impacts their work effort, we learn that we should involve them in future decisions to raise employee morale.

The danger of not learning from our past is that we are more likely to repeat the same mistakes. There is a saying that expresses this type of behavior very well: "There are none so deaf as those who will not hear." Do you remember how many times your parents warned you that something was going to happen – and it actually did? Since they are more knowledgeable and experienced in life, they are able to recognize patterns and therefore predict similar behaviors and situations. However, let us remember that each person is different. Similar experiences can bring different types of lessons. If something goes wrong or not the way we want, it is still an incredible learning opportunity. Let us not reject it and be grateful to be able to take responsibility for it and learn accordingly.

The most challenging part at the beginning of the self-discovery process is to look inwards, since we hardly pay attention to our internal self. Growing up, we were not taught to develop our self-analysis skills and were not even made aware of its value to our personal development. Unless we directly face and address our inner thoughts and feelings, our ability to learn from experiences and reach our maximum potential in life is reduced.

Some questions we can ask ourselves to help facilitate this process are: *When we think of this person or event, what feelings immediately come to us? What are they pointing us to? What are they trying to teach us? What are we experiencing – internally and externally? Why do we think we feel this way? How can we better manage these feelings in the future?*

THE PROCESS OF SOLVING OUR PROBLEMS WITH OTHERS

- *JAMES: I want the orange.*
- *CATHERINE: Me too.*
- *MOTHER: Boys, do not fight. Stop! Take a banana too. There is only one orange. Do you want to draw lots?*

When we have a problem with somebody, the first thing we must decide is whether or not we want to actually solve it, or to keep fighting and arguing. Many times we instinctually want to fight without realizing that we do not seek a solution. So, whenever we face a conflict with somebody, let's think: *What do we really want to do? How do we want this to end, if at all?* Do we really want to solve this, or are we just trying to fan the flames and make the problem even bigger and last longer?

To find a solution, the first step is to decide not to continue fighting and instead seek the path to understanding. The second step involves asking a lot of questions to discover the source of the problem and why the other person disagrees. At this point, we try to recognize and understand the other perspective, and then engage in an open, respectful and honest conversation to discuss each other's viewpoints. The goal is to mutually arrive at a solution. If both parties want to resolve the situation, there is a great likelihood of reaching a beneficial compromise. The third step is only used when there is no way to reach an agreement, since sometimes there is compromise. In this case, it is better to just leave it there and "agree to disagree."

If we reject compromises or solutions to instead pursue fighting and conflict, we run the risk of escalating the situation with feelings of anger, resentment and even rage. We start to justify our negative feelings and even feel entitled to them. This all leads to a downward negative spiral, which causes greater suffering. Think of about it: Is not taking the time and effort to resolve a conflict really worth it in the end?

Mind over Matter

Having bad feelings is a luxury that no one should have, that is why they say "mind over matter." Matter, the physical body that includes the instincts, reacts very strongly when it does not get what it wants. Therefore, whenever we stay angry, we are giving our consent for anger to control us. Our mind controls our bodies, and if those thoughts and feelings are negative, then it will cause negative responses. The consequences (karma) of having bad feelings and anger are very strong.

Learning to ask and not assume can be difficult, especially when we have been taught not to think for ourselves (and have instead relied on obeying others) and have not acquired yet the communication strategies that can promote understanding and comprehension. What if, for example, that due to our limited consciousness, we are never able to recognize whenever we make assumptions or judgements? What if we did not understand the impact of our words or the possibility of others' misinterpretation of them? This can occur when there are gaps in our knowledge base that cause us to rely on instincts rather than logical reasoning when reacting to someone or something. However, once we move up the Pyramid of Consciousness, we start to fill in these knowledge gaps and learn how to consciously assess a situation before responding to it. Assumptions mask reality and often lead to false judgments as well as unproductive or negative behaviors.

At home we practice this by playing a specificity game that helps children learn not to make decisions based on assumptions. Children will ask me, for example, "Can I have a soda?" "Yes," I answer, and then when they go to the fridge to get it, I ask, "Why are you taking the soda now? You did not specify today. Also, which kind did you want? The flat or carbonated kind?" This role-playing game teaches them to be specific when they talk instead of making general assumptions. Over the years, I have enjoyed teaching this concept to children, and they quickly understand it and even like to play it with me. This game was adapted from the example of the airplane and the parachute that was discussed earlier in this book. Now they have learned that if somebody is not specific about a request or a subject, they know to ask the right questions to get the right information – without making any wrong assumptions.

CONSUMERISM

- Honey, wait, I'm going to buy other shoes I need.
- Really? But our closet has no more room for anything else, and
* you have others that are very similar.*
- They are not; they have a different heel.
- Why do you want to buy a pink pair when you don't even have a
* matching dress?*
- You're right. I will also need to buy a new dress.

Normally when human beings suffer and maybe are sad, hopeless or angry, they try to compensate by doing other things that give them instant pleasure and keep them entertained (or distracted). For example, people who have anxiety or stress might pursue "retail therapy" where they go on a shopping spree and buy a lot. Or, some may binge eat or seek some type of tangible reward. These behaviors might temporarily distract people from feeling pain, stress or misery, and bring artificial joy or pleasure. However, it is a vicious cycle in that, like a drug addict who seeks an extreme "high," the behavior or act will temporarily provide relief but will then be followed by an extreme "low." The person will crave more and more, but will ultimately receive less and less.

We can see these types of behaviors every day around us. Some are addicted to buying or collecting clothes, cars, watches, shoes or anything else. This consumption of goods (consumerism) can generate moments of pleasure that can make us feel instantly better for a period of time (like euphoria) but then disappears leaving us feeling emotionally empty. It is like trying to nourish ourselves by excessively drinking alcohol, but actually harm our bodies instead. The effects of this substance on our health are negative because no matter how much we take in, it does not nourish us but harms us.

Out of Sight, Out of Mind

Because we can focus so much on external behaviors, we can lose sight of what is happening internally. One's actions are often manifestations of how he feels inside, yet some of us do not even consider what is happening on the inside because we cannot physically "see" it. In these cases, "out of sight becomes out of mind." Rather than facing and addressing those feelings that make us feel uncomfortable, we seek to replace them with new feelings – ones that make us happy, even if only for short time. But just like how a pleasant buzz from alcohol can wear off or turn into a hangover, the pleasure we get from certain behaviors wears off and makes us just as conflicted or miserable as before, maybe even worse. And so we again try to seek the next high to counterbalance this by buying more and more things, which perpetuates an unhealthy cycle of unfulfillment and discontent.

As we advance up the Pyramid of Consciousness (POC), the strong desire to convulsively buy and possess even more begins to calm down as we learn that objects cannot solve problems or remove inner conflict. Material things cannot nourish our mind, our heart and our soul. The more conscious we become, the more our desperate quick-fix thoughts transition to logical and responsible thoughts like: *Why do I need this?* The lighter our luggage (physical, emotional and mental), the better we feel. Today, I can happily tell you that I have discarded many of my possessions, which has inspired feelings of relief. Gone are the days of my meaningless shopping habits. And because of it, I feel much lighter and freer.

FIFTH PYRAMID LEVEL: CONSCIENCE

"He who overcomes others is strong,
but he who overcomes himself is powerful."
Lao Tse

WHAT IT IS TO FLOW

- *I had a great time talking to Sarah yesterday. She is so kind and always has something to say that we end up in a lively debate about the education of children. I believe that these meetings with friends help us to get rid of small talk and instead lead to more interesting and engaging conversations that reveal different points of view and enable us to learn from each other. We could do another one next weekend. How about it?*
- *Of course, dear. We will. Will you call everybody? I'll bring some drinks and snacks. Let's meet at the same place as always.*

To "flow" (being in our zone) means that we give each person enough importance to remain in the consciousness of others. In other words, it is our mental state in which we immerse ourselves in an activity while feeling energy, focus, presence and enjoyment. It is like if we are at a party and are enjoying talking to people and having a good time, but we are also getting what we need from it. Think of a fish swimming downstream in a natural and harmonic way. As the fish overcomes all the obstacles it finds in its way, like stones or trunks that have fallen into the river, it nonchalantly continues swimming without stress towards its ultimate destination: the area of the sea offering the food the fish needs.

Empathy Required

The qualities necessary to flow are not physical traits like being handsome or smart, but rather just being ourselves and present in the moment, without attracting attention. Empathy can be defined as the ability to put ourselves in the shoes of the other in order to think and feel like him. To flow, we need some degree of empathy that forms a kind of emotional and meaningful bond with people as we interact with them. When empathy is activated, individuals usually connect through love (compassion, tenderness, or gratitude), and may even perceive, in some cases, what the other person feels. We cannot force flow in life; we need to naturally just be. We need to "go with the flow." That is, we should focus on "what is," instead of wasting time thinking of what should be or what will please others.

When a truly empathic person is in a group, we can feel his energy, his flow. He can relate with others in a natural and intuitive way in that he knows when to talk and when to let others talk, without jealously or conflicts arising. People who go with the flow tend to easily get along well with everybody without even trying. Like a natural spring when water just flows, it simply happens.

It has been my experience that when we migrate from a base of fear to one of love, and continue to ascend the Pyramid of Consciousness, we can develop genuine empathy and reduce much internal conflict. This inspires a sincere desire to connect in deeper and more meaningful ways with others who cross our path in life.

In order to flow, we do not have to always be extroverted. There are individuals who are more introverted and yet know how to give the necessary support and say the right words when required. These people give love all the time through their facial expressions and body language; their gestures speak for themselves. They also have a great capacity for listening and connecting with people, but on a different level. We do not always need to be the center of attention to talk with others. Some individuals are very empathetic (can understand and share feelings with others), but prefer to hang out on the sidelines. However, they too play an important role in personal relationships. In this case, the communication methods are just a bit subtler.

Finding Joy in the Moment

The physical expression of empathetic people is most visible in those who are already at the near end of their lives. Most of them have fully lived their lives and achieved their goals, and now they just enjoy being present in the day-to-day and reflecting on and talking about their lives. Through their expressions, posture, gestures and mannerisms, they wear their flow – their content, their peace – and are fulfilled just being able to share space with those they love. They are happy to just be. In this final stage, they do not seek to have new experiences or to buy more things; they simply appreciate small and simple moments of joy. They embody love and kindness, which they delight in sharing with others, even with the seemingly smallest gesture.

To the casual observer, these people might look like they are introverts since they are not outwardly energetic or loud communicators. But, in this last stage of life, they do not need to demand attention or try to impress. By now, they have very little ego and have understood that life is not as one wants it to be, but that it is as it comes. Life has become a lot more precious, and is bigger than them. They have learned that life should be lived to its fullest, and be enjoyed, appreciated and celebrated. They know they cannot control time and physical changes in their body, but they can very much influence their attitude and outlook on life. They have figured out which battles to fight and which to let go so they can have inner peace. Understanding this life balance should be a goal for everybody.

People who reach the highest levels of the pyramid are also mediators. These are usually trained to assimilate into any group, connect with the individuals, immediately identify pain points, recognize the source of conflict and act responsibility. They do not force anything but instead empower others to just let go so they can collectively move the ocean current (energy). For this reason, conscious empathic individuals know what to do and say in typical situations, without having to think or try hard. They make everything flow naturally and may even have the ability to captain the group since they have likely earned the trust of the members. Not needing to feed their ego, they see themselves as equal to the others in the group and sincerely seek the overall good. They do not have to stand out by being funnier or friendlier or more talented; they just know how to surf the wave and get others to join them for the ride.

ETHICS: LET'S DO THE RIGHT THING FOR THE RIGHT REASON

> *- We're going to tell Mom to sign us up for painting class, and then we'll have the perfect excuse to be able to come home later and do whatever we please.*
> *- Yes, but we will not have time. We have a lot to study this year.*
> *- I know, but I don't care if I get bad grades.*
> *- I don't think what you are doing is the best strategy.*

Ethics has its origin in reason and reflection, and refers to behavior. This is where the principle of "do the right thing for the right reason" comes into play. However, morality, which is itself part of ethics, is the innate capacity we have to differentiate and choose between good and bad; however, this comes with certain prejudices.

Making decisions is easy, especially if we let ourselves be influenced by what we want. When we wish things to happen a certain way, we can leverage our intelligence to create situations that turn our desires into realities. For example, if we want to get good grades, we may have to consistently study hard during the school year. However, life does not always turn out the way we want or planned. Maybe our parents, teachers or bosses are not as we would like them to be, or maybe our best friend does not always behave like we want. There will be times when we can move the pieces by manipulating situations according to our needs. We can exercise our free will, but at what price? Are we really doing the right thing? Are we acting ethically?

If we say that we are going to help our grandmother with the shopping, or tutor our brother for the math exam, it would seem like on the surface that everything is ethically good because we are doing something positive (helping others). However, if we decide to do something to make a profit, such as looking for a tip, or helping somebody so that we can avoid doing something else, the integrity of our actions is compromised. Of course, if we were upfront in terms of our real objective behind our "benevolent" action, then it would be less of an ethical issue since there is a type of exchange between the parties and everyone is informed.

From the ethical point of view, everything we do should be with the internal motivation to help "*per se*" and in the best interest of the other person to help him expand his knowledge base and grow. If there is something that we receive from it, consider it a gift and enjoy! Yet, let honesty and integrity always be part of us. An example of unethical behavior would be if we purposely tried to befriend a classmate who always earned very good grades, but our intent was to use the friendship as a means to be able to copy her exams so we can also get good grades. On the surface, it appeared we were just being friendly, but internally, we wanted to profit at her expense. It was the wrong reason.

Therefore, the ethical principle of "do the right thing, for the right reason" is very important. We should always examine what our real intention or internal motivation is before we do something, and reconsider our action plan if our personal interest goes beyond helping or doing good for others. As we climb the POC, our fine-tuned ethical sense makes us question precepts that society accepts; some we will find to be reasonable, and others we will determine are not. Although our ethical judgment was heavily shaped by obedience, as we become more conscious of our own thoughts and feelings about morals and values, we will eventually evolve our understanding of ethical principles, independent of what others believe is right or wrong.

Sometimes not intervening in a relationship or situation can be an easy decision, which means that there is no learning that will happen, and that we are using it as an excuse for not doing what we find is challenging or uncomfortable. Before we respond or act, we should ask ourselves if what we are doing is the right thing for the right reason, and if our response is because it is the comfortable thing or the responsible thing.

It has been my own experience that once we have learned this knowledge, are trained in consciousness-building techniques, and can manage ourselves more responsibility and compassionately, we will be able to respond and make decisions in more difficult situations while remaining calm, cool and collected.

HARMONY THROUGH CONFLICT

- I'm telling you to leave me alone.
- I don't want to. Let's solve this problem here and now.
- Okay, whatever you want, but things are not done with bitterness.
- So, what are you saying? You like to act like the victim and not to be responsible for your actions. You chose the worst path to take, instead of becoming stronger because of it, you continue to behave like a moody child.
- What did you say? This means war! We'll see who wins.

Conflicts can be created for many reasons. Some start simply from somebody not liking how somebody else is talking to them or behaving with them. Some occur when people differ on opinions or ideas. Others are due to people's negative emotions taking over and leading to negative results. We can also deliberately use conflict to manipulate others to get what we want. Although somebody's conflict might have nothing to do with us, we sometimes take it personally. The less conscious and evolved we are, the greater control that conflict has over us. If we do not do introspection and learn how to channel negative thoughts and feelings into positive behaviors, our conflict can continue or repeat.

A *conflict* is a clash between two opposing sides (people, philosophies, opinions, etc.). It is why wars are typically started. A war has only one objective: to produce a winner. Each side decides they want something, and so they fight for it. When they agree that war is the only option, what they really are saying is that they do not want to solve their differences according to logical reasoning. The fight continues until one side loses, typically after their reserves are depleted and they need to settle. At this point, any solution is valid since now war no longer makes sense.

Negotiations, if carried out respectfully with common sense, can avoid many conflicts. A good negotiation strategy is to start with asking questions instead of making general assumptions (remember, "question our version of the truth"). The lens should be as objective and bias-free as possible, while dismissing popular stereotypes or inherent prejudices that can sometimes negatively influence us. During the negotiation process, we need to discover what is really important to the other party, along with why and what for, so that we have a more informed lens from their point-of-view. Eventually each side should arrive at a general consensus or compromise in terms of a solution that is agreeable to all parties. Ideally, no conflict should ever be needed to remedy a problem, but in many cases we endeavor to resolve them this way.

In personal relationships, the "from harmony through harmony" formula is much more evolved, but implies that one of the parties must have the knowledge to relax its position as many times as necessary when the level of conflict is very high. It is like a kind of temporary retreat, until there is a new opportunity to return to understanding and dialogue. This prevents one side from fanning the flames from the other side and making the entire situation much worse.

There is yet another way to achieve harmony without conflict: through a neutral third party or a conscious arbitrator who can listen to and counsel each party what they really need when there is a dispute. Mediation has been shown to be quite effective in helping disputing parties resolve the dispute on their own.

WE NEED MORE CONSCIENCE (AND CONSCIOUSNESS) TO EVOLVE

- What are we going to do this summer?
- I won't do anything. I'll stay by the pool and have fun.
- Right, I would like to learn something new that requires working with my hands. We have a lot of time. I'm thinking of taking a cooking course.

Individuals need a broader understanding of everything in and around them in order to be able to rise from our operational level (mental, emotional and physical) to a higher level called evolution. However, because our body is always seeking comfort in homeostasis, we are naturally inclined to reject expanding our knowledge base so that we can keep things as they are. Therefore, there are times when we forget particular information on purpose because we can have "selected memory" due to the way we filter (intentionally or unintentionally) the information (consciousness) we perceive and the associated feelings and experiences that come with that. Therefore, on certain occasions our body could be manifesting its desire to ignore because the information received will probably make us think and/or work on it. As previously stated, the body has two rules of conduct in the following order of importance: survival and reproduction. It typically does not instinctually crave anything beyond that.

Likewise, change involves effort, and the mind and body do not like to work towards change or goals, unless they are well-trained. As long as our conscience (and consciousness), is at the level of the body, stubbornness will dominate and control. There are cases in which stubborn people who have a low level of consciousness can begin to operate with more of their mind and emotions, but it takes work. Generally, a person with the highest level of stubbornness is one that lives at a lower level of consciousness, that is, in the bodily consciousness.

Typically, consciousness is whatever stimuli and information we can take, receive and perceive from our inside and outside world. Equally, consciousness allow us to analyze and reflect with the data or information stored in our memory. So whatever conscious status (thinking, perception or emotions) a living human being can have, that is consciousness. Additionally, Consciousness leads the path to make better decisions with conscience's help by building your personal ethics, moral and values.

Our internal compass orients and guides us, but it needs to first be developed and fine-tuned. Initially, our conscience is imprecise; it lacks both the knowledge and experience to accurately direct us. However, the more insight we gain, the more introspection we do, and the more life lessons we seek, the more powerful our conscience and consciousness becomes. Life is a complex system that teaches us to make better decisions through experience and mistakes. To learn from these experiences, we must go through the discernment process and use logical reasoning to form conclusions. Discernment requires the conscience to use the information from one's internal database. Without discernment, there is no development of consciousness nor conscience and no path to enlightenment.

Generally, Conscience is part of the consciousness process. It is related to the discerning of the good and the bad, fair and unfair, etc., within each person ethics guidelines or control points. I like to look at it as if it was the adult/father/kid role in us, – depending of our POC level – who in the end make all the decisions. Therefore, we use the info – learned – in your consciousness and then we make decisions according to our parameters or control points that are very important for us and decide our path and purpose in life.

Consciousness helps us to be aware of what is happening in and around us. Responsibility, which is relative to an action, allows us to respond to a concrete circumstance that happens to us. Sometimes consciousness and responsibility develop together, although usually the development of conscience (along with consciousness) goes first followed by responsibility. Individuals handle different levels of unconsciousness all the time. By focusing too much on something we can lose consciousness of what is happening around us. Remember that consciousness (along with conscience) and responsibility are infinite – we should never stop learning.

WHAT OUR WORDS SAY ABOUT US

- Hello. Are you going to the game?
- I am not. Are you going? My daughter is going by herself.
- Yes, my son usually does too, but his car was damaged and I have
  to take him.
- I'm going to Pilates on Thursday. Are you going to come to class?
- Yes, I am. I really like it.

We are always communicating and supplying information, even about us. Words can show how we treat ourselves, how we feel, or how we think. Using certain verbal forms may allow us to identify the role we are dealing with (adult-parent-child), the motivation with which we do it (obedience or responsibility), and the likelihood that we have to reach our goal or phase ("I'm going to" or "I have to"). If we add other visual clues, such as noticing how she walks or analyzing how she dresses, we could collect much more information and get a clearer idea of how she feels and what may be happening inside them.

Let's suppose we have a driving test on Thursday, and we have studied five hours a day for the entire month to prepare for it. We have also done many tests that will help us be even more ready for the exam. However, our expression and mannerisms will likely convey the degree of confidence we have to pass the exam. That degree of confidence in turn will be a reflection of our level of integration in this regard. True knowledge stimulates the alignment of our fundamental bodies, such as the heart and the mind, supported by the effort of our studying.

When we say, "I would like to pass the exam tomorrow," we indicate that we are thinking hypothetically. "I would like to pass" is much different than "I will pass." If we are very confident about our chances of passing, our statements would reflect that. When we express our preference rather than our resolution to do well on the exam, it shows ourselves (and others) that we are doubting ourselves. Even if we said, "I have to pass the exam tomorrow," it would mean that we are giving ourselves an order (using the father role), but are still not convinced that we will pass, although we have obviously put a lot of pressure on ourselves to do so. At this point, our verbal statement indicates that passing the exam is something we would like to do and we know that we have worked for it, but we are doubtful. There is still no responsibility.

However, declaring "I will pass the exam" means that we not only want to do it but we *will* do it. We are confident that we will do well because we know we have studied a lot and worked hard for it. In this case, our five parts (the physical, emotional, mental, spiritual and the aura) are aligned, integrated, and collectively focused on the same point. We consciously believe we will. We feel we will. And we know we will.

In summary, an in-depth analysis of the way we speak can give us additional insight into how we are feeling, whether we are integrated and/or the level of responsibility. To think it is one thing, but to speak it can be completely different. Sometimes we need to actually say and hear our thoughts in order to assess whether we believe them. To begin observing our own words and changing them accordingly is part of our personal learning on the road to evolution.

HOW TO INTEGRATE OURSELVES FROM THE "LOWER SELF"

> *- Hi, Nicole, you're dressed very formal today. Where are you going?*
> *- I'm going to try to get the rent reduced for the apartment that I'm going to sign today. I hope to convince the apartment manager with this dress, my charm and good girl ways. Uuuugh!!! I want to finish and take off these clothes!*

The "lower self," as we already know, corresponds to behaviors similar to those found on the bottom level of the Pyramid of Consciousness, and is based on instincts, desires and feelings while focused on itself. On the contrary, the "higher self" deals with a broader, responsible, integrated adult, and leverages compassion and understanding to pursue the overall good.

Our perception and comprehension of circumstances and experiences depend on whether we are using our "lower self" (unconscious) or "higher self" (increased consciousness). As we evolve, we learn how to integrate both parts of ourselves, with them being guided and piloted by the one with the superior level of consciousness, that is, the "higher self." This means that regardless of what we do, there will always be an integration of the two parts from the point-of-view of the "higher self." For example, if somebody instinctually reacted to something (utilizing his "lower self"), the experience would be processed from the conscious integrated perspective of his "higher self." What is important is not only what we do but how we do it and learn from it. Higher consciousness means operating from our "whole" self and not fragmenting ourselves. Regardless of what we do on an instinctual or emotional level, our "higher self" can observe, interpret and process it.

For example, let's say that while you are sleeping, two strangers break into your home and attack your family. In that moment, you grab the closest weapon to defend yourself and protect your family. You are acting in an integrated way and from the "higher self." Even if you pull the trigger and kill someone, which is using your "lower self," your action of protecting your family can be done in an integrated way. Therefore, it is not what we do, but how we do it (either with our integrated or disintegrated self) that matters.

It is important to have the necessary consciousness to manage what we do in an integrated way, whatever it may be. Focusing from the "higher self" while being integrated is like using a responsible guide that helps us to do what is required as efficiently as possible. Another example: Imagine that we want to have crazy sex one night, which plays into our instincts and desires, but if guided with the "higher self," it could also be treated in an integrated way. Here, again, it is not what we do but how we do it integrally.

By integrating your upper and lower selves we can have our cake and eat it too – literally. Rather than automatically stressing about the dessert's calories, we can eat it responsibly, which means choosing to do so without remorse and without counting calories. We will accept that we like it, and therefore occasionally eat it and enjoy it from all our senses, without feeling guilty. When we let guilt stand in our way, our responsibility disappears. To cope with that guilt, some of us fragment and try to forget that fact we indulged in dessert.

Both the "higher" and "lower self" are fundamental parts of us. The pieces become harmonized when we are integrated, but not all the time. When we ascend to the top of the Pyramid of Consciousness, we also integrate our more animalistic side so that both parts of us complement each other perfectly in order to evolve more harmoniously. Such union is not normally present all the time in people; it comes and goes, since it is not completely and consistently stable in people. Earlier I used the example of how a person's constantly changing state affects their moods. It is the same with integration of the body. We are continuously fluctuating as we respond to external factors (people, environment, etc.), which means that sometimes we will be integrated, and other times we will not.

The Holy Trinity is a mystery or dogma that deals with the belief that there is only one God in three different beings, hence the reference to the

Father, Son and Holy Spirit. Applying this to the concept of integration, when people are in the "higher self," (holy spirit), it means that they are also integrating the other two parts, which are the one of the Father (soul or mind) who is working on the emotions by imposing itself, and the one of the son, (instincts) where our pleasures are. Therefore, the Holy Spirit is the union of the three together, and they at the same time connect with the energy (similar to the World Wide Web).

LEARNING TO BECOME CONSCIOUS

- What did you decide to play: clarinet or piano?
- I have not thought about it yet.
- Haven't you taken the test classes yet? We have to do the
registration today. What if later you don't like it? I don't really
understand how you can take life so lightly; it's your future and
what you're going to be doing in life.

Becoming conscious is the origin of everything. It is a function of the mind that leads us to think about something according to these three questions that relate to introspection: *What, Why* and *What For*.

1. What: Refers to understanding exactly what (facts, events) transpired
2. Why: Refers to the possible reason, purpose or explanation; describes the intended motive behind the act
3. What for: Refers to the ultimate payoff or goal or benefit of why something happened

Here's an example using these questions to describe my personal situation:

1. What: I am living in Madrid
2. Why: (various reasons) Because I want to reconnect with my family and the world in which I grew up; or, I need to do the routine annual medical checkups since last year I did not do them; or, I do not need a visa to live in Europe; or, I need to have time to write this book
3. What For: Living in Madrid will allow me to be more available for potential job opportunities; or, writing this book has helped me learn more about myself and clear up a lot of misunderstandings I had about life; or, this is where I belong and now have to accept things as they come

Answering these three questions when examining (and understanding) our lives from different perspectives will help us put together life's puzzle and have more clarity and vision in terms of the lessons that life brings. In the first stage of introspection, we may not have recognized or understood our experiences, but through perseverance and learning how to observe, analyze, discern and reflect, we will gain more wisdom and comprehend the law of cause and effect.

We Decide our Life's Path

Introspection allows us to be wiser and humbler, and teaches us that life has greater meaning and is bigger than ourselves. It does not allow us to play the victim or poor-little-me role; rather, it challenges us to think higher and act higher while developing more consciousness and compassion. Accepting life means that we should try to understand it through comprehension. We need to liberate ourselves from the overbearing rules and expectations that might have weighed us down throughout childhood and adolescence. Expanding our minds and seeking experiences that will challenge and grow us will help us see that mistakes, pain and suffering can teach us valuable life lessons. It is how we will eventually calm our minds and souls (acceptance) to find inner peace. We must always remember that we are empowered with choices in life. For example, we can choose to let guilt overwhelm and defeat us, or we can leverage it to learn, accept and embrace who we are.

Let us take ourselves seriously and pursue our mission and purpose in life – before we get too old and miss out on all the incredible experiences life can inspire. Let us not live a life in which we will look back someday and regret with sadness. Right now is the perfect time to chart your new course and follow it. As we grow older the opportunity to gain the knowledge we need through experiences is usually shortened and therefore the difficulty increases. So, don't wait. Just like surfers, we want to catch the wave as soon as it comes; otherwise, we might find ourselves waiting for that next perfect wave for a really long time and miss out on so much in the meantime.

If we wait too long before proactively changing our life, it is very probable that we will not have time to learn from and leverage the necessary experiences and the teachings that will enable us to be better so we can live better. Procrastinating on your journey of self-discovery and enlightenment is like trying to cram four years of college into the last semester. It will be overwhelming and will not set you up for success.

Step by Step

According to my experience, once you start on the path towards consciousness it will probably be very difficult to leave it because everything that moves within us will surely surface. We will have to work intensely with introspection to clean and change learned thought and behavior patterns, the way we process feelings, thoughts or behaviors, among many others. It is a new and freer life without rules and is based on discernment and knowledge acquired through life experiences. This road is not a hobby. It is not a dream. It is not a hypothetical. It is one of the biggest challenges that we will face, but it is the most inspiring and rewarding. In today's world, the way forward is the only option, even if we occasionally zigzag or take three steps forward and two steps back. Our biggest challenge will be … ourselves. Our ego will not want to bend, our bodies will want to stay in homeostasis. But, if we can integrate ourselves – mind, body and soul – and persevere, we will overcome.

The thorniest struggles are against ourselves, but through introspection and analysis we can bring to consciousness what we dislike about ourselves, even our worst behaviors or twisted thoughts. Accepting, understanding and processing them can eliminate them or help us manage them in a better way that will reduce their power over us and enables to develop understanding and responsibility. We will integrate more and more. And as we are able to be more conscious and transform as a result, we will find that we will detach from people, things and habits that bind us and hold us back, and become more energetic, extroverted, compassionate, joyous, and laugh even more in life because of it.

SIXTH PYRAMID LEVEL: ENLIGHTENMENT

"When you're experiencing one of those days when you feel you are fully aligned, and you can press life's gas pedal and go anywhere, then that is when the magic happens. Only then can you feel that you are truly connected to life's World Wide Web, and you feel so empowered that you know that nothing can stop you. You can do or achieve anything because the limits disappear, your mind expands into unlimited possibility and you do not see anything else ... except when the routine brings you back to what we call "reality" and you cannot remember where you put the keys."
An apprentice of how life works.

NOTE: With regards to this part of enlightenment I have addressed only five topics in the following pages. Nevertheless, it is an infinite and complex step, with many layers. There may not be one, but several pyramids within this step in which each person enters the path where he will be discovering on his own through study and experimentation of new knowledge.

From this point forward, a big part of one's life that embodies a high level of consciousness is focused on helping others. Because life is no longer only yours or your family, it belongs to the world and to others. Through consciousness, we are all connected to one another. Therefore, our mission should be to help others by paying it forward. The following provides some guidelines to help us do just that.

THE WORLD OF CAUSE AND EFFECT

*- Connor, do not pull the rubber waist of the pants so hard – it can
break.*
- Yes, Mom, you're right. It's already broken. I am sorry.

Cause is the origin of something, and *effect* is the consequence of that
origin, to which physical energy has been applied to create something
concrete. Expressed in a very simplified way, we would say that to build
a closet, we would have to get the material, the tools, and make a plan. In
the end, after adding the necessary work, the result will be a newly built
piece of furniture.

The moment a baby is born, we know that he or she will be different
from the rest of the people on Earth, a complete original just like a fin-
gerprint. Our DNA is like an amazing cocktail, composed of numerous
ingredients that make us truly unique and special. We possess physical
characteristics similar to those of our parents and ancestors, in addition
to a host of new traits. Many of us will also resemble relatives in our mannerisms and the way we think and act – even though we have never met
them.

On the other hand, we also know that each of us has a soul, which
comes to us when we arrive in this physical world and leaves our body
when we die. It is said that the soul lives within us, eventually becoming a spirit when it returns to where it belongs after we pass. The spirit is in charge of organizing a route plan for our life. Therefore, causes
are organized at the level of the spirit, not of matter, which means those
events and experiences we encounter throughout our lives were intended
to serve a purpose. Sometimes the soul, when aligned with our physical,
mental and emotional bodies, reveals valuable information to us so that
we can learn from it.

Each person has a different programming and a different explanation
why it might not be working in their favor on a certain day. Ever heard

this saying? *Today I got off on the wrong foot or the wrong side of the bed.* Well, for some, this is how they infer they are having a bad day; others would say that the stars aren't aligned. Why else would one day be different from another? The latter group believes that the movement of the stars and changing positions of the planets affect us on a daily basis, just like the Moon and the Sun are known to control the sea tides.

The world of effects is material and can reveal the consequences of what happens to us. However, sometimes we will not see all the causes for those effects. For example, if we notice that the tornado devastated the city, we can understand what happened and its outcome, but we do not know the spiritual reason for this to happen. The world of causes is abstract and can be difficult for us to understand and to line up an effect with its cause. This can lead to us dismissing certain things that happen to us simply because we do not understand why or how they happened.

Any type of conflict, including the rejection of something, has the specific purpose of overcoming the resistance that prevents us from learning. Our life plan is the sum of our experiences, resources (support) and challenges planned at the spiritual level. Hence, these experiences, and the lessons gained from living them, will increase our knowledge, which is our ultimate goal in life. Therefore, continually rejecting or dismissing something that we do not want to happen or do not like is merely procrastinating the inevitable. It is a missed learning opportunity that will eventually find its way to us, and sometimes even through greater suffering.

Human will is undeveloped and inexperienced if we compare it with divine will, which is infinitely mature. As long as human will exists, it will mean that we have not evolved enough since there will continue to be a clash against divine will, which creates inner and external conflicts (suffering). This battle of the wills will eventually tear us down to a point when we surrender. It is only then when we will cease fighting what life hands us and instead accept and grow from the lessons.

HIGHER AND LOWER MINDS

- I do not know why you insist on working for that company.
- Its business vision is what attracts me the most.
- Yes, but if you are not hired, you will not have a job and then will financially struggle. I have applied to fifteen more companies. Maybe you're not making the best decision right now, don't you think?

The "lower mind," which refers to the tangible mind that is focused on producing effects, should not be confused with the "lower self." The "lower mind" is composed of the "higher self" and the "lower self." However, the "higher mind" operates in the abstract world, which focuses on the world of causes. The "higher mind" has no "self" since at this point we are part of the energy that connects everybody. Therefore, the "lower mind" strives to produce effects, while the "higher mind" focuses on the causes that produce these effects.

The Spirit is that which is not material and which is at the level of energy like light, heat, intuition or "the writing on the wall." Something spiritual has a higher level of consciousness that operates in an abstract world, that is, with our "higher mind."

The union of the material world (which is perceived by the senses) and the spiritual (the flow of energy) in the "lower mind" creates causes that are understood only at the level of the "higher mind" since through the "lower mind" consequences are only enjoyed or suffered.

The lower mind observes and can operate in any of the following states:

- **Unconsciousness:** We do something but do not realize it. We have our mind in something else. For example, we accidentally step on someone's foot yet do not notice it because our mind is distracted.

- **Consciousness after the fact:** We do not realize it at the moment, but only after some time do we recognize and process what happened. We realize we stepped on someone's foot moments or minutes after the fact.
- **Real-time consciousness:** We are aware of what happens at the exact same time that it is happening. Here we have a higher level of consciousness. On this occasion, we step on someone, notice what our foot did, and immediately apologize.

Conscious people generally fluctuate between real-time consciousness and the higher mind.

THE OBSERVER

- I do not want to talk to you again. I'm tired of something always happening whenever we are going to meet. I am leaving.
- Come on, Jack, you know I have many obligations. You know if my kids get sick I have to go pick them up at school and take care of them all day. It's not like I plan those things. Well, we'll talk about it some other time. I'm sorry I could not go with you to the party. I didn't mean to, I apologize.
- Don't count on me for the next one. Bye.

The observer is a point of view that moves away from the scene in order to view it in a more panoramic way and be able to see and hear everything that is happening. It is not a physical process but is rather like metaphorically stepping outside of ourselves so we can see all around us. It is a way to leverage the higher mind and view reality in a more objective, non-judgment way. Think of a spectator at a sporting event or a cameraman filming a movie; they watch and record but do not actually participate in the event. An important point of differentiation is that the observer does not use the information collected during this process, but instead passes it to the mind as a valuable resource.

In addition to receiving information from the observer, the individual is also having his own experiences interacting with the people and using his senses to respond to stimuli. Therefore, two types of information are being collected by this person: the panoramic details from the observer point-of-view, and also the thoughts and feelings he is personally experiencing as he goes through the experience. This is enabling him to perceive and approach the experience from his "higher mind" in that he is conscious of internal and external factors from different angles, and thereby has a more holistic view of the situation.

An example of the leveraging the observer lens might be if I am currently having a conversation with a work colleague. However, at the same time, I decide to launch the observer so as not to judge and add more information to my interaction. In this case, I am consciously collecting and interpreting bits of information as I survey the external scene and environment while also engaging in an interpersonal dialogue.

As discussed in the previous lesson, the lower and higher minds are oriented toward different goals, with the first focusing on achieving effects (outcomes) and the second focusing on finding the causes (influencing factors). Technically yes, one could start the observer and be present at the same time talking about something, but it is an immense and almost impossible job, since it requires an extraordinary effort. The transition from the "lower mind" (which focuses on what we can perceive) to the observer view (which is largely abstract) involves tremendous amounts of focus and energy. The true observer goes "beyond himself" and represents full consciousness.

NEW ABILITIES AND PERCEPTIONS

- Mom, why does that man carry a cane if he seems to be walking well?
- Because he cannot see, son.
- It must be very difficult to walk without the sense of sight.
- Yes, of course, but he seems to be doing well. However, his perception
of the world is probably very different from yours.
-Yes, I wonder what it is like.

This section about new abilities and perceptions is based on the processes and experiences that I personally have lived, which does not mean that other individuals could not have different manifestations during their own self-discovery process. We each have our own starting point, which influences the pace at which we go and the milestones or levels we reach. Everybody's journey is unique and special.

Climbing a new level in the POC (Pyramid of Consciousness) is essential for further development. Therefore, the process of putting into practice all that has been learned, identifying what we must improve or modify, and leveraging any other resources we collect along the way is fundamental to our continued self-evolution. We must always keep in mind our purpose in life and strive to develop ourselves to our maximum potential. To do so, we should experiment throughout life, make mistakes, seek learning opportunities, align our bodily systems, and persevere.

Challenge Yourself to Change Yourself

Expect the journey to be uncomfortable and difficult. If we start on the two lower levels of the pyramid, we are likely comfortable living in our black-and-white world that feels deceptively safe and secure. Creating a multicolor world for ourselves will include some challenging brushstrokes, and some of the changes will be initially hard to accept. It can be unsettling to move from a world of rules and limitations to one that promotes freedom and expression. But always remember: If it does not challenge you, it will not change you. You will learn how to better understand and manage those challenges, and it will be incredibly worth it.

We have basically two lens we can choose from to perceive reality. One lens shows a grey world, which is very similar to the "lower self," where there is hardly any enjoyment or contentment. In this world, we begin to look for all kinds of intense and euphoric sensations so that we can feel alive in the short-term. But, we also look for distractions, which compel individuals towards addictions, due to their deep level of unconscious suffering. The other lens shows life in full color, the "higher self" world, and enables us to pursue long-term goals that provide intrinsic rewards, emotional stability, fulfillment contentment and inner peace. Adding colorful variety to our world is not the last level, however. Once we reach a higher level of consciousness and have deepened our spirituality, we will enter a stage in which where our perception and abilities will multiply. At that point, we will probably be more in touch with the abstract world.

It has been my personal experience that when we start from ignorance on the POC, each step we take towards the top introduces new knowledge through our experiences, which alters our perception of reality. At first, it is very difficult or confusing to see things as they are because ignorance and our internal conflicts have distorted our lens. But as we learn more about how life works, our lens expands and becomes clearer and multi-dimensional. We recognize and interpret experiences that we would have previously ignored or rejected. We are more aware of our own thoughts and feelings, and become more conscious of how those are manifested in our responses and actions.

From Black-and-White to Multi-Dimensional Color

Learning and practicing this knowledge will allow us to look deeper within and analyze our state of mind. We can better manage our inner conflicts by accurately interpreting our thoughts, feeling and emotions in any given situation. Utilizing the lessons presented in this book will help us even more to know what we need to look for and focus on in terms of our overall personal development. Our old mental "software" has to therefore be modified because it no longer serves us as we have "upgraded" from a plain black-and-white world to a bright colorful one. We need the knowledge and the skills to decode this new multicolored reality we have discovered – and also a more advanced version of ourselves to experience and learn from it.

I have personally found that this journey of self-discovery and climbing the POC will add much depth to how we perceive ourselves, our world and others. The higher we go towards consciousness, the more will not see things as they were before; instead, they will appear to be more complete, rounded and meaningful. Our perceptions and abilities will increase as they are no longer blocked or hidden. We will realize what we did not understand. What seemed like problems to us will no longer matter because we will be able to see them through a more informed, more compassionate lens.

I have experienced firsthand how feelings and emotions we never knew were inside of us will surface. It is similar to wearing glasses, which help us see things near and far, but there is always more we can be observing and analyzing. Yes, those glasses can show us many things. But, a microscope or a telescope can reveal things we never knew existed. There are thoughts and emotions you have that might be daily influencing your attitude, mood or behaviors. Consciousness helps you to get out the microscope and investigate in more detail what is truly underneath.

Unlocking our Potential

Therefore, raising one's consciousness might mean unlocking or revealing his intellectual capability. The greater the consciousness, the greater the abilities with respect to our potential. The higher up we go on the POC, the more experiences and information we collect. In cases where we were previously situated on the lower area of the pyramid, we may happily discover intellectual abilities or gifts that we did not know previously. When we reach the top of the pyramid, we can increase and leverage those abilities to help others in profound ways.

In the multicolored world, we will need to continually challenge and motivate ourselves to seek new experiences and learning opportunities. This will require a positive attitude, strong commitment, enthusiasm and much passion for what we do. Being able to understand how life works – and then leverage that understanding to grow mentally, emotionally and spiritually.

In general, we will need to learn to discover, again, how the software that manages our brain works, as it expands and changes. Sometimes this can be frustrating since we will have to acquire new knowledge and practice new techniques to learn seemingly simple things. However, we must invest a great deal of time in our rediscovery process and consciously train our mind and body to live more consciously and be more integrated in each moment.

As mentioned before, once we reach a certain degree of consciousness and have deepened our understanding of spirituality, it is when the "magic" happens. Our bodies become more aligned, we experience emotional stability, we practice an attitude of gratitude and we benefit from inner peace. We can then focus on continually evolving by: capture other, more subtle information where we can occasionally:

- Translate the energy that people transmit more clearly and feeling what others feel (developing empathy)
- Receive more information from intuition and much more you cannot imagine...

As we raise our level of consciousness (and intelligence), the world we live in will be transformed before our eyes and we will begin to uncover the powerful awareness of what it means to be enlightened, empowered and inspired. We will open ourselves to incredible experiences whose lessons can teach us how to improve our mind, heart and soul. We will be able to perceive and understand people, situational dynamics and our interactions with the world in ways others cannot. Because each of us has different backgrounds, personality traits, inherent biases and support resources, your journey will be different than mine. But, your path will be in the same direction in pursuit of the same goal: forward towards the light. It is there where we can eventually fulfill our life's purpose and become stronger, wiser, healthier and happier people.

PUTTING IT ALL TOGETHER:
Integrating Morals, Ethics, Conscience, Consciousness, Internal War, Love, and Passion

- Hello Rob! How are you? Hey, what happened to your friend? It seems like he's a different person. Where is his strength, vitality and joy? It's as if all these years have negatively changed him.

- Yes, he is different. It all started with him having a bad conscience. A lot of things were weighing on him. He's had to work really hard to financially support his family, which meant that sometimes he had to sacrifice his morals to get ahead in work. Not feeling good about the bad things he's done and the people he's hurt along the way has caused him to become depressed. His health has suffered. And even though that was two years ago, it seems like's he's gotten worse since.

- I understand that he can't go back and change that, but don´t you think it could help if he talks to the people he hurt and asks for their forgiveness? I know a three-step technique that can help him right his wrongs and might even guide him on a spiritual level. Want to try it? I think it will comfort him and give him some peace of mind.

- Let's do it!

Generally speaking, when we're taught what our morals should be, but are not encouraged to thoroughly analyze or reflect on them, they're likely located at the lower part of the POC. Usually they're influenced by our own cultural, economic and/or political contexts. Moral values that are shaped and reinforced merely by rules and norms can often be associated with traditional education, especially if there is no personal analysis. Equally, moral codes can be influenced externally by others and require strict obedience, such as following the Ten Commandments (as part of the Christian teaching), which in black and white declares exactly what one should or should not do. At a lower level of consciousness, rules allow those with non-developed minds to live in a society with just a few directives.

According to my experience, if you are at this instinctive POC level and were not taught to think for yourself about what you believe and value, it is possible that you did not learn how to practice good discernment on your own. Consequently, you do not know which rule to follow when situations are not in black and white – and instead are in shades of grey. This might mean that you may not fully understand the given moral values, or know how to apply them in real-world scenarios, or be able to confront and deal with difficult or unusual circumstances. When you do encounter an important issue, but do not know the 'rule' or moral code to help you discern what to do, you become stuck or instinctually react. For example, if that issue concerns somebody you know, you might feel so conflicted about what to do, you become paralyzed by your own mind. Or, if you do not know the person, your instincts in the situation might cause you to lash out. This perpetual inability to perceive moral values and react accordingly can create a fertile breeding ground for bad feelings to grow and manifest into all types of abuse.

When ethics originate from individual analysis – and you pursue a quest for the Light – you will likely need to examine your life and work on improving yourself from the inside out. Ethics include not only one's moral study but also one's behaviors and actions. Always focusing on your ethical progression will lead to fine-tuning your personal values with precision and excellence. This will help you to pursue the needs of the Light (spirit), which are: 1) the common good, and 2) the higher self within you. If you follow this path of enlightenment, you will be better able to interpret situations, make the right ethical calls, and feel both content with and proud of your responses. The ultimate personal benefit is that you will ultimately feel more complete, humble, blissful, strong and compassionate. I see this as you reaching a new enhanced life level, as though your avatar is playing the game of life and is starting to exponentially collect all the points (gold coins) from previous personal enrichment. The "enlightenment level of the POC" is where you start to understand yourself and gain a better idea regarding the vision of your life's purpose and manifestation. You recognize the dots of your past and start connecting them in ways that help you understand your life in order to clearly make better and more informed predictions about what is ahead.

While observing others, I have found that if we do not consistently follow our moral convictions and ethical guidelines – that is, our version of what is right/better or wrong/worse – we will inevitably find ourselves on a lower life level with an altered (half-truth) reality. When issues or situations are imposed on us (or, when they conflict with our inner self and moral center), there's the potential to steer us off our ethical path and cause us to lose our way. Sometimes, it's difficult to find our way back to that path. The control points (guidelines) that are related to our personal morals and ethics, together with a consciousness full of feelings and emotions, can make us extremely powerful and strong; however, they can also weaken us. There is the likelihood that we can morally deteriorate and experience the negative consequences from the fallout if we do not respect our inner judgement or behave in ways our higher self will not approve. What can start our moral decline is the presence of a bad conscience in the form of an ongoing war that rages within due to us feeling bad and sacrificing our personal integrity.

These personal ethical values, guidelines or control points that were already approved and defined internally sometimes cause struggles within our conscience whenever new situations or others' expectations are imposed on us. In certain cases where our integrity is at risk (maybe due to societal / peer pressure, etc.), our moral nature and conscience can break into pieces and create opposing forces. If prolonged, this internal struggle can start to break down our entirety of self. This war is between what we called the 5 *Bodies*, especially the upper ones, since they do not agree to dismiss what was previously built and accepted in us. This can move us into a lower state of the POC where personal mental blockages, emotional conflicts or issues may appear and also lower our capacity to wisely reason, discern and react in an ethical and beneficial way. Ultimately, the body will be fighting an inner continuous battle every day and night, and after a while, will cause us to stray too far away from where we once were morally. However, the more evolved we are in terms of knowing who we are, and the more we understand what our values are, the more responsibility we have for our behaviors, and the more intensity and impact the internal consequences will create.

Here's how I see it: During this period of inner war, our physical appearance (facial expressions, mannerisms, body language) might look like everything is seemingly fine and "normal," but deep down, our mental and emotional capacities (our energy) have diminished. If we want to return to our previous POC position – when we were functioning from a higher self in an ethical, responsible way – we will need to essentially 'earn it' by working hard to build ourselves up again. Just like in a video game, to get to the top level, we need to persevere and work hard to repair the damage we did and to navigate through higher levels of awareness and insight, which is different for each person.

In most cases, I have observed that highly evolved people have, by the end of their existence, been put through a series of extreme life tests that have brought great insights but have also demanded a great amount of mental and emotional strength. These people have had to fully integrate all aspects of themselves – mentally, physically and spiritually – in order to continually learn and evolve. This integration is key to enlightenment, consciousness and empowerment. For example, if you do not commit fully with your heart when making decisions and instead rely predominantly on your brain (mental), you might find yourself conflicted about your decisions or behaviors. Sometimes, the situations and conditions you will face in life at this level could be risky, challenging and/or uncertain. As you age, this ability to respond ethically and wisely from an integrated perspective will become even more important, especially towards the end of your life. The older you become, the less time you have to repair any negative effects from your moral discretions or integrity violations.

While we are at the lower level of the POC, our inner judge in the form of our conscience usually does not come into play. This is probably due to a couple of reasons: 1) our conditioned response to following rules and the ethics imposed by the society, and 2) our worry of what others will say or do or think of us. Unfortunately, those reasons drown out the importance of our own self-perception and feeling of self-worth.

When you climb the POC, a new understanding of previous concepts presented in this book appears, and you begin to experience the benefits. For example, the agape love I experience in life now is totally different than before. This love feels integrated and complete. It also shifts love's gravity center to the middle of the chest, just where one's hands are typically located when praying, or where the heart chakra is located, or where the images of Jesus show His heart. The higher you climb, the more you realize that the love you used to know was more related to fear or instincts; you notice that it beat faster when you experienced anxiety or that it related to things you thought may or may not happen. But today, having worked on my own self these past years and climbed higher on the POC, I can tell you that I experience love more fully and more deeply now and that it is like waves of emotions have encompassed my entire body.

At the top of the POC you start learning more in depth what agape love really is and how it has nothing to do with us individually but has everything to do with the common good of everyone and everything. With this change, the negative emotions and outbursts you may have had in the past start to diminish and dissolve. Now I am able to better interpret and adjust my responses using the approach of love and kindness. After learning how to ascend the POC, I am now more in tune with my own thoughts, feelings, emotions and behaviors, and can recognize very quickly when I steer off course or make mistakes. Instead of responding with insults or anger, like I used to, I can better analyze the situation, become more empathetic and respond more compassionately. Just like a learning language requires practice and skill development, so does this thing called life. There are various levels of enlightenment, and the only way you can achieve them is by committing, focusing and practicing.

The ability to recognize and experience love changes at this higher POC level, and so do many other things related to it. For example, I also found the sweet spot of recognizing and embracing my passions that elevated my drive and enthusiasm to levels I never was in touch with before. It has led to this full love and zeal I have for life now, regardless of the day of the week or the circumstance. I experience love and life in ways I never have before – within my soul, and up and down my spine. When I was in the lower part of the POC, I used to work off mere adrenaline (which was a conditioned response to fear), but after my spiritual awakening, the adrenaline eventually disappeared. For a while, I struggled with decisions and behaviors, but I persevered on my path towards light and consciousness until I finally found and understood better what others call "passion." Even today, I continue to work on myself and search for a more complete Truth, as I know that this is just my first step in this infinite search for Light.

CONCLUSION:
OUR PERSONAL ODYSSEY

The person who begins this journey into the unknown can use this book's principles and techniques, which are based on the Pyramid of Consciousness, as a guide to enlightenment and empowerment. He should expect to face all kinds of tests and setbacks, as it happened to Ulysses in Homer's Odyssey. The difference is that he will evolve and develop from the inside and that his warriors are the pages and lessons found in this Basic Guide for How Life Works.

During this process of change or metamorphosis, you will probably go through situations that you have never faced before and that you will perceive as uncomfortable, unfamiliar and even heart-wrenching. However, in the worst moments, when you think that you have hit bottom, you might look down and see a deep, dark hole. You will consider giving up on the process. But remember, if you want to advance in life, there is only one way – through great effort and perseverance. So, in these times, look up. Find your support ropes and start climbing. The only way to truly find the light is to pull yourself up.

If you have had internal wars (struggles), it could be because your body armor was too restricted and did not let anything in or out. You bottled your feelings and emotions, even your voice, while shielding your heart and soul from anything uncomfortable or painful. You fought hard, and yet you did not quite know who or what you were fighting. You could not yet see what you had internalized all these many years.

In critical moments, your ego will probably make it even more difficult, by raising your resistance considerably, and you will seek seemingly logical reasons to support your transformation. If you persevere and follow the path to the end, you will likely discover a different truth in the way of life, which will feel more complete, genuine and gratifying.

At other times, when you have learned part of the way and you know something more about how life works, you may believe that you are strong, brave and smart *enough*, and therefore do not feel the need to continue. Here the ego returns, just as Ulysses did in revealing his name to the Cyclops in his escape, and it will continue throughout the process. But there is no such thing as "enough." We can always learn and always grow. Humility and acceptance are crucial throughout the whole transformation to combat pride, ego and stubbornness. In this case, the most important challenge is the fight against yourself.

However, once you start on this path, you will likely not turn back because as everything within you starts to surface and you discover your own source of power, the only logical thing will be to continue advancing. While you observe more and more what you like and do not like about yourself, you will learn how to accept *all* of you, rather than leverage only part of you. Consciously looking inward will be necessary to understand who you are so that you can progress into who you want to become.

During this process, expect to shed the excess layers of yourself that prevent you from growing, and to seek compassion and humility that will allow you to accept, enhance and integrate all your constructive traits. Therefore, the warrior will have to temporarily leave so that he can learn, but then he will eventually return to his home, just as Ulysses did in the Odyssey by going back to Ithaca.

So, if you commit to this self-discovery process and decide to let go of your former self, the weight that has burdened you for so long will finally lift. It is like when something dies and is then raised from the ashes into its stronger self, like the Phoenix, and gives way to the new rebirth of the person. You will be reborn. The individual, through the acceptance and integration of oneself, rises to a new level of evolution and greater consciousness where he can look directly at the Sun. At last, he will discover what he is truly looking for... himself. At this point, the butterfly appears as its metamorphosis is finally complete.

From this moment on, the person understands and is able to recognize similar characteristics and behaviors that were part of his past and that have since dissolved. He now has empathy for those who are currently like how he was, and therefore rather than judging them, he consciously views, respects, understands and genuinely approaches them from his heart – with love.

When one internally exposes himself to unimaginable experiences and battles, he understands that, as noted by J. Donne, "no man is an island," for everybody relies on each other. We are all part of the essential whole. Therefore, we need other people to also develop a greater consciousness and achieve happiness and harmony. It is why we should collectively promote gratitude, compassion, kindness, humility and love. Always.

If you truly desire self-improvement and are willing to put in the time and work to rediscover yourself, you will be successful in creating a better version of yourself and your life. It requires that you go through a process of personal and spiritual discovery and transformation. It will probably be the most important test that you will ever face, because it is the one that will give you the most peace, happiness and harmony in your life. Throughout the entire journey, continually ask yourself: *How do I feel? How has my path been so far? Do I feel that I've found what I am looking for? How can I help others?* Your answers will continue to challenge you, and will hopefully inspire you.

LIVE CONSCIOUSLY, THE REST IS EASY

I am very grateful to have gone through this process that has brought (and continues to bring) new knowledge and new experiences that enable me to live a new life – a life that is more meaningful, more productive and more fulfilling.

ABOUT THE AUTHOR: PENELOPE MORCILLO

Penelope Morcillo holds a degree in European Studies, Master's degrees in both Financial Management and International Foreign Trade, and a Master of Business Administration (MBA). Most of her professional career has been dedicated to working as a marketing specialist in the telecommunications industry.

Morcillo is committed to raising the human consciousness and promoting the personal development and the stability of individuals. Learning and teaching how life works is one of her personal passions. She enjoys learning by observation and experience, and has an immense curiosity about human behavior and mental processes.

Since 2013 she has developed an expertise and experience in open-heart techniques, the practice of Buddhist meditation, and intense personal introspection; she has also been instructed in other healing techniques.

Published by The Royal Hispania Group © 2018

Printed in Great Britain
by Amazon